The Kokoda Trail

A History

For

Sarah and Kate

The Kokoda Trail

A History

Stuart Hawthorne

Boolarong Press

Also by Stuart Hawthorne:

Port Moresby: *Taim bipo*

PO Box 182,
Kedron Qld 4031.

Website: http://www.stuarthawthorne.com

ABN 19 688 236 083

First published in 2003 by Central Queensland University Press.
ISBN 1 876780 30 4.
Reprinted 2003.

This edition (with minor corrections, reset and re-indexed) published in 2012 by:
Boolarong Press
PO Box 308,
Moorooka Qld 4105 Australia.

Telephone: +61-7-3373 7855
Email: publish@boolarongpress.com.au
Website: http://www.boolarongpress.com.au/

ABN 60 009 754 929

Cataloguing in Publication data:
Hawthorne, Stuart, 1948–
The Kokoda Trail: a history / Stuart Hawthorne
Bibliography:
ISBN 9781921920202 (pbk.)
1. World War, 1939–1945 – Campaigns – Papua New Guinea.
2. World War, 1939–1945 – Participation, Australian.
3. Kokoda Trail (Papua New Guinea) – History.
4. Kokoda Trail (Papua New Guinea) – Description and travel.
Dewey Number: 995.3

Printed and bound in Australia by Watson Ferguson & Company, Brisbane.

Contents

Acknowledgements

The Kokoda Trail in Papua New Guinea became well known in Australia during the war in the south western Pacific in 1942 and the term 'Kokoda Trail' has been in popular use in Australia since then. While this term was not unknown in post-war Papua New Guinea, in PNG the Kokoda Trail was more generally known as the 'Kokoda Track'. In October 1972, when the Place Names Committee of the PNG Administration gave notice they intended to officially call the route the 'Kokoda Trail', a vigorous public debate, extending over several months, arose in Papua New Guinea concerning the 'correct' name of the overland route.

At the height of this debate, I suggested to my late father Ronald Hawthorne, who was then President of the Port Moresby Returned Services League sub-branch, the matter could be easily settled by 'looking up the history' to ascertain the provenance of each term. He thought this a good idea and promptly co-opted me into doing the looking up for him. But after I made enquiries at the RSL's headquarters in Australia, the Mitchell Library in Sydney and at university libraries in Queensland and New South Wales, I began to suspect this route had never been 'officially' named. Indeed, it did not seem as if any account at all of the origins of the Kokoda Trail had ever been compiled.

Acknowledgements

This book has evolved from my original quest and is an attempt to fill this surprising gap in both Australia's and Papua New Guinea's recorded histories. In regard to the origin of the route's name, it is hoped my comments in Chapter 17 will satisfy, once and for all, all those involved in the Track/Trail debate.

Research for this book has taken over thirty years of spare-time enquiry in Papua New Guinea and Australia. In this, I have been fortunate in having spent much of my early life in Papua, and later as an adult, living in or visiting many of the places mentioned in this book. This, together with my access to ex-soldier's accounts through my father's contacts, have proved providential for my work since I was exposed from the age of eight years to many stories and yarns spun by World War 2 ex-servicemen. Many of these people served in New Guinea during 1942, and many were 'B4s', or pre-war residents of PNG. I am indebted to these gentlemen for sparking my interest in the history of Papua New Guinea.

Given this, my research could be said actually to have started back in the 1950s. On several occasions in the 1970s, I followed up an item of information or interesting lead with one or more of these people, based on a story I could recall them telling me years before. Much of my background information therefore was accumulated over a considerable time and, initially at least, in quite a casual manner. For fear of omitting someone, I am reluctant to attempt to list the many people who helped in this way. To all those people concerned, thank you.

It would be quite wrong however, not to mention the encouragement and assistance freely given by the late Fred Turner of Port Moresby. Turner was the champion of a group which supported the official adoption of the name Kokoda Track and, before his death, made available to me a substantial file of information he had gathered on the route's wartime background. I also must mention my gratitude to the late Herbert Kienzle, then of Kokoda and who was a friend of my father's, for his encouragement and advice at the very start of my project. His prophetic insights into the effects of the war, and the Kokoda Trail campaign in particular, on the post-war development of Papua were extremely helpful in placing events in a wider context. I am grateful too, to members of the Vidgen and Jardine-Vidgen families of Brisbane for their time spent in attending to my enquiries. A debt is also owed to Stuart Inder, formerly of Pacific Publications in Sydney, for his help on publishing.

I am most grateful to Joe Foley, Bill Kelly, Bill Peckover, Wally McPherson, Nance Oakly (nee Sefton) and Colin Sefton for their assistance in confirming details of the overland mail service as it was immediately after the Second World War.

The wartime portion of my research was helped enormously by Bill McKell, Fred Cranston, John Chalk, Alan Hooper, and Duncan McDermant, all previous members of the 49th or Papua Infantry Battalions. I am very grateful for their comments on and recollections of the southern end of the track before July 1942. I am particularly appreciative of the assistance afforded me by Mr McDermant, who generously allowed scrutiny of his personal diaries and photograph collection compiled as a member of the 15th (later 49th) Battalion in Port Moresby from 1940. I am similarly indebted to Norman Affleck for his comments on the operation of the 1st Independent Light Horse unit, which operated at the southern end of the track during 1942. Another soldier of the time, Myles Powell of Brisbane (ex Signals Corps) was based at Alola in 1942, and I much appreciate his reminiscences on the state of the track during this time.

As to earlier periods in the track's history, the passage of time has denied the opportunity for many direct accounts. I have depended principally on official government reports, gazettes and dispatches. It is fortunate that until the 1920s, the history of Papua was almost solely the history of the overland track and, as a consequence, there are many dusty documents containing a wealth of first-hand reports, observations and comments on the northern goldfields, the areas inland of Port Moresby, and the track that lay between. The official view has been supplemented with published works of private individuals, some unpublished papers, and with newspapers of the day. It would seem nearly everyone who visited British New Guinea in the late 1800s and early 1900s, no matter how short a sojourn in the country they had, felt compelled to publish a book on their travels. I was fortunate to obtain access to many of these rare works in the New Guinea collections of the the Papua New Guinea National Library, Ela Beach Public Library (since destroyed by fire; the portion of the collection that was saved is now with the PNG National Library), and the University of Papua New Guinea, all in Port Moresby, and in the Fryer Library of the University of Queensland in Brisbane.

Given these sources, this work is very much a white man's explanation of events. I leave it to others to set down history as perceived from other perspectives.

The biggest problem in handling all the material over such a long period has been to stay closely aligned with the topic, since the fascinating past of Papua New Guinea makes it easy to become side-tracked. In the end, some severe revisions were necessary to restore the focus but I have reinstated some of the removed material in the form of footnotes. It is hoped these are found of interest but do not intrude too much into the main story.

For knowledge of the overland route as a geographic entity, I have depended on my own experiences of several years bushwalking experience, on the track itself, on Hombrom, Varirata and Sogeri Plateaux, in the Laloki Valley, and around and along the banks of the Brown, Goldie and Musgrave Rivers.

Besides the libraries in Port Moresby, I have utilised the services of others over the past years. My thanks are offered to the many library staff who cheerfully undertook to attend to the sometimes obscure demands I made of them. Libraries used are: *Port Moresby*: the Ela Beach Public Library (New Guinea section), the Papua New Guinea National Library, and the University of Papua New Guinea (New Guinea Collection). *Brisbane*: the State Library of Queensland, the University of Queensland (Main, Fryer and Geological Libraries), the Royal Geographical Society of Australiasia (Queensland), the Commonwealth Archives, Santos House, Brisbane, and the library of the Department of Resource Industries, Minerals and Energy House, Brisbane. *New South Wales:* Mitchell Library, Sydney. *Victoria:* the State Library of Victoria.

Special thanks is due to Mary-Lyn Warden of the University of Queensland for her assistance in locating Stuart-Russell's map of the 'first Kokoda Trail.

For advice and help with many of the photographs used in this book, I am indebted to Bill Ilic and Ian Clarke, both of Port Moresby (in 1977), and Craig Shaw, photographer with Queensland Newspapers Ltd, and Tony Forsyth, both of Brisbane. Their technical skill and knowledge of photographic processing has enabled many poor quality 'originals' to be included. Thanks also to Len Vicary of the University of Queensland's Photographic Unit for his excellent work on the old maps reproduced in this book.

The stanza cited at the beginning of Part 2 is an extract from 'Via Kokoda' by 'Decimvir', first published in the *Papuan Courier*, 13th January 1928. This poem, as far as I am aware, has not ever been re-published. The lines cited at the beginning of Part 3 are from 'The Owen-Stanley Track' in the anthology *Musings of a Moresby Mouse* by Howarde Tilse, published by Barker's Bookstore, Brisbane in 1944. The poem was first published in Cummins & Campbell Ltd, *Monthly*, Townsville, Queensland, in July 1943.

Stuart Hawthorne

Brisbane.

General maps

The Kokoda Trail and adjacent districts. *Author.*

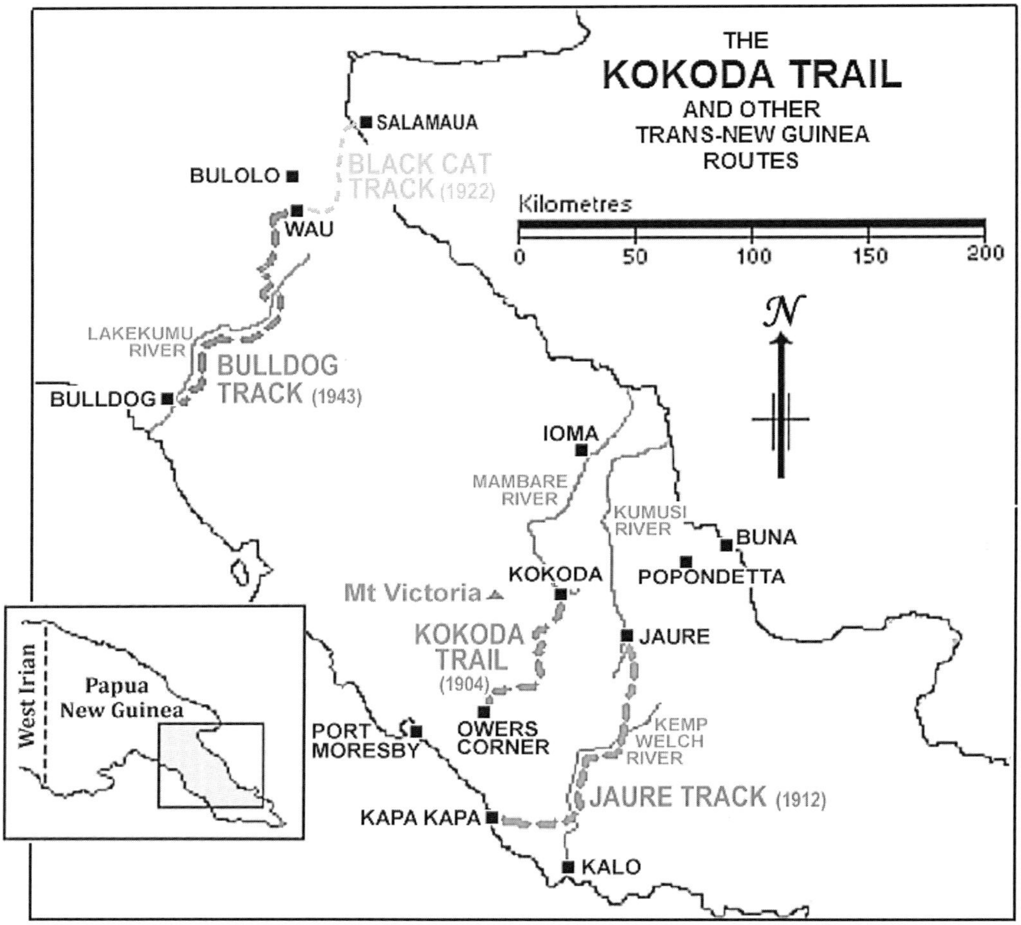

THE
KOKODA TRAIL
AND OTHER
TRANS-NEW GUINEA
ROUTES
Kilometres
0
50
100
150
200
N
SALAMAUA
BULOLO
BLACK CAT
TRACK (1922)
WAU
LAKEKUMU
RIVER
BULLDOG
TRACK (1943)
BULLDOG
IOMA
MAMBARE
RIVER
KUMUSI
RIVER
BUNA
POPONDETTA
KOKODA
Mt Victoria
KOKODA
TRAIL
(1904)
JAURE
OWERS
CORNER
PORT
MORESBY
KEMP
WELCH
RIVER
JAURE TRACK (1912)
KAPA KAPA
KALO
West Irian
Papua
New Guinea

The Kokoda Trail and other trans-New Guinea routes. *Author.*

UBERI
IORIBAIWA
NAURO
MENARE
KAGI
TEMPLETON'S
CROSSING
ALOLA
OWER'S
CORNER
EFOGI
ISURAVA
IORA
DENEKI
MT VICTORIA
4072 metres
KOKODA
HOMBROM
BLUFF
MT
BELLAMY
2286 metres
PORT
MORESBY
IMITA
RIDGE
MAGULI
RANGE
BUNA
South coast
96.4 kilometres
North coast

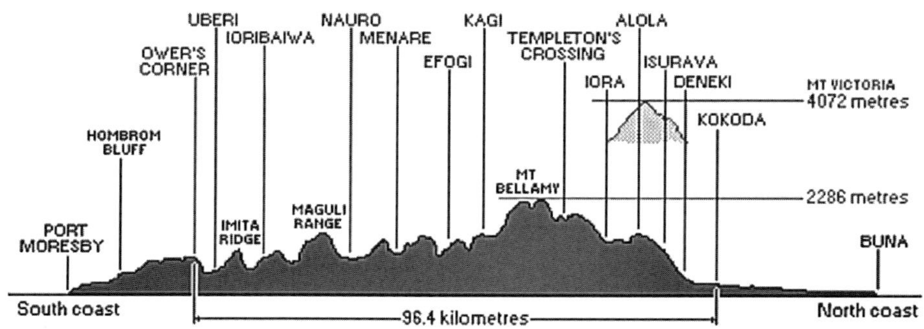

Cross-section through the Kokoda Trail (looking approximately west-north-west). *Author.*

Part 1

Early Days

1874-1899

It is evident the difficulties of
travelling in this country are not trifling.

George Ernest Morrison, 1878

The Owen Stanley mountains in 1876, as seen by the first settlers from Moresby Harbour.

The Owen Stanley Range was the barrier to overland travel explorers faced in their attempts to travel inland. The highest peak shown is Mount Victoria, then known as Mount Owen Stanley. The peak immediately to the left of Mount Victoria is Mount Douglas.

Sir William MacGregor succeeded in climbing Mount Victoria in 1889 by first ascending Mt Douglas so as to enter onto the spur that connected the two mountains. All earlier attempts at scaling Mount Victoria had been made from the right and all these had failed.

PNG National Library.

1

First steps (1874–1878)

In the early 1900s, a walking track reached from one side of the New Guinea island to the other. This track was about 200 kilometres long and joined Port Moresby on the southern coast with Buna on the northern coast. Between these two towns lay the Owen Stanley Range, the massive backbone of eastern New Guinea. Since those earlier times, portions at either end of this track have evolved to become motor roads but the remainder, about half the original distance, remains accessible only to foot traffic. This constitutes what is known today as the Kokoda Trail.

The Kokoda Trail crosses areas of the country so rugged that even at the beginning of the 21st century, a feasible route for motor traffic has yet to be found. Modern bushwalkers find it a daunting prospect to walk the 96 kilometre Trail, and this is with good maps, a defined track and lightweight equipment. In the late 19th century, the country and its inhabitants presented such formidable impediments to travel, white exploration was not able to penetrate more than 60 kilometres inland in the first thirteen years of white settlement. As late as 1887, so little was known of the interior of the country it was seriously supposed monkeys existed there.

The lack of knowledge of the interior was not for the want of effort or enthusiasm by the early settlers. Many expeditions, official or private, were to set out with the aim of crossing from Port Moresby to the northern shore. In the way however, some 80 kilometres inland, rose 4,072 metre Mount Victoria and her attendant ranges, which rise to over 3,600 metres. A route across this barrier just could not be found.

Mount Victoria seemed to hold a peculiar fascination for the early white population, attracting the attention of many who desired to reach its summit, if only because it was the highest part of the range visible from Moresby Harbour. Also, Mount Victoria lay on the most obvious route to the far side, that is, to the north-east. It was felt an explorer successful in ascending it would have an 'easy' downhill walk to the sea on the other side. This view was found later to be far from the truth.

The first permanent white residents of Papua New Guinea were the Reverend Doctor William G. Lawes and family who arrived at Moresby Harbour on 21st November 1874. They represented the London Missionary Society. The Lawes family joined four Polynesian members of the Mission who, 12 months earlier, had established a station at the village of Hanuabada on the shores of Moresby Harbour. Lawes was not a keen explorer but in the course of his work he went inland in early 1875 to the summit of Hombrom Bluff (then known as Mount Vetura or Vaturu) where he succeeded in making friends with the Koiari people, occupants of the area.

Though disinclined towards the physical demands of exploration, Lawes nevetheless had a special aptitude for establishing amicable relations with the natives. It was his early success in this regard which facilitated much of the later exploration of the Moresby Harbour environs, as well as significantly contributing to the establishment of Port Moresby township in the following decade. Unfortunately, the value of his standing with the natives, and of the advantages it presented to explorers, were either initially not recognised or, subsequently, taken for granted. It was not until many years later, following a complete breakdown of relations with people living a few kilometres inland from Hombrom Bluff, that Lawes' expertise was fully appreciated. But by then, the initial harmony and trust had gone and it took almost two decades to rectify the damage.

Despite the short Hombrom Bluff trip being the only direct contribution made by Lawes to the story of the Kokoda Trail, he must be credited as the person to make the first tentative steps inland. His was the first recorded crossing of the Laloki River by a white man and that of his wife, Fanny, the first white woman.

The Reverend Doctor Willian George Lawes of the London Missionary Society.

Lawes, with his wife Fanny and young son, were the first permanent European residents of the New Guinea island. Lawes was the first white man to cross the Laloki River and the first to ascend Hombrom Bluff.

Lawes left New Guinea in February 1906 and died in Sydney on 6th August 1907.

PNG National Library.

For his work about Port Moresby, Lawes was made a Fellow of the Royal Geographical Society in 1876.*

Close on Lawes' heels came other explorers. A visiting geologist, Octavius C. Stone, who had arrived in the Ellengowan with colleagues Lawrence Hargrave† and Rendall Broadbent, departed the harbour settlement on 22nd November 1875,, initially following Lawes' track. It seems probable he left this at some stage to follow the course of an as-yet unnamed river, a tributary of the Laloki, which tracked to the north-east of, and past, Hombrom Bluff. Stone's limit was a village he recorded as 'Munikaira'. 'The total distance from Anuapata [Hanuabada]', he wrote, 'is 18 miles [29 kilometres] and the height above the sea is 1200 feet [366 metres]'. Taking into account the probable transposition of 'r' and 'l', which is common in Papua New Guinea, this village is most likely that of Munikahila. Munikahila is not shown on modern maps but an 1887 Royal Geographical Society map does have this point marked as a feature of 1100 feet (335 metres). However, the available copy of this map has a scale too small to make other than approximate calculations. Even so, it is accurate enough to indicate the point reached by Stone is consistent with either what is shown on contemporary maps as Mount Mumkainala, a 412 metre feature 32 kilometres from Port Moresby, or the nearby village of Uberi. If either assumption is correct, Stone would have been the first white man to cross the Goldie River, the first stream to be crossed on the Kokoda Trail today. Mount Mumkainala is about three kilometres north of today's Uberi Village and to reach this point, Stone would have had to ascend the southern slopes of Imita Ridge, site of the Kokoda Trail's torturous 'Golden Staircase' of the war years.

---

* Lawes recorded the name of this stream as the Laloke, and others as the Larogi, Laroge, Lilogi, Tarogi, Laluka and the Stanley. It was, and still is, called the Iarawari on the Sogeri Plateau, above Rouna Falls. Some late 19th century maps and official records refer to it as the Usborne River. The present name and spelling, Laloki, has been in official use before the end of the 19th century.

† This was the third of four expeditions Hargrave made to New Guinea, the first being on the *Maria* which sunk off the Queensland coast, the second, with Macleay on the *Chevert* and the fourth with d'Albertis on the *Neva*. Hargrave later became a pioneer of aviation in Australia.

Stone made only three trips away from the Moresby Harbour settlement, the one of 22nd November being of the greatest distance inland. He departed New Guinea on 26th January 1876 but it seems he liked the country and had at one time entertained the idea of staying, for he had purchased a parcel of land at Hanuabada. He may have been disinclined from making further trips inland since he had had some difficulty in obtaining satisfactory service from his carriers. In the light of the well-documented efforts of the 'Fuzzy-Wuzzy' carriers on the Kokoda Trail in 1942, it is of interest to note Stone's observations of those he had recruited as porters:

> They are not accustomed to bearing loads as the women do it for them; and it became evident that they didn't intend to carry more than they could help on this occasion. With some difficulty, we made the four men carry 20 lbs [9 kilograms] each and the others a smaller load in proportion to their strength …

In 1876, Andrew Goldie, a Scots naturalist employed by a London nursery firm to gather exotic botanical specimens arrived at Moresby Harbour. On this occasion, he lasted only six months in the country, malaria forcing his return to Australia. While in Sydney, he organised his own expedition and returned to the Moresby Harbour settlement on 19th July 1877 in his twelve ton lugger *Explorer*. He was accompanied by three assistants, Shaw, Blunden and Morton. They established a field camp on the Laloki River about 13 kilometres downstream of the site of the Lawes' first crossing. The search for new specimens carried Goldie and his team in ever-widening circles as they gradually exhausted the possibilities of the areas adjacent to their campsite. Shaw climbed Varirata Plateau's seaward slopes, to find open bushland with nomadic inhabitants. This Plateau is now the site of a National Park. It was then, and later, variously known as Mount Astrolabe, Wariarata, Variata or Warriraba.

Later the same year, on 22nd October 1877, the schooner *Bertha* arrived at Moresby Harbour to put ashore an assistant for Dr Lawes. This was the Reverend James Chalmers. While Lawes preferred the quieter pursuits, Chalmers was the complete opposite. 'He keeps everybody alive and has an inexhaustible stock of energy', wrote Lawes of Chalmers. In his own vein, Chalmers expressed: 'I prefer any amount of hard work … travelling or otherwise, to writing letters or reports'.

Andrew Goldie, after whom the Goldie River is named, was principally responsible for the Laloki River gold rush of 1878. This drew attention to the largely unknown country of New Guinea, which in turn led to accelerated exploration of the New Guinea interior.

Goldie opened the first commercial store in New Guinea in 1880. He left the country in 1891.

Drawing by Basia Boratyn, 1976, from a photograph in the collection of the Office of Information, Port Moresby.

The Reverend James Chalmers, colleague of Lawes', was the first man to attempt a crossing of the New Guinea island. He was a keen explorer and much of the initial exploration along the southern coast of Papua was his doing. The author Robert Louis Stevenson, who had befriended Chalmers in Samoa, described him as 'restless as a volcano'.

Chalmers was killed while on missionary work in the Gulf of Papua in 1901.

PNG National Library.

Within three days of his arrival in New Guinea, he had cajoled Lawes and Goldie into taking him inland. Included in the party accompanying him on the now well-worn path to Hombrom Bluff was Lawes, Goldie, and one of Goldie's New Caledonian *kanaks*, Jimi. Two days after their return to the coast, Jimi approached Goldie and handed over what he believed was quartz with gold in it. He had found it during the inland walk with Chalmers but he feared the *Bertha's* crew, at the time enjoying shore leave, might discover his find, hence his telling Goldie. Lawes wrote in his diary Goldie

> seemed excited about it and expected that we should be. I knew of auriferous quartz being here, but I hoped that nothing would be known of it yet ... Mr Goldie gave me a specimen piece. The gold in it is not visible to the naked eye but they say it is very evident with a microscope. If there is a rush of white men with gold fever on them, the natives must suffer.

These misgivings of Lawes' stemmed from the London Missionary Society's paternalistic view of native society. Lawes himself had found gold in the area the previous year and had sent samples to Sydney for assaying. He was told the gold in his samples was 'quite payable' but fearing there would be an uncontrolled rush of miners should this become known, he had decided to keep the knowledge of his discovery to himself. In doing this, he remained consistent with the London Missionary Society's class-bound attitudes, typical of late 19th century England. The Mission's view was 'except under proper control the greatest evils will probably arise from the lawlessness of the classes by which gold digging has been usually undertaken'.

In their guise as self-appointed protectors of the local people, the Mission had been pushing, from as early as 1876, for the British Government to physically extend the jurisdiction of the Fiji-based Commissioner for the Western Pacific to New Guinea. The idea of this was to ensure outsiders could be prevented from entering the country, or people already in the country could be subjected to the constraints of British law. In their efforts to convince the politicians in far-away London, the Society regularly painted the worst possible picture of New Guinea life. In 1878 for example, in *anticipation* of an influx of gold miners to Port Moresby, the Society wrote to the Colonial Office urging immediate action to be taken on the basis miners, 'in entire ignorance of the language ... are likely to come into most serious collision with the native tribes'. As well, it was pointed out, the place was a 'thoroughly tropical country which has proved to be exceedingly unhealthy' and therefore miners would be exposed

to 'the most terrible risks of health and even life'.

These claims were unfounded at the time they were made. There was no evidence at all 'most serious collisions' between miner and native would occur. Furthermore, while it was true malaria was rampant, and there had been deaths amongst the missionary group, the purported '*exceedingly* unhealthy' environment was not consistent with the fact of continuous white settlement at Port Moresby for the preceding five years. But, irrespective of whether these arguments were justifiable or not, the Society could not convince the Colonial Office to establish formal control over New Guinea.

Principally through Goldie, news of the gold discovery leaked out and by May 1878, five prospecting expeditions, including one from New Zealand had been mounted. The largest, and first to arrive in New Guinea, was a group which sailed from Sydney on 27th March 1878 on the schooner *Colonist*. Within three months, over eighty prospectors had arrived and had moved some kilometres inland from the mission to set up their camps. Much interest was shown in the Laloki tributary Octavius Stone had first ascended three years earlier. This flowed into the Laloki from the north, the junction being about 13 kilometres to the west of Hombrom Bluff. Andrew Goldie travelled up this stream, reaching a point he estimated to be about 65 kilometres in a straight line from Moresby Harbour. 'At this point', wrote Goldie in his journal, 'the country changed entirely; instead of open grassy land it became dense bush, intermixed with numerous climbers, the timber very light, and the banks of the river very steep which made travelling very difficult'. Goldie estimated a further 16 kilometres upstream was managed before a shortage of food forced their return.

The Laloki River immediately upstream of its junction with the Goldie River, at the place where Lawes made the first crossing by a European in 1875.

This photograph was taken in 1912.

PNG National Library.

Goldie's party may well have cut across the ford where the Kokoda Trail passes between Owers' Corner and Uberi today. Certainly, the journal description fits the country a few kilometres downstream of the present crossing and the distances he claims would take him past this point. Of the gold, Goldie recorded 'the black sand of the river yielded gold at every prospect' although, he thought, not in payable quantities. Of the river, he reported to the Royal Geographical Society he had named it the 'Goldie' River, declining to elaborate on whether it was named after himself or because the river was 'goldy'. There has been some confusion over this.

Up to the late 1950s, there was a belief among many Port Moresby residents the stream's name described the contents of its sands. Frank Clune, in his *Prowling Through Papua*, which was published in 1943, may well have been influenced by this viewpoint when he wrote of Goldie's early exploration of this area: '... they obtained flaky colours of gold from the drift and gravelly deposits in the banks of the river ... Appropriately, the stream was named the "Goldie River"'. The confusion about the origin of the name is reflected in use of the term 'Goldi' (with an initial capital but without the terminal *e*) as an adjective in the *South Pacific Post's* editorial columns in 1957. Despite this, the official, and correct, interpretation has always been the stream was named after Andrew Goldie. On this matter, one can cite no more informed viewpoint than that of Sir Hubert Murray, who recorded in 1912 in his *Papua, or British New Guinea,* 'Mr Goldie did a lot of collecting ... on the river that bears his name'.

In addition to Stone's and Goldie's initial explorations of the Goldie River, a prospector named John Hanran, who had been with the original *Colonist* group, reported in May 1878 a party of four men penetrated about 50 miles (80 kilometres) from their inland camp (which was 27 kilometres from Port Moresby), up the r Goldie's right (southern) bank, at which point they found 'the river heading to the south-east in a half-circle'. They returned overland to the inland camp in a journey of 35 miles. Another expedition, which left on 28th June 1878 under Frank Jones, leader of the *Colonist* group, which left on 28th June 1878, further extended this penetration inland. According to Hanran who was with Jones, 'after travelling in a south east direction [for] four days, [they] came to the tableland [Sogeri Plateau]'.

The distances Hanran provides seem excessive and do not plot easily on a modern map. However, to enter onto the Sogeri Plateau from the Goldie one would have to be a considerable distance upstream. As well, it is reasonable to assume Jones and his group would have remained with the river so long as it continued in a south-easterly direction, leaving it to head south towards the Sogeri Plateau only after the Goldie had swung away, as it does, to the east and then to the north-east. Given this, it seems likely, as with Andrew Goldie, they would have traversed the ford on the Goldie which links Owers' Corner and Uberi village on today's Kokoda Trail. The straight line distance of this crossing from Port Moresby is 40 kilometres (or 25 miles). The point ostensibly reached by Stone is about 3 kilometres further to the north of this point.

A Koiari tree house.

The Koiari people, occupants of Hombrom Bluff and the Sogeri Plateau, regions first visited by Lawes and Forbes in 1875, lived in tree houses as a means of protection against surprise raids by the Uberi and other groups who lived to the north of the Goldie River.

This photograph was taken in 1885 by J. W. Lindt, photographer for Sir Peter Scatchley.

University of Papua New Guinea.

But in September 1878, it appears from a further report from Hanran, the prospectors travelled even further inland via the Goldie. Hanran reported a party of 28 made up from men of the *Colonist, Emily* and *Hibernia* groups decided to ascend the Goldie 'for the purpose of prospecting the creek that runs into the Goldie from the north-east'. It seems likely this creek is Ua-Ule Creek. One of the members of the party, James Willey reported on his return a distance of 40 miles (64 kilometres) upstream was accomplished. Again, the mileage claimed seems to be over-estimated—Ua-Ule Creek is at best only about 20 kilometres long from source to Goldie junction and none of the miner's reports indicate the head of the creek was reached. Nevertheless, given the party travelled for five days to track end, it seems probable a fair distance was covered. They would only have to have travelled 15 kilometres (about 10 miles) for them to be some three or four kilometres further north of the place supposedly reached by Stone in 1875 and it is reasonable to assume at least this point was attained. This then, would be the furthest inland point reached by any white explorer up to December 1878.

Besides the Laloki and Goldie Rivers, interest was also shown in a much larger stream about 20 kilometres to the north of the Laloki. In August 1878, a group of 15 from the *Colonist* and *Emily* expeditions, including one Peter Brown, travelled overland to this stream, known then by its native name of Manu Manu (or Mana Mana), but which is known today as the Brown River. This stream was so named on 26th August 1878 during the burial service of Peter Brown. He had drowned while attempting to swim to the opposite bank. Coincidentally, the waters of this river are normally a muddy brown but its naming was meant as a mark of respect to the unfortunate Mr Brown, and had nothing to do with the water's colour. Given Brown's death, and a further incident in which a misunderstanding with the natives led to another member of the group being speared, it was doubly unfortunate the area showed poor prospects for mining. As well, the steep riverbanks and dense scrub made access to the stream difficult. Accordingly, the miners gave up on the Brown River after three weeks and returned to their Laloki camp.

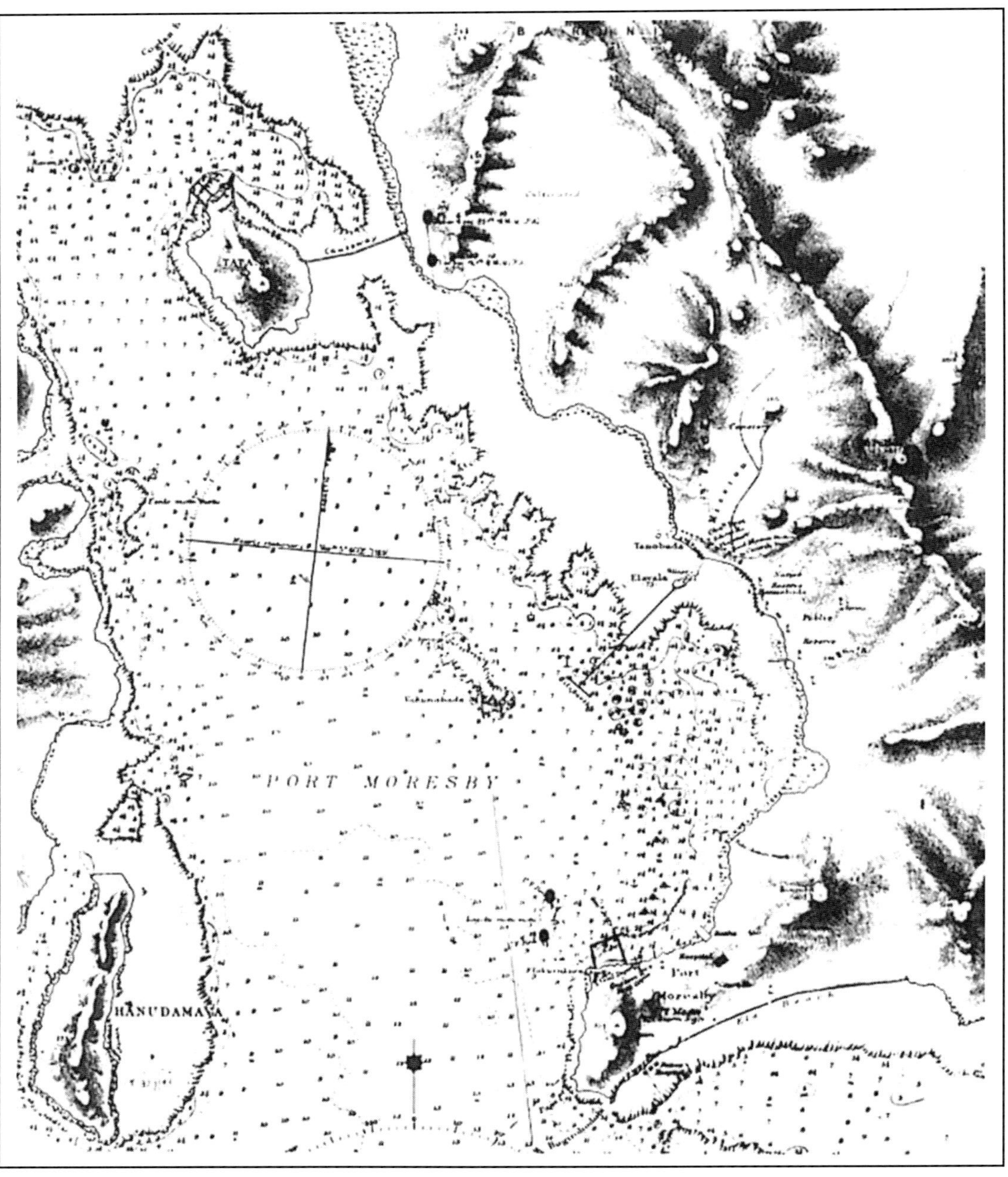
TATA
PORT MORESBY
HANUDAMAVA

This portion of a naval chart of Moresby Harbour, originally published in 1885, shows the locations of some of the original tracks leading inland from the London Missionary Society's coastal settlement. Though faint, the main track to the Laloki River can be discerned passing through the cemetery and crossing the coastal hills north of the peak now known as Mount Pullen and down into June Valley via country occupied today by the Port Moresby suburb of Hohola.

The resolution of this chart is poor because it is a reprinted copy. Useful maps were in such short supply at the outbreak of the Pacific war in 1942 that this chart, at that time already 57 years old, was copied and re-issued with more recent naval information included as overprinted features. The oil berth and pipeline to Elevala Island, and the causeway to Tatana Island (top left), stem from this time.

University of Queensland.

The intensity of the 1878 gold rush to the Laloki and other rivers declined quickly, mainly because the gold was not present in the rivers in sufficient quantity to make mining economical. As well, the wet season had been unusually late in 1878 and the prospectors found the swollen rivers difficult to work outside of the lower flood plain reaches. The well-watered scrub made cross-country traffic difficult and exhausting, and the swampy ground gave rise to swarms of fever-carrying insects. Thus, with uncertain prospects of finding their fortune, with the harsh conditions, high prices and food shortages, and with sickness prevalent, a drift of disillusioned men out of the country began. From a maximum of about 100, by mid-September 1878 only about 60 men remained, and this had fallen to less than 10 by the year's end.

The rush did have two significant outcomes. The first was, in line with the London Missionary Society's long-standing pleas, an 'official' presence was finally established in the country. But, as if trying to make up for lost opportunities, not one, but three, 'appointments' were made. The first of these was William Bairstow Ingham, who was appointed as a 'mining warden' in February 1878 by the Queensland Government. Ingham's powers to issue mining leases, approve surveys, and to conduct all the other aspects of his position were never clearly regularised and it is probable he had no legal authority in New Guinea at all. In any event, Ingham's tenure in office was to be only a short one. In November 1878, while on the island of Utain, about 160 kilometres east of Samarai, he met an untimely end at the hands of the island's inhabitants.

The appointing of a 'legal' government representative was left to the British Colonial Office. Initially, the Office proposed to send Henry Chester, the Queensland Government's police magistrate on Thursday Island, to Moresby Harbour, suitably empowered as a Deputy Commissioner for the Western Pacific. But it was realised on his own he would have been powerless to enforce any direction or order he may have issued. Instead therefore, *HMS Sappho* was sent to Moresby Harbour, arriving on 27th July 1878 'to do what might prove to be necessary in the event of disturbances having arisen', the *Sappho*'s captain, Commander Noel Digby, holding the warrant of Deputy

Commissioner originally intended for Chester. But Chester, anyway, had already arrived at Moresby Harbour on 16th July, having been sent by the Queensland Premier John Douglas to ascertain the situation at the settlement.

Ingham, Chester and Digby all found by mid-1878 the 'rush' had stalled due to the wet weather, sickness and the harsh country. Surprisingly though, the missionaries' predictions of a breakdown in relations with the natives were not realised. In fact, notwithstanding some isolated incidents, the reverse seemed to be the case, as Chester reported in July 1878:

> It is with pleasure I am able to report that the friendly relations with the natives inaugurated by Mr. Ingham remain unimpaired. Men go and come between the camp at the Laloki and the port, a distance of 12 miles, entirely unarmed, and have no difficulty in getting carriers for their goods. The example set by those who arrived in the 'Colonist' is worthy of all praise, and has given a tone to the rest.

Chester also recounts the views of the prospectors which demonstrated a collective outlook on life mightily different from that envisioned by William Lawes and the London Missionary Society:

> [The miners] ... spoke in high praise of the kindness shown by the natives to the sick and to those who had been temporarily lost in the bush. The general desire on their part is to live in harmony with the people. They expressed themselves as most anxious that someone with sufficient power to repress lawlessness should reside among them, and promised to support his authority.*

Though this seemed to augur well for the immediate future, the British Colonial Office saw the circumstances differently. They reasoned the departure of most of the miners indicated a

---

* The discipline of the prospectors in 1878 was evidence of a self-imposed code of conduct that was to be consistently displayed by miners as a class over the following years. Almost two decades later, Sir William Macgregor was reporting almost the same observations of the miners as Chester had in the 1870s. In the Annual Report for 1896/97, MacGregor noted the reaction of the miners when expected conduct levels had been transgressed:

> The conduct of the old miners … has been good. They have generally dealt justly and fairly with the natives, and they have been law-abiding. But amongst the men that came … last year there was, as might have been expected, a margin, probably a small one, of a different complexion. By these some acts of robbery were committed on natives … These acts of violence were … met with universal condemnation on the part of the great majority of the men themselves. The old hands who have worked with the natives for years spoke of one voice in terms of indignation.

decline in interest in the country. Therefore, a permanent official appointment to the country was not required and a visit by a warship was all that was necessary should future events require official attention. Be this as it may, the important outcome was the seed of formal control had been planted and though this was to germinate only slowly over the following half-decade, it eventually led to a Port Moresby government being established.

The second important consequence of the gold rush was, as we have seen, much new ground about the present site of Port Moresby was opened up, though exactly how far inland the miners went is not clear. Two governors of what was later to become British New Guinea and later, Papua, Sir William MacGregor and Sir Hubert Murray, both found difficulty in ascertaining the actual limits reached by the early prospectors. MacGregor cites Ingham as referring to 'a party of prospectors working under Mount Victoria' but MacGregor thought 'that may have been twenty or thirty miles [32 to 48 kilometres] from Mt. Victoria'.

Though there were different groups of miners, usually identified by the name of the vessel which carried them to New Guinea, a sort of 'main' camp became established on the Laloki, about 19 kilometres from the coast and about 4 kilometres downstream of the Goldie River junction. This was not a particularly sophisticated place, in July 1878 consisting of a rudimentary log hut roofed with bark, and a few tents. From about September 1878, the settlement was known as 'Camp Chester'. The 'dray-road' to the camp seems, from the reports of Ingham, Chester, Digby and others, to have been well defined and well travelled so it is likely the land which this route traversed, between the Laloki and the coast, would have been well explored.

Further out, we can be certain the Brown River, 32 kilometres from the coast, had been reached, with dense scrub stopping further progress to the north. This appears to be the greatest distance to the north that was reached. However, the longest journeys, and the greatest distances inland from Moresby Harbour, seemed to have been made up the Goldie and Ua-Ule Creek to the north-east. And, importantly, all this was accomplished without any friction developing with the natives.

Karema Village on the Brown River, first reached by miners in 1878. This photograph was taken in 1957.

Author.

We know too, in addition to the river-based exploration, Hombrom Bluff and the Varirata Plateau, the Sogeri Plateau's two massive westerly spurs, had been reached overland from the south and south-east with, again, friendly relations established with several villages. As well, despite the single-mindedness of the bulk of the white population in seeking gold in the local rivers, there was the first stirrings of an interest in an overland route, as evidenced by a report of Ingham's in July 1878:

> The natives say that about 40 miles [64 kilometres] inland from Port Moresby, at a height of 2,000 feet [610 metres] above the sea, it is only five sleeps to the big water on the other side, so that, should it ever be required, there is little doubt that communication could be obtained with the north-west [sic] coast, through the great gap between Owen Stanley [Mount Victoria] on the west and Mt. Obree on the east. The absence of ports on the north-west coast renders it not unlikely that a large portion of it may have to depend upon Port Moresby for supplies.

The Port Moresby rush of 1878 was not a success. Nevertheless, it became the pivotal event which triggered, or upon which were hinged, later significant developments. It forced official notice to be taken of the country for the first time and lay the foundation for better things to come. It ensured wide publicity for New Guinea and a continuing interest by the white man in the country. The rush demonstrated, against all predictions, friendly relations between black and white could be established and maintained. Most importantly, it brought about the beginnings of determined exploration of the interior. It opened up the areas adjacent to the settlement, and left the way to the unexplored country beyond there for the taking.

Hanuabada village on the shores of Moresby Harbour (photo taken between 1938 and 1942), much as it would have appeared to Lawes and Chalmers in the 1870s.

After World War 2, following a 1944 fire that destroyed most of the village, Hanuabada was re-built using European building materials and corrugated iron roofs.

Judy Ryan.

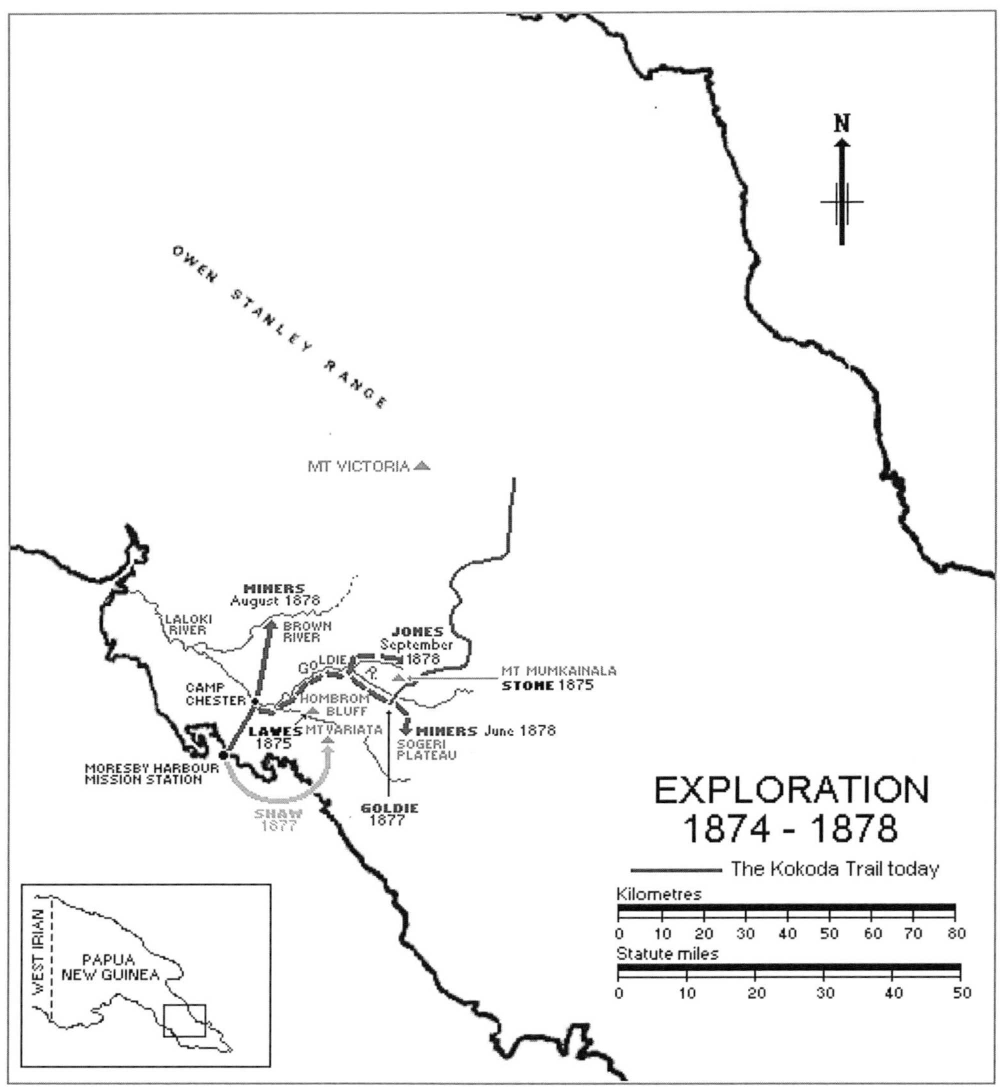

Summary of exploration 1874–1878. *Author.*

2

Overland attempts (1878–1887)

The first recorded attempt to cross the eastern half of the island of New Guinea appears to have been made by the Rev James Chalmers. Chalmers had not set out with this in mind, intending only to establish sites for mission schools but it seems he went further than planned.. While this attempt did not succeed, the venture was of value because it added significantly to the limit of white exploration while maintaining friendly relations with the native inhabitants..

Chalmers left the LMS station on 15th July 1879. After crossing the Laloki a short way upstream of its junction with the Goldie, he followed the latter's right bank , ascending the Sogeri Plateau's north-western slopes to emerge at Uberi Village, to the north of the Goldie. This retraces the track taken by Stone, Goldie and Frank Jones. Several accounts corroborate Chalmers' venture to this point but there are doubts on his later movements. Lawes recorded in his diary Chalmers formed a base camp on a ridge near the village. 'From this starting point', wrote Lawes, 'he made an excursion east-north-east across the Munikahila [probably Ua-Ule] Creek which flows west and falls into the Goldie ... In the hope of reaching the opposite coast of New Guinea, Mr Chalmers went along Mount Bellamy until he found it ended abruptly and was distinct from the Owen Stanley Range'. Lawes added Chalmers also visited 'a mountain he called Mount Nisbet'.

This account sounds very optimistic—Mount Bellamy (2,286 metres) is definitely not 'distinct' from the Owen Stanleys. This mountain forms the north-western corner of the valley known as The Gap, through which the Kokoda Trail runs. As well, once either Mount Bellamy or Mount Nisbet has been reached, the main range has virtually been crossed. Cuthbert Lennox, in his *James Chalmers of New Guinea*, cites an unnamed source as saying Chalmers, on this journey, 'visited many native villages, and explored the mountainous country along the course of and between the Goldie and Laloki Rivers'. This is a more likely version of Chalmers' adventures although it is apparent some time was spent north of the Goldie. Entries in both Chalmers' and Lawes' diaries refer to the establishment of friendly relations with the Ebe or Eburi (Uberi) people, whose regions lay on the river's inland side. Though Chalmers does not claim to have reached the summits of Mount Bellamy or Mount Nisbet, it would seem he probably did cross into the country north of Ua-Ule Creek.

Chalmers also is credited with making the first recorded attempt to ascend Mount Victoria, about nine months later, though, again, he fell short of success. In fact, he reached nowhere near his objective, Sir William MacGregor finding Chalmers 'never reached the Brown River'. Chalmers admits the lack of success was due to a miscalculation on his part. Before leaving the coast, he decided the party would travel lightly, the intention being to live off the land by killing wild game. But once away from the coastal grasslands and into the jungle proper, it was found edible animal life was 'exceedingly scarce', and so they had run short of food. * Over 50 years later, in much the same area, it was this need for travellers to carry their own

---

* Although the little above is the total of his contribution to the story of the Kokoda Trail, the efforts of James Chalmers in other parts of the British Possession in the following 21 years were to make him the most highly regarded and respected New Guinea explorer of his day. In one expedition alone, he led a party through 800 kilometres of unexplored country. Unfortunately, he spent little time in the districts where the Kokoda Trail passes today. One can only conjecture how the story of this route may have been altered had Chalmers confined his talents to these areas alone. Chalmers was ambushed, killed and reportedly eaten at Dopima on Goaribari Island in the Gulf of Papua on 7th April 1901.

supplies that imposed such telling restrictions on Australian and Japanese military operations.

Three years were to pass before the next expedition of any serious intent was to set out from Moresby Harbour. This one was unique because it was the first to be organised outside New Guinea. It also differed from other ventures in that it appeared to be organised solely to obtain publicity for its backer. An Australian newspaper, the Melbourne *Argus*, sponsored it and it was an attempt to cross the island. The *Argus* expedition left the Moresby Harbour mission settlement on 14th July 1883. The expedition's destination was Dyke Acland Bay on the north coast, about 50 kilometres south-east of today's Buna township. The leader of the group was William Edington Armit, formerly an officer of the Queensland Native Police. Armit's companions were Robert Hunter, Loftus Irving and George Belford.

Hombrom Bluff with the Laloki River in the foreground.

William Lawes was the first European to cross the Laloki and the first to ascend Hombrom Bluff in 1875.

Author.

In the first two weeks, Armit closely followed the Laloki River upstream and by the 28th July had reached a position a little further inland of Sogeri village. From this point, he swung to the north, striking inland to eventually come upon the Goldie River. Here, after the death of one of his party from snake bite, Armit abandoned the attempt to cross the mountains and spent the next four weeks exploring the northern and western areas of the Goldie River basin. The party returned to Moresby Harbour on 3rd September 1883. Although Armit's original aim was not achieved, and he made no advance on distance inland, his venture was later considered by MacGregor to be 'of special value', since Armit mapped a good deal of the course of the upper Laloki for the first time.

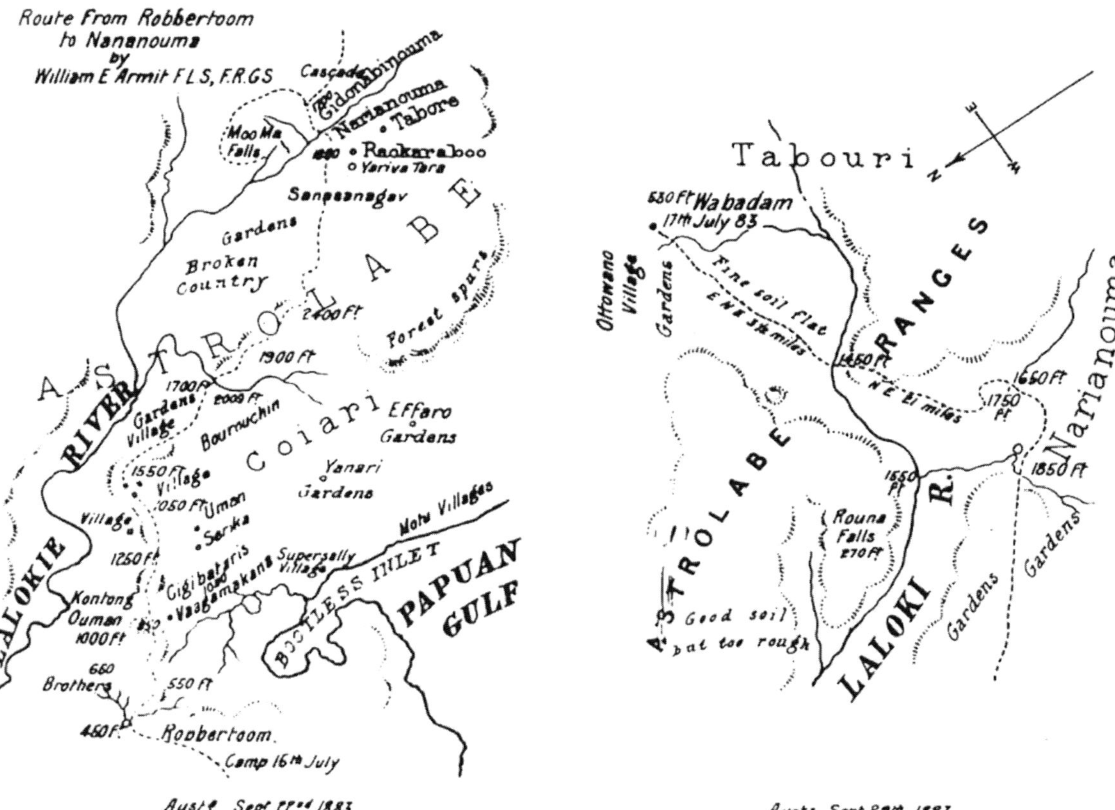

Two of the first maps of the upper Laloki River system prepared by William Armit, following his *Argus* expedition of 1883.

Ela Beach Public Library, Port Moresby (New Guinea Collection).

Not to be outdone, another Melbourne newspaper, the *Age*, had sent their own expedition to New Guinea, also with the intention of crossing to Dyke Acland Bay. This expedition was certainly the best appointed ever seen in the country, much planning and money having been expended to secure the latest in equipment and accoutrements. The expedition's stores, which included among other things, 180 kilograms of salt, soldering irons and 37 dozen plates, weighed over four tonnes. The party's leader was George Ernest Morrison, a twenty-two year old Australian adventurer and medical student who had failed his university studies. After two false starts, he and his group left

William Armit, leader of the 1883 *Argus*-sponsored attempt to cross New Guinea. Armit's expedition got no further than the Sogeri Plateau.

Armit later joined the colonial government of British New Guinea and was Resident Magistrate of the Northern Division when he died of malaria, aged 52, at Tamata Station on 3rd January 1901.

Ela Beach Public Library, Port Moresby (New Guinea Collection).

the coast on 24th July 1883, 10 days after Armit. Morrison elected to follow the course of the Goldie River upstream and then possibly branch off to the north or north-east. He reached a point somewhere near the village of Ginianumu, in the same area where it seems likely Chalmers had peacefully entered in 1879. Unlike the missionary however, Morrison encountered an openly hostile reception. This culminated in his being ambushed by a large party of natives.

Sir William MacGregor, who did much research into the early days of New Guinea, found it was 'not quite clear' why there was such a radical change in the natives' behaviour. However, the late Cyril Pearl, in his biography of Morrison, provides plenty of examples of Morrison's brutish and uncaring attitude towards the local inhabitants. Morrison is reputed to have shot a native thief. Whatever the actual trigger may have been, the outcome was Morrison and his men were attacked and compelled to retreat, he himself suffering wounds to the face and body. In their hasty departure, the expedition members found it necessary to discard the bulk of their fine provisions and superior kit and it was a dispirited rabble that reached the safety of the white settlement on the coast on 15th October.

For Morrison, the expedition was a personal disaster. He was so dejected by the whole affair he destroyed all his records of the venture. Vowing to never mention it again, he packed in haste and left the country at the end of October 1883. Morrison, who resumed his medical studies to gain degrees in Medicine and Surgery from Edinburgh University, Scotland, was later to achieve considerable fame in China as 'Chinese' Morrison of Peking.

It was unfortunate the attention given to the outfitting of the party was not extended to the selection of the leader, for it was the inexperience and behaviour of Morrison which caused the expedition's failure. Morrison had a deserved reputation in Australia, having travelled solo 2,500 kilometres down the Murray River in a canoe, and having walked alone some 3,300 kilometres from Normanton in the Gulf of Carpentaria to Geelong in Victoria. It seems these admirable feats (The *Times* of London observed about the latter venture, it was 'one of the most remarkable of pedestrian achievements'), were considered sufficient qualification to obtain sponsorship and to lead an expedition across New Guinea. It was not Morrison's lack of success that was to matter in the end but rather, the consequences of his clash with the natives. The incident was of particular concern to James Chalmers. 'His chief concern', recorded Cuthbert Lennox, 'arose from reports of hostility on the parts of natives in which he had established friendly relations with the people'.

Accordingly, on 4th December Chalmers went inland himself, returning a week later. He was unable to contact the group which had attacked Morrison, the best he could do being to leave a message. Chalmers was able though to ascertain 'certain signs, recognised by most travellers, had been given by the villagers, but Morrison had not understood them, and had stumbled on to his fate'. Though he had to leave it at that, Chalmers was far from happy and the wide-ranging consequences following Morrison's expedition soon after, and later, justified his concern. Morrison's venture, in fact, virtually destroyed in that area all the good relations which had been carefully nurtured in the previous nine years by the missionaries and miners.

George Ernest Morrison at the age of 19. At 21, Morrison was the leader of the disastrous *Age* expedition of 1883, the consequences of which affected exploration in New Guinea for over 20 years.

Morrison left New Guinea in October 1883 and in 1897 went to China reporting for the London *Times* where he was later to achieve fame as 'Chinese' Morrison of Peking. Morrison died in England in May 1920.

PNG National Library.

Official condemnation was quick to surface. In November 1883, the month before Chalmers had gone inland in his attempt to settle the peace, Hugh Hastings Romilly, who was then a Deputy Special Commissioner for the Western Pacific, but was later to hold goverment office in New Guinea, had reported his view of both Armit's and Morrison's expeditions:

> The two so-called exploring expeditions have done no good. One of them has unfortunately done much harm ... . These private expeditions, led by men of no experience, will do much harm if any more should be organised.

On top of the debacle, several other events were to take place which would eventually force the British Government to take an active interest in the country's status. The publicity from the *Age* and *Argus* newspapers kept popular attention focussed on the country. Previously, the legality of the pre-emptive attempt by Queensland police magistrate Henry Chester to annexe south-east New Guinea for Queensland in April 1883 had been denied by the British Government, which at the time did not have any intention of taking over the country. Chester's move though was consistent with the views of, and was later supported by, all

Australian colonies as a means of confirming a British presence in an area where other European countries were showing increasing interest, a fact which the British seemed strangely reluctant to accept.

In addition to the problems Morrison had generated was the uproar surrounding the attempted purchase in July 1883 (the same month of the Morrison furore) of 12,000 acres (about 4856 hectares) of native land to the north-west of Port Moresby for a total of about £190 (less than 8 cents a hectare). The purchaser was John Cameron, a Sydney businessman. Cameron's colleague in effecting the deal was Andrew Goldie. Though Lawes and Chalmers were either involved in the negotiating process preceding the sale, or at least seemed to indicate their condonation of the sale by their non-interference, the missionaries later publicly attacked Cameron for taking unfair advantage of the natives. But there is a suggestion it could have been the other way around. William Armit, who remained in the country after returning from his Sogeri expedition, and who investigated the event for the *Argus*, found:

> that the white men were deceived I have no doubt whatever. Neither of them was ever there before, and knew nothing of the dialect, and only one of them knew Motu, and that very, very little.

Yet, for those pushing for a government presence in the country, the situation demonstrated perfectly the need for government protection of the natives—the political opportunity was heaven-sent—and Lawes, Chalmers and Armit, each to their own ends, lobbied the Colonial Secretary in Brisbane for action to be taken. In doing so, they simply omitted to give equal emphasis to the fact it was Cameron who had been tricked. In a letter to the Queensland Premier about the land deal, Armit wrote, in reference to Chester's annexation of New Guinea, and in apparent contradiction of his *Argus* article, that

> there is great ferment among the natives, who never knew that the trade [the transaction] was for land. Your action in annexing has drawn the attention of the whole world to New Guinea, and England cannot hold aloof now, but must protect the natives from designing whites. ... All dealings between individuals and natives should be strictly prohibited, and some officer should be sent over, pending the decision of the Imperial Government. If something is

> not done at once, I foresee grave complications, whereas peace and friendly relations can be easily maintained by prompt and energetic action.

Though the transaction between Cameron and the natives was later reversed, the point had been made and the wider issues highlighted by the attempted sale had been successfully placed on Colonial Office desks. So by late 1883, with British western Pacific interests being crowded by the Germans in northern New Guinea and by the French in New Caledonia, (and with the Dutch in eastern New Guinea, though they were not considered a threat to Australian interests), with continuing pressure by the Australian colonies and New Zealand for annexation of south-eastern New Guinea, and with local Port Moresby events subtly giving rise to questions of duty and responsibility, the Colonial Office in far-away London finally came round. Though it was to be another eight months before the matter went through the British Parliament, the decision was taken to annexe the south-east coast of New Guinea. This resulted in Commodore James Erskine formally taking possession of what became the Protectorate of British New Guinea on 6th November 1884. Sir Peter Henry Scratchley, a major-general of the Royal Engineers, was appointed the first Special Commissioner and arrived in New Guinea on 28th August 1885 to commence his governorship.

Scratchley had been briefed on the events of two years earlier and the first thing he did on arrival was to put into practice the sentiments expressed in Romilly's report. The effect was an immediate official curb on exploration although as Scratchley's biographer C. Kinlocke Cooke (later Sir Clement) was careful to point out, 'it was a prominent feature in his policy to encourage exploration when conducted upon a proper footing and under recognised leaders'. A conservative and methodical man, Scratchley was appalled by the debacle of the Morrison expedition. He was determined to preserve any positive gains, such as those made by the London Missionary Society, so

> rejected every application for a permit to explore, where he was of the opinion that the attempt would not only result in ruin to the applicant, but might cause a breach in relations with the natives, which it would possibly take years to heal.

This portion of an 1887 map of New Guinea produced by the Royal Geographical Society indicates how little of the interior of the country was known up to that time.

Explorers attempting to cross the island were entering literally uncharted territory, particularly if relying on charts like this since they recorded some geographical distortions. For example, Sogeri ('Sugairi') is placed almost on the slopes of Mount Obree and the Goldie River lies to the *south* of Mount Mumkainala (shown as 'Munikahila'). The stream indicated by 'Goldie R.' on this map is actually Ua-Ule Creek, a tributary of the Goldie.

Some features are described by names that are no longer in use. The Vanapa River is shown as the Edith River, the Laloki River as the Usbourne River, and Mount Victoria as Mount Owen Stanley.

The words written in capital letters in various places indicate language groups.

Ela Beach Public Library, Port Moresby (New Guinea Collection).

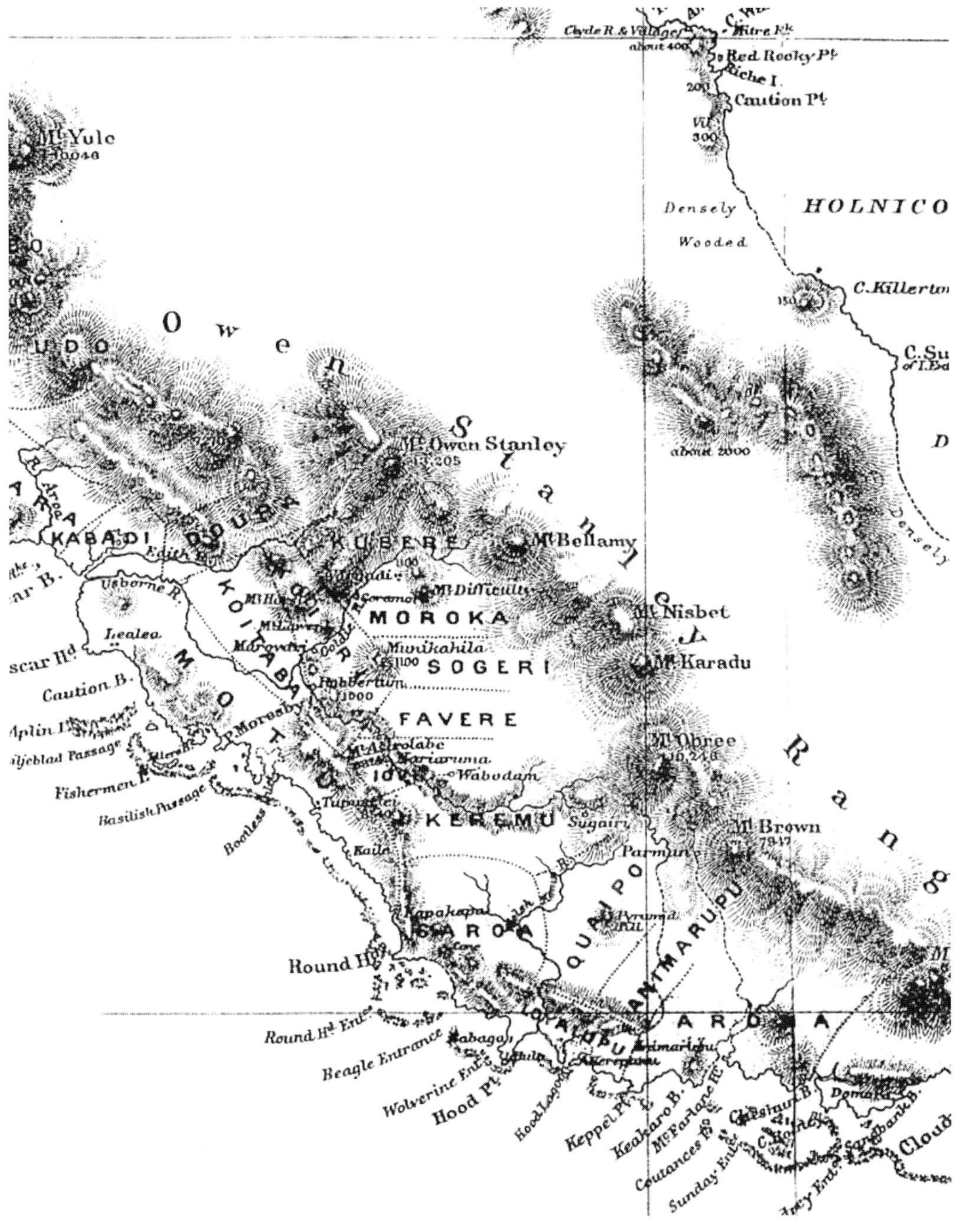
Red Rocky Pt
Caution Pt
Densely Wooded
HOLNICO
C. Killerton
Mt Yule
Owen Stanley Range
Mt Owen Stanley
13,205
about 2000
KABADI
KUBERE
Mt Bellamy
Usborne R.
Lealea
Mt Difficulty
MOROKA
Mt Nisbet
KOITAPU
MOTU
SOGERI
Mt Karadu
Caution B.
FAVERE
P. Moresby
Mt Astrolabe
Mt Obree
10,246
Wabodam
Fishermen I.
Basilisk Passage
KEREMU
Sugairi
Mt Brown
7947
Parmuri
QUAIPO
SAROA
Kapakapa
Round Hd
MARUPU
AROMA
Round Hd Ente
Beagle Entrance
Kabagai
Wolverine Ente
Hood Pt
Hood Lagoon
Keppel Pt
Kealraro B.
McFarlane Hr
Coutances Pt
Sunday Ente
Chestnut B.
Domara
Cloudy

(Interestingly, like Ingham, and despite being officially appointed, it does not seem as if Scratchley really had the authority to make such decisions or enforce such actions. It appears too this was recognised before Scratchley even got to New Guinea. While in Australia prior to taking up office, he had sought clarification of the extent of his powers. A memorandum of 15th May 1885 from the Colonial Secretary's Office in Brisbane, signed by the Queensland Premier Samuel Walker Griffith, noted Scratchley was not 'possessed of legal jurisdiction unless Her Majesty [Queen Victoria] should issue some further Order in Council ... No such Order in Council has been issued'. Griffith's view was Scratchley 'has no power to make any regulations having the force of law ... or otherwise to exercise any legislative or judicial functions in the Protectorate').

One person who who Scratchley received favourably was Dr Henry Ogg Forbes, a scientist who had been given passage from Brisbane on the *Governor Blackhall*, the vessel which had delivered Scratchley to New Guinea. He was one of the first white men to be authorised to take up land in the country and did so near Sogeri Village, on the Sogeri Plateau, where he established his field station. He was soon absorbed in his specialist pursuits but as MacGregor later found, 'though he added considerably to our knowledge of the natural history of this region, he did not visit any new area of the country or make any addition to the already known geography of the place'. Scratchley was impressed with what Forbes had achieved and in December 1884 had obtained directions from the Colonial Office to the effect he should 'give all assistance in his powers [to Forbes] and if [the] Australian Gov[ernmen]t approve of his making a pecuniary grant he is at liberty to do so'. He had mentioned the possibility of government assistance to Forbes but he was never able to follow through with the offer. Some weeks after visiting Forbes at Sogeri in November 1885, while at Samarai (then Dinner) Island, he contracted a severe bout of malaria. A hurried voyage to Townsville was made, but Scratchley died on board on 2nd December 1885, shortly before the vessel reached port.

The Special Commissioner's death did not mean the end of the controlled exploration policy, for the two succeeding administrators elected to continue with it. The day after Scratchley's death saw the appointment of Romilly as the Acting Special Commissioner. It was unfortunate for Romilly, who had been Scratchley's senior deputy, that he spent most of the next three months in Queensland suffering from malaria, leaving Anthony Musgrave, the resident Deputy Special Commissioner, in charge of the country. Romilly therefore had little chance of securing permanent placement in the position, but Musgrave, who coveted the appointment, was also to miss out. On 27th February 1886, the Honourable John Douglas, Premier of Queensland from March 1877 to January 1879, also a Deputy Special Commissioner for the Protectorate, but who had been stationed at Thursday Island as a magistrate and Queensland Government Resident Officer, was appointed to succeed Scratchley. He arrived at Moresby Harbour on the schooner *Governor Cairns* on 28th June 1886 to take up his duties.

Sogeri Village in the mid 1890s, little changed from how Henry Forbes found it in 1885.

University of Papua New Guinea.

An unidentified government official (with sidearm) on horseback at Sogeri Village c. 1902.

It was adjacent to this settlement that Henry Forbes first settled on the Sogeri Plateau. The *sawn* tree stump (at lower left) gives an indication of how European ways gradually pervaded all aspects of traditional village life.

University of Papua New Guinea.

Concurrently with Douglas' arrival was the return to the coast from Sogeri of Henry Forbes. Forbes had reckoned he could reach Mount Victoria by following the Goldie River's course back into the mountains and was determined to lead an expedition to her summit. He was on his way to Australia to seek sponsors for his attempt but Douglas pointed out this would take him into the unsettled area to the north-east of the Moresby Harbour settlement. As passage into this area was still officially prohibited, he would not be able to approve the proposal. Apparently not one to miss an opportunity, especially one of his own making, Douglas hastened to invite the scientist to fill the vacant post of Government Agent at Samarai, an offer Forbes accepted.

Some twelve months were to pass before the next move was made to cross the island. Douglas had little hesitation in approving the proposed expedition as the intended route was to be across the ranges about sixty kilometres to the east of Moresby Harbour, well away from the restricted area to the north-east. George Hunter, brother of Robert and a self-styled 'trader' who acted as Government Agent at Rigo, and Carl H. Hartmann, a botanist from Victoria, had concluded a traverse to the northern coast was possible by following the course of the

Kemp Welch River back into the ranges, across the high ground to the sources of the rivers flowing to the northern coast, and then by following one of these down to the Coral Sea. They departed Hunter's Kemp Welch camp on 1st July 1887 and followed the river 65 kilometres upstream to the Mimani River junction. No map record of this journey appears to be available but it seems from this point, the explorers worked their way onto the slopes of Mount Obree (3,055 metres).

On 6th July 1887 at their journey's end, Hartmann scrawled a draft of a report to the Geographical Society in Sydney on a scrap of paper: 'I have much pleasure in writing [... ?] at the top of the Owen Stanley Ranges July 6/87'. In a formal report written on 17th July after his return to Port Moresby, he stated he and Hunter had 'been right at the top of the main Owen Stanley Range, between Mounts Obree and Brown'. There does not seem to be any documentary evidence Hartmann or Hunter actually claimed more than what was reported—indeed, Hartmann admitted 'we intended to go further; but the excessive rain every evening drove us back'. However, Hartmann's somewhat metaphoric claim of reaching the 'top' was interpreted as his having reached the summit of Mount Obree. This view persisted for over 40 years, with J.N.L. Baker, in his *History of Geographical Discovery and Exploration*, published in 1931, recording 'Hartmann and Hunter reached the summit of the Owen Stanley Range', and with the *Pacific Islands Monthly* of 19 July 1932 running, in similar vein, an article entitled 'How Hartmann climbed Owen Stanley Range in Papua'. (The summit of the Owen Stanleys, in the context of white settlement at the time, was Mount Victoria).

Actually, the extent of Hartmann's travels was challenged only a month later. A scientific expedition had left on 2nd August 1887 to cover the same route he had taken and reported Hartmann and Hunter had not climbed higher than 2300 metres. This second expedition, led by Walter R. Cuthbertson, a surveyor from South Australia* and which included, again,

* A year before his Kemp Welch expedition, Cuthbertson had surveyed and planned the town of Granville. Granville was the original name for Port Moresby.

George Hunter, in turn claimed to have reached the summit of Mount Obree on 30th August 1887 but the validity of this ascent too was later challenged by Sir William MacGregor in 1889.*

As well as the difficulties posed by the weather, Hartmann reported 'the country on the whole of the eastern side [of the Kemp Welch] is more steep and rangy than the southern'. A continuing problem seemed to be the native tribes, Hartmann noting 'a great difficulty is to get through the mountain tribes; very hostile, guarding the mountain range very carefully against intruders ...'. Perhaps for any one of these reasons, nothing ever came of these journeys as a basis for an overland route and there was no official action taken at the time to consolidate the exploration.

George Belford, one of the most experienced New Guinea explorers of the late 1800s and early 1900s.

Belford originally came to New Guinea in 1883 as a member of Armit's *Argus* expedition. Belford accompanied Sir William MacGregor on the first ascent of Mount Victoria in June 1889, and crossed from Buna to Port Moresby along the Kokoda Trail with Royal Commissioners Mackay and Herbert in 1906.

PNG National Library.

Not that it is impossible to cross over to the northern coast here, though it took a quarter of a century to establish such a route. In 1912, a track from Kapa Kapa, just to the west of the mouth of the Kemp Welch, to Jaure on the headwaters of the Kumusi River was recognised. This became known as the Jaure Track (also the Kapa Kapa Track). There is little evidence of regular use of it by white people and the local people supposedly stayed away because of the belief it was, as Hartmann reported, 'the secret Saramogoro, the abode of the departed spirits'. In October 1942, when 250 men of the 2nd Battalion of the United States 126th Infantry Regiment under Captain Alfred Mendendorp crossed the Owen Stanleys by this route during the Allied offensive against the Japanese forces at Buna, there had not been a white person on the Jaure Track since 1917.

By 1887, and though the government ban on white travellers entering the Uberi people's territory was still officially in place, the urgency and reasons behind the original 1883 prohibition had lost much of their impetus. There had been no incidents in four years and a complacent attitude had redeveloped among the whites in Port Moresby. Indeed, one prospector, George

* The persistent misinterpretation of Hartmann's report, which easily could have been corrected by Hartmann at the time had he been able to, is explained in a curious sequel to his expedition. Hartmann had had an obsessive fear of dying in Papua. While he did not die there, he became seriously ill in Port Moresby on his return from Mount Obree and died at the age of 53 only days after his return to Brisbane.

Belford, who had originally come to New Guinea as a member of Armit's 1883 *Argus* expedition, completely ignored the restriction. In mid-1887, Belford travelled to Sogeri, then without disclosing his intentions, set off northwards. No written record of this venture was kept, but MacGregor, from his research, believed Belford was 'the one who seems to have got furthest inland'. MacGregor, who thought well of Belford for his exploratory prowess, estimated a point 'some half-score of miles [16 kilometres] further inland from Ginianumu was attained'. Ginianumu, it will be recalled, was the scene of Morrison's defeat, although Belford went and returned without incident. MacGregor's estimate would put the termination of Belford's journey near the present site of Kagi Village.

Belford's peaceful venture was seen as an encouraging sign the situation had improved. Only a matter of weeks later, in September 1887, Douglas recalled Henry Forbes from Samarai to finally allow him his ambition to lead an expedition to Mount Victoria. Forbes was to be the leader of an official expedition Douglas had planned to ascertain 'if Mt. Owen Stanley [Mount Victoria] could be ascended from the head of the Goldie'. Belford's earlier conduct seems to have been condoned as he was appointed to accompany Forbes, as was Dennis Gleeson, another experienced New Guinea explorer. Forbes, as we have seen, had spent several months exploring the Sogeri district and had been the Government Agent at Samarai for over a year, acquiring much practical knowledge of Papuan bushcraft. MacGregor later formed the opinion 'this expedition was ... as rich in experience as the Morrison expedition had been the reverse'.

Forbes' party left Port Moresby on 1st October 1887. After crossing the Laloki River, they worked their way up the southern bank of the Goldie River to a point about 32 kilometres from the coast where they established their base camp. Leaving the bulk of their supplies here in charge of two of their men, Forbes, Belford and Gleeson travelled overland to Ginianumu where they attempted to obtain carriers for the next stage of the journey. However, they found the villagers sullen and unwilling to help. Meanwhile, their base camp had been attacked. Fearing for their lives, the two men left in charge fled back to Port Moresby, leaving all the expedition's supplies to be ransacked.

The expedition of Henry Ogg Forbes at Hanuabada Village (Moresby Harbour) in October 1887.

Forbes, at far right leaning on the tripod, left New Guinea in 1890 to take up a position as director of a New Zealand museum. Next to Forbes in the light coloured clothes is William Lawes and next to Lawes in the dark coloured clothes is Anthony Musgrave. (Lawes and Musgrave were not members of Forbes' expedition).

The man to the left of Musgrave in the dark jacket and light coloured trousers with the rifle is Dennis Gleeson. Gleeson originally came to New Guinea during the 1878 Laloki River gold rush and later became the Government Gaoler. Gleeson committed suicide in Port Moresby on 26th July 1893.

Department of the Prime Minister, Port Moresby (A/H/110).

Forbes and his companions were faring no better. Appreciating their situation, they had tried to withdraw quietly, but ended up being chased from the area. They had to leave most of their equipment as a distraction for their pursuers, being fortunate to reach the coast uninjured.

Sir William MacGregor wrote (in 1898)

> it was impossible that the expedition of Mr. Morrison should greatly increase the risk to which Dr. Forbes' party was exposed; but this risk was very greatly increased for future travellers by the expedition of Dr. Forbes, as it not only confirmed the hostility of the Ebe or Eburi confederation [Uberi people], but animated the more powerful and more warlike Baura [the Nauro people, who lived further inland] with analogous feelings. That part of the country has consequently been regarded as unsafe, but until lately* there was nothing to tempt Europeans to enter it, and it was therefore left alone.

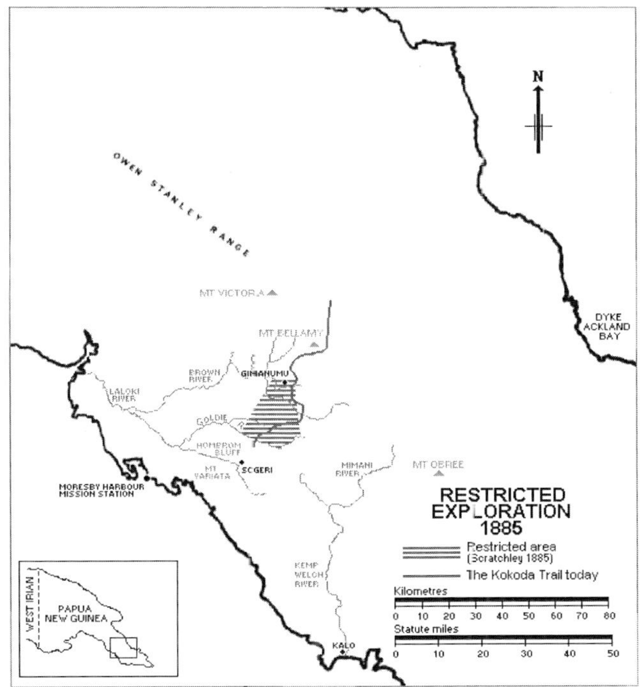

Restricted exploration area imposed by Scratchley in 1885.
Author.

* MacGregor is referring here to his time of writing, 1898, which is eleven years after Forbes' expedition.

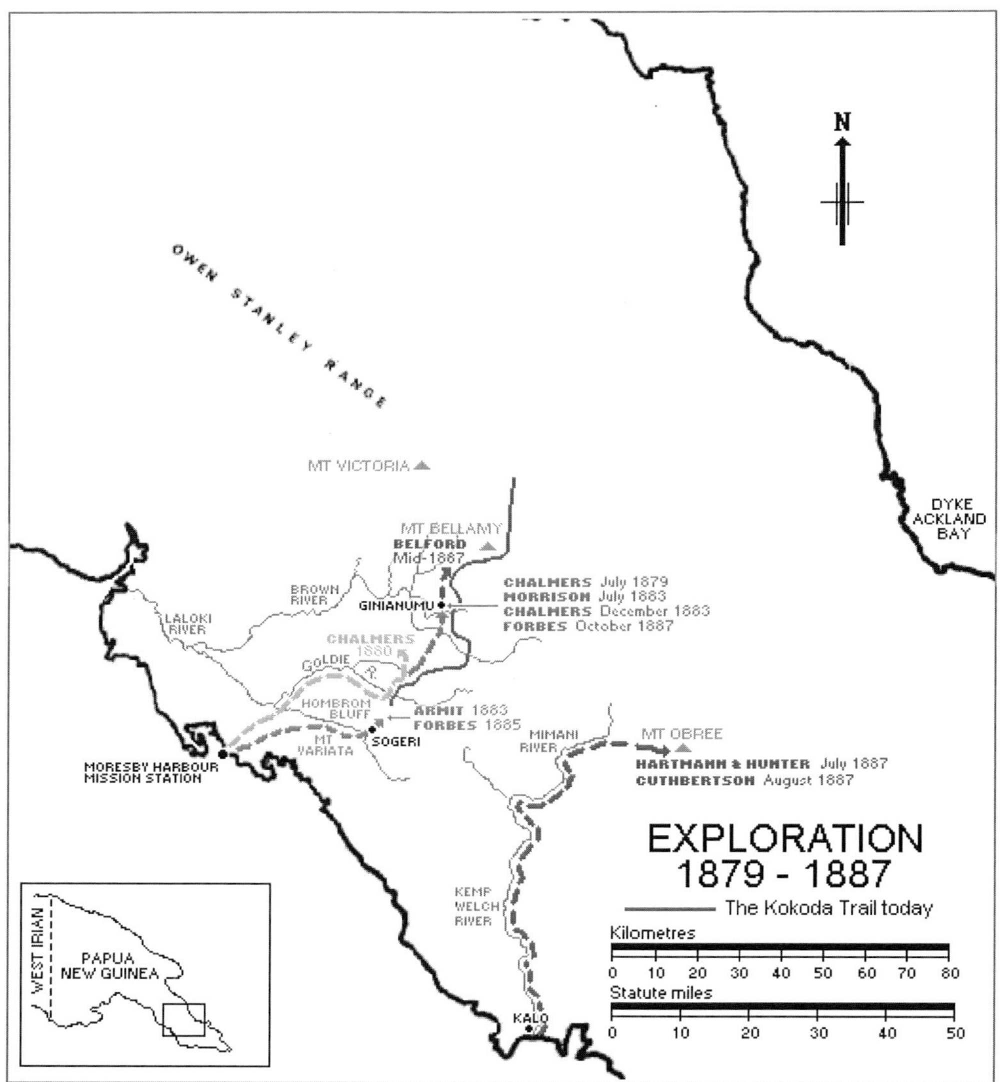

Summary of exploration 1879–1887. *Author.*

3

Mount Victoria and the Mambare (1888–1896)

Despite Commodore Erskine's declaration of a Protectorate in 1884, it had taken place only after an unenthusiastic British Government had been pressured by the Australian colonies. By early 1888 however, interest in New Guinea had heightened considerably. This resulted in a decision to have New Guinea declared a Crown Colony (until this time it had been a 'Protectorate'), and Douglas was replaced as governor. The man selected for the new position of Administrator was Sir William MacGregor.* He arrived on *HMS Opal* on 4th September 1888, and his first duty on New Guinea soil was to conduct the formal ceremony elevating the status of the country to one of Queen Victoria's Dominions. The new Colony was to be known as British New Guinea.

Considerable credit is due to MacGregor for much of the significant early exploration of British New Guinea, particularly that which led to the establishment of the overland route to the northern coast. Time after time, his resourcefulness, determination and persistence rewarded him with success where others had failed. MacGregor was a fascinating and

---

* The official title held by Scratchley and Douglas was Special Commissioner. MacGregor's initial title was Administrator but was altered in 1895 to Lieutenant-Governor.

complex person and was, in all respects, a self-made man. He was born on 20th October 1846 at Hillockhead, Towie Parish, Scotland, the second of nine children of a poor crofter. The Scottish government, progressive for the times, felt strongly its obligations to provide a sound education to all who desired it and MacGregor, who was a competent student, succeeded in gaining scholarships allowing him to complete his education. Had it not been for the ready availability of schooling and his own capacity for hard work, it is doubtful whether he would have risen above the station of his birth, for his family had no money and no influence.

Sir William MacGregor, Lieutenant-Governor of British New Guinea from 1888 to 1898.

After leaving New Guinea, MacGregor gained a series of vice-regal appointments—Governor of Lagos (1899–1904), Governor of Newfoundland (1904–1909) and Governor of Queensland (1909–1914)—but he always yearned to return to New Guinea. He was a strong contender for appointment to Papua following the 1906 Royal Commission, being personally favoured by Alfred Deakin, the Australian Prime Minister. However, the strong public sentiment that the governor of the new Australian Territory of Papua should be an Australian prevailed and Hubert Murray was appointed instead.

MacGregor died in Aberdeen, Scotland on 3rd July 1919.

State Library of Queensland.

MacGregor graduated as a doctor from Aberdeen University in 1872 and in the next 16 years served in various medical posts in Scotland, Seychelles Islands, Mauritius, and Fiji. In Fiji, where he held the offices of Chief Medical Officer and Health Officer, his capability as an administrator became apparent and in June 1887 was offered the appointment in New Guinea. While there was some opposition to his being chosen, the news was generally received with approval in government circles. A British army officer, Major (later Major-General) B.F.S. Baden-Powell,* who visited New Guinea in 1889, described the Administrator as 'strong, hardy and active', and thought it was 'an instance of the right man in the right place'.

Within eight months of his arrival, MacGregor had mounted an expedition and set of inland in an attempt to scale Mount Victoria. This provoked considerable agitation among those who had opposed MacGregor's appointment, the main contention being MacGregor was more interested in adventurous expeditions than in governing the country. Strictly speaking, it was not so much MacGregor's motives that were under attack, but his timing of the venture. At this time (April 1889), MacGregor's presence at other places in New Guinea would have been desirable, at Milne Bay, Samarai and nearby islands for example, where frequent clashes between the local natives and white miners were taking place. There was some truth in

* This was Fletcher Baden-Powell, younger brother of Robert Baden-Powell of the Scouting Movement. Fletcher Baden-Powell was private secretary to General Sir Henry Norman, Governor of Queensland, at the time of his visit to New Guinea.

these allegations which MacGregor admits, but it was also, in a classic piece of lateral thinking, MacGregor's way of alleviating another pressing government problem. This was the Uberi people's hostility to white intrusion into their territory. In 1912, 23 years after the event, he wrote in the 'Introduction' to Sir Hubert Murray's *Papua, or British New Guinea*,

> Exploration as apart from administration was indulged in only once. It has been shown by experience that exploring expeditions, sent from Australia or elsewhere, too frequently ended in collision with the natives, and it was decided that a Government expedition should proceed to the top of Mount Victoria, which it was thought would put a stop to others from outside. This had the desired result. All other explorations were on an administrative basis ...*

Unlike earlier attempts, MacGregor's expedition to Mount Victoria completely avoided the Uberi area, leaving Port Moresby on 20th April 1889 by boat to travel 48 kilometres north-west along the coast to enter Galley Reach in Redscar Bay. Galley Reach is the outlet for several streams including the Laloki (into which flows the Brown and Goldie Rivers) and the Vanapa (then Edith) River. (According to Octavius Stone, the first white man to explore Galley Reach was a Swede called Thorngren, who in 1875 travelled up the Laloki to as far as the Brown River junction). Within a week, a base camp had been established 65 kilometres up the Vanapa, and on the 16th May, after having determined his line of march, MacGregor led his party of 42 persons, among whom was George Belford, further inland. The many streams and water-courses and the sodden terrain made travel tedious but there were no difficulties at all from that area's native inhabitants. In fact, it was not until they were camped at 1,500 metres on a ridge of Mount Musgrave the first contact was made. A submission to the Royal Geographical Society reported:

---

* In MacGregor's defence, he had been in New Guinea only two weeks when he was forced to choose between what he would have liked to have done—explore the interior—and what he saw as his duty—the need to go to the eastern islands. In the minutes of the Executive Council meeting of 19th September 1888, the clerk Basil H. Thomas recorded that 'the Administrator intimated ... that it was his intention to have visited the interior but felt it his duty under the circumstances to proceed to Sudest Island'.

> The expedition was visited by a number of these mountain people during its stay in the locality, and the relations throughout were of the most friendly character, a circumstance which rendered the operations of the expedition agreeable, and the services of the natives of great value in the supply of food.

From Mount Musgrave, MacGregor sought a connecting ridge but was obliged to descend the northern slopes of Mount Musgrave and cross over at a lower level. A new camp was established at 1,300 metres but most of the party were in such poor physical condition due to the exhausting pace MacGregor had maintained, he was obliged to leave most of them here, continuing on with only Belford, two Polynesians and six natives from Port Moresby. They crossed the Vanapa and worked round to the base of Mount Knutsford. Mount Victoria was now less than five kilometres away, yet MacGregor could not find an accessible route before him. Accordingly, he opted to re-cross the Vanapa and to ascend Mount Knutsford to get onto the spur connecting with Mount Victoria.

On 6th June, after having further reduced his party by four men, and after an exhausting climb MacGregor attained the summit of Mount Knutsford. From here, he and his men were

The bridge across the Vanapa River constructed of bush materials used by MacGregor's Mount Victoria expedition to make the first European crossing of the stream in May 1889.

This illustration is taken from the official report..

able to traverse Winter Height, then onto Mount Douglas (where they picked wild strawberries), then to Mount Victoria proper. At 11am on the 11th June 1889, MacGregor reached the south-east peak, the actual 4,072 metre summit of Mount Victoria. This is one of five peaks, all over 3,660 metres, which form the apex of the mountain. Belford climbed the north-east peak where he left a powder flask containing a record of the ascent, and a statement declaring MacGregor had given to the mountain, which previously had been called Mount Owen Stanley, the name of Mount Victoria. On 13th June, they departed the mountain, and after collecting the rest of the expedition, reached the coast on 25th June.*

MacGregor was to have much to occupy his attention on his return from the interior, particularly with the activities of gold miners in the colony's far eastern parts. Prospecting there had had its origins about six months before his arrival in New Guinea, in April 1888, and his predecessor, Douglas, had been directly involved. Douglas had been at Thursday Island in Queensland when a pearl-shell diver called David Lindsay White had sought his assistance. White informed the Special Commissioner he had discovered 'some gold-bearing reefs on Joannet'. (Joannet, also Johannet or Janet, known today as Misima Island, is in the Louisiade Archipelago, about 225 kilometres east of Samarai). He admitted he knew next to nothing about mining as he had had no prospecting experience, but he felt sure there was much gold to be won and asked to have the island declared a protected area. Douglas could not accommodate this request, but he actively encouraged White to carry on with his venture. With this official sanction, White and seven more experienced prospectors left Cooktown in North Queensland on 23rd May in the cutter *Juanita* bound for the island.

Following in their wake was another group of 16 miners, under Harry ('German Harry') Christensen. White's group arrived on the 10th June 1888 and they, along with Christensen's men, quickly established only one of White's claims was

* The summit of Mount Victoria was not visited again for over 41 years, being next climbed in December 1930 by Patrol Officer S.E. Smith.

true—that he knew nothing of mining—for his reef was 'a "buck" reef (by which is meant a quartz reef not bearing gold), which never had carried gold and never would. In fact there was no trace of gold on the whole island'.

They were to have more success on a nearby island, Tagula (then known as Sud-Est or Sudest), where they obtained over four kilograms in eight weeks. Somewhat naively, they let the master of the *Griffen*, Christensen's schooner, return to Cooktown and speak of the finds on the island. The news spread rapidly and precipitated a rush to the area. Tagula and nearby islands were well picked over but, though some reasonable finds were made, there was not enough to satisfy all. Many of the miners came ill-prepared in their hurry, lacking suitable equipment, clothing, food and medical supplies, and there were many deaths from tropical diseases. Like the Laloki River rush of 1878, the majority's enthusiasm soon faded and from a peak of 400 in early 1889, numbers fell sharply, to 150 in 1890, and to 70 a year later.

Some prospectors returned to Australia, but many joined general drift towards the New Guinea mainland. Because of its proximity, the Milne Bay area received most of the initial attention. The native inhabitants there were more aggressive than those on the islands, and there were clashes resulting in deaths on both sides. This did not deter the increasing numbers who were being drawn there as the early good finds had been well publicised. This influx resulted in the population of Samarai, the principal town of the area, swelling to a total larger than Port Moresby, the seat of government.

The district could not contain them all and further exploration for gold spread along both the southern and lesser-known northern coasts. MacGregor had first inspected these shores as far as Mitre Rock in August 1890. (Mitre Rock was a nine metre high rock offshore from Cape Ward Hunt. Known locally as Duie, it was then regarded as indicating the border between the New Guinea territories of Great Britain and Germany). A few kilometres north-west of the Rock was Mambare (also variously called Clyde, Duvira or Traitors') Bay, the outlet of the Mambare (then Clyde) River. A German scientist, Dr Otto Finsch, made the first recorded discovery of this stream in April 1885 but the water level was low at the time and he explored only its mouth. It was left to Sir William MacGregor to take the first close look at the river proper and on a second expedition into the area in March 1894, he travelled about 83 kilometres upstream before shallow rapids stopped him. Nearby, he found 'traces of gold', a fact he mentioned in the Colony's Annual Report of 1893/94.

George Clarke, an experienced miner from the Charters Towers field in Queensland, noted this report with interest when it was released in Australia . Clarke organised a party of twenty miners and arrived in New Guinea on 10th April 1895. While en route through Samarai, his group was reduced to six men. The smaller size of the party was to prove fateful for Clarke, and the basis of an unsettled start to white settlement on the north coast. Clarke and his men left Samarai on 20th June 1895 in the schooner *Seagull*. They first tried Bartle Bay, on the north coast about 32 kilometres north-west of the head of Milne Bay but finding the prospects poor, journeyed further up the coast to the Mambare. The party had no trouble making friends with the occupants of Clyde village at the mouth of the Mambare, and purchased canoes from them to help in transporting their supplies upriver. The party also had a whaleboat from the *Seagull* and had no difficulty in navigating the stream until they came upon a rapid reach, about 56 kilometres from the coast. To lighten the whaleboat, all the white men save Clarke went ashore and the local Binandere natives were recruited to assist in hauling the boat through the rapids by means of a long rope.

Halfway through the rapids, the natives either cut or let go of the rope, allowing the whaleboat to be swept quickly downstream. It is not known if this was part of a plan but several canoes containing armed warriors were downriver. As the whaleboat closed on them, they leaped aboard and began taking the supplies. Clarke either fell or jumped overboard and was killed in the water by either a spear or club. There was little the other white men could do since their rifles were on the boat, but eventually succeeded in driving off the attackers with revolver fire. But it was too late for Clarke, whose body had sunk. The five white men recovered the boat, and quickly left for the coast.

Before they reached the river's mouth, they met a small cutter, the *Mayflower*, proceeding upriver. On board was a party of seven prospectors led by William Simpson. The two parties joined forces and returned upriver where they made a futile search for Clarke's body. In revenge for Clarke's death, they torched all the village houses they could find and destroyed all the native property they came upon. They travelled a further 24 kilometres inland where the increasing number of rapid reaches made further boat travel impossible. This was about 15 kilometres further than the point reached by MacGregor. Here, on the eastern bank, about three kilometres upstream of the Mambare's junction with what is now known as Green Creek, they constructed a strong log stockade and named it 'Clarke's Fort', after their late colleague. Leaving this base in the care of two of their number, Clunas and Elliot, the remainder went still further inland. The country was so rough it took them three days to travel eight kilometres but they found indications of gold everywhere. They returned to Clarke's Fort to collect Clunas and Elliot, and then to the *Mayflower* on the coast. As soon as they could replenish their supplies, it was intended to re-enter the area and commence mining in earnest.

When news of the circumstances of Clarke's death, and the aftermath, reached MacGregor, he organised a well-armed party of twenty-three men under his own leadership to go to the Mambare. On arrival in the Government steamer *Merrie England*, he went inland to determine for himself the attitude of the people and the situation of the white miners. He managed to get past the earlier rapids and got to as far as Clarke's Fort by boat. From here, MacGregor scouted about in all directions but saw no natives. They had literally taken to the hills. However, while camped at the Fort, he was attacked by a large force. In the ensuing melee, six of the attackers were killed and six taken prisoner. Of this, MacGregor's official report boldly claimed 'the natives were soon vanquished in a thorough and complete manner'.

However, MacGregor was concerned at the miners' reckless behaviour. Another instance of the Morrison episode on the south coast was the last thing he wanted. The unrest in the region was not a good start to white settlement there, particularly in view of his government's inability, by virtue of distance to act quickly from Port Moresby if similar incidents should happen again. The problem was the miners in this area preceded the Government or missions. (The Anglican Church established the first mission station on the Mambare in October 1898). The miners, MacGregor realised, were not much concerned with long-range government policy—their sole aim was the rapid accumulation of their fortunes and the securing of their personal survival. (As with the miners on the Laloki in 1878 however, the prospectors on the northern goldfields were to demonstrate over the next 20 years a consistently responsible attitude in their dealings with the local inhabitants). These objectives, even in a peaceful country, were likely to lead to trouble. In British New Guinea, with effectively no restrictions in place, and with attacks by aggressive inhabitants providing ample justification for white retaliation, the potential for serious trouble was high. But, in a country governed by an administration with a grossly under-strength establishment, there were advantages in new mining fields opening. Prospectors spread white influence, they generated wealth, they provided work for native indentured labourers, and they spurred the creation of supporting industries. MacGregor could not afford to ignore these benefits.

What was needed was an official presence in the region. To this end, MacGregor established a new Government Station at the junction of the Mambare and Tamata Creek. The officer appointed to man this post was John Green who had previously been employed as a Government Agent at Cloudy Bay on the south coast. Green's staff consisted of 18 members of the Armed Constabulary. Another British New Guinea officer, Charles Arthur Whitmore Monckton, who himself served in this area in later years, thought highly of Green: 'This officer was, for native affairs, absolutely the best man the service of New Guinea ever possessed ... he was absolutely fearless. John Green was ... the most valuable man for a difficult post in the New Guinea service'.

Tamata Station, or Tamata Junction as it was also known, was indeed to prove a difficult post, for the task entrusted to twenty-nine year old Green required much tact and personal courage, and was eventually to cost him his life. The miners welcomed Green's appointment and much of their exploration, though initially for their own ends, assisted the Green in contacting new villages and establishing a tenuous peace. Simpson, Clunas, Elliot, as well as William McLelland and Sam McLaughlin were prominent in entering new country inland of Clarke's Fort, across and along the Cherima River and streams now known as Simpson's Creek and McLaughlin River, all the way to the slopes of Mount Scratchley. Later, they shifted their attentions to the region between the Mambare and the Kumusi River further to the east.

Tamata Creek in 1906.

PNG National Library.

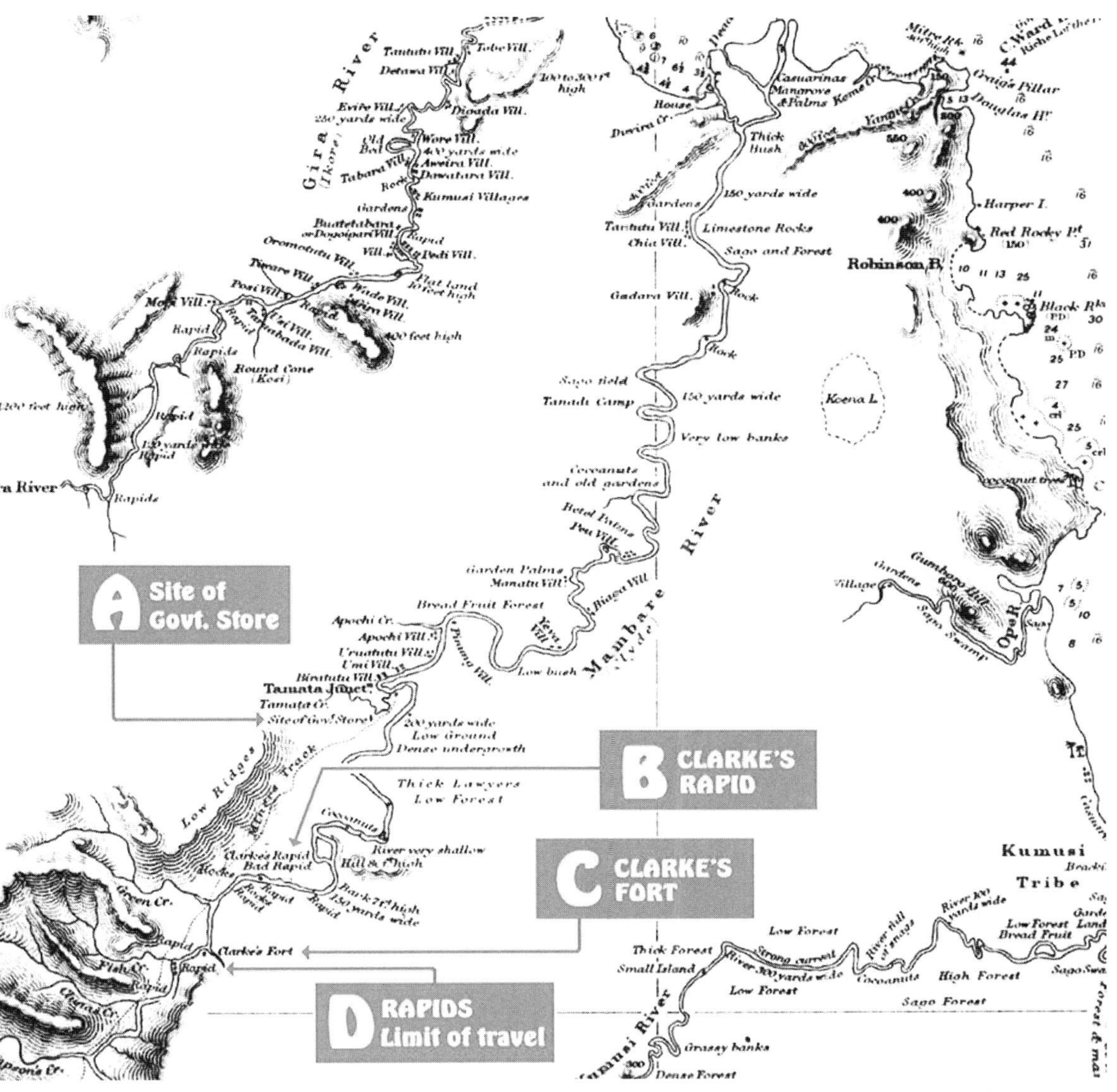

Detail from a British Admiralty chart shows details of white settlement on the Mambare River up to December 1898.

George Clarke was killed at Clarke's Rapid (indicated at B). The rapids just upstream of Clarke's Fort (at C) adjacent to the junction with Fish Creek (indicated at D) was the limit reached in the whaleboat by the original group of miners led by William Simpson in July 1896. John Green and Corporal Sedu were killed at the 'Site of Govt. Store' location adjacent to Tamata Creek (indicated at A) (see Chapter 5).

Author

In March 1896, when news Simpson and his men had obtained 200 ounces of gold in three weeks on McLaughlin Creek was received in Samarai, something of a rush developed and many vessels carrying hopeful souls set out from Samarai. But the country, climate and native inhabitants presented such unforgiving impediments only 30 men were on this new field by November 1896. The unrelenting hardships deterred the majority from staying and at one time there were just as many men going down the Mambare as coming up it. Simpson cut a track from Tamata Station about 16 kilometres inland along the course of the Mambare to establish a stronghold on high ground overlooking the river. This camp became known as Simpson's Store and was used as a base by prospectors working nearby. MacGregor later used this route himself and despite his 'official' view private parties were not to enter unexplored territory, he was impressed enough to record in a formal dispatch 'the cutting of this path is from the point of view of the explorer and the geographer by far the most important work ever performed by any private exploring party in this country ... It is an undertaking that reflects very great honour and credit on Mr Simpson and his companions ...'.

This was the furthest point reached from the northern coast to date, yet this was passed only months later by John Green. In July 1896, Green cut a new track from Simpson's Store inland to Neneba on the slopes of Mount Scratchley. Neneba was 112 kilometres from the mouth of the Mambare. This point put Green only ten kilometres from Winter Height, which had already been reached from the south coast by MacGregor on his expedition to Mount Victoria. The traverse of the New Guinea island had almost been achieved.

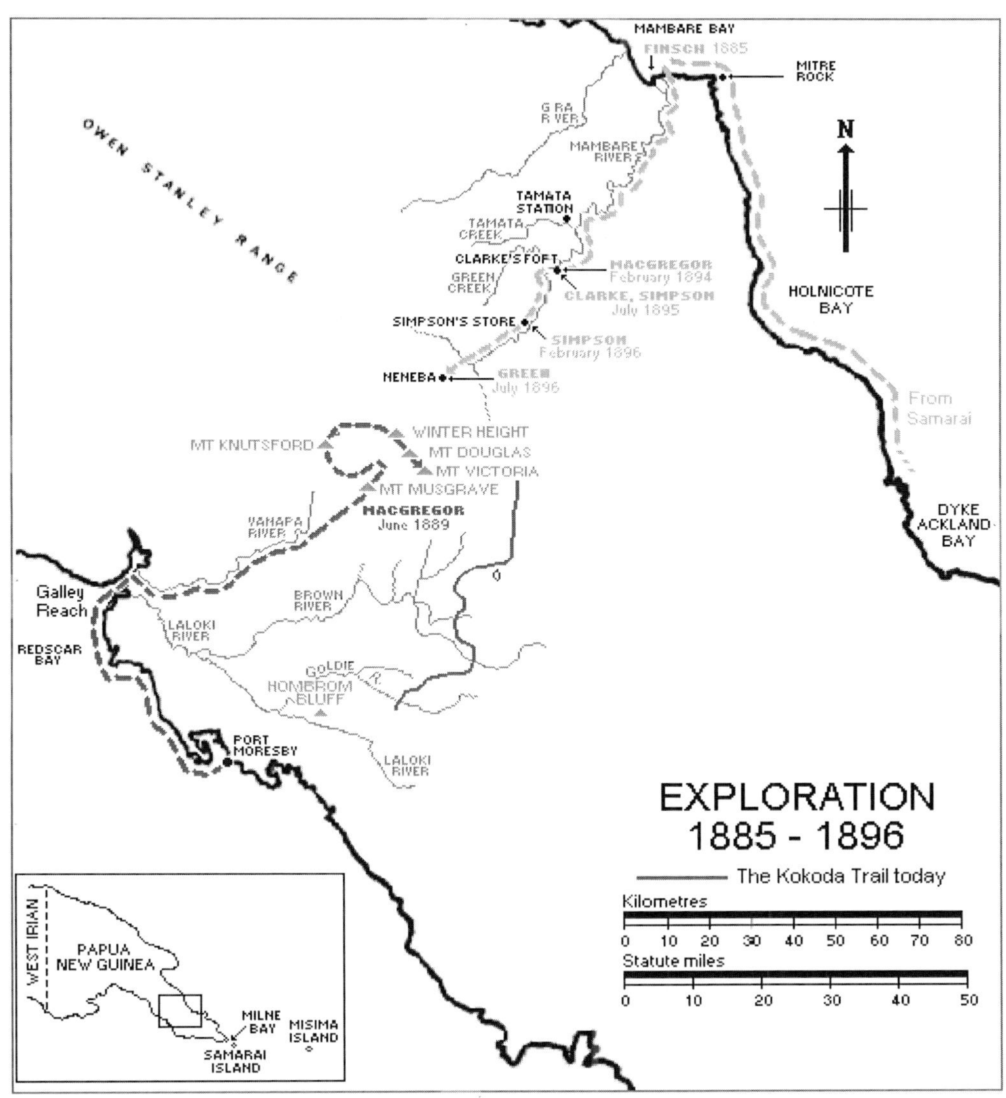

Summary of exploration 1885–1896. *Author.*

Across the New Guinea island (1893–1896)

MacGregor's actions on the Mambare in the first half of the 1890s were motivated in large part by a determination to avoid the type of problems Morrison's expedition had bequeathed to the country in 1883. Yet any influence, persuasion or government edict he could bring to bear upon exploration north-east of Port Moresby had no real meaning to the natives of this region and the difficulties therefore persisted. In fact, they were to get worse before they got better.

Henry Forbes' expedition in 1887 had been the last official attempt to penetrate the area inland from Port Moresby and his assailants, the Uberi people, were of the same group that had attacked and repulsed Morrison four years before that. As MacGregor had feared, these continuing defeats of white explorers, coupled with a rich bounty of discarded expedition supplies, had a stimulating effect on the confidence of the warriors. It led them to the belief their prowess in battle was exceptional and if no white man would come to their villages to fight (because of the government ban), they would go to the white man, or at least to other, friendlier, native tribes associated with the white man. Accordingly, they began to attack their weaker neighbours and 'killed of most of the small villages around'.

In 1891, they mounted a raid down the Goldie and into the Laloki valley where they killed two natives of a peaceful tribe. Two years later, on 27th September 1893, they ventured even further, this time striking at a coastal village of the Baruni people near Port Moresby. In this raid, they massacred thirteen people, including several children. Frank Ernest Lawes,* the Resident Magistrate for the government's Central Division (which included Port Moresby) conducted an investigation into the attack. He reported:

> This forenoon [28th September 1893] I visited the Barune villages and saw the wounded chief Audabi and a woman wounded in the head. Kava village is totally deserted, and the dead bodies, some half-charred by fire, are left in the remaining houses ... I still hold it is useless to go after them unless with a strong reliable force, who will not return until punishment is effected. That to go now with a party of Koitapuans [Papuans living near Port Moresby] quite unused to such work, would be risking the prestige of the government.
>
> With my experience of bush natives I do not anticipate seeing any of the bush raiders. In that case they will be more boastful still, saying we went after them and could not find them. On the other hand, if they attack us, I firmly believe our carriers will drop their swags and run. I know the country and it is particularly rough and we will have no chance of hunting them down.
>
> However, if you instruct me to go, I have recruited twenty Barune natives, who are willing to accompany me if they are allowed to go armed. Six or seven of them state they have used a shotgun before. Besides Mr Butterworth [the Government Storekeeper] I shall require three trustworthy Polynesians and rations for fourteen days.

Wisely, the prudence of Frank Lawes, who MacGregor regarded as 'a man of excellent judgement', was heeded and he was not sent inland. Shortly afterwards however, another volunteer came forward and offered to go after the murderers. MacGregor was away from Port Moresby at this time and Anthony Musgrave, now Government Secretary, agreed to this proposal. This man, a Malay, 'long resident at Port Moresby, a man of integrity and of remarkable ability and courage',

---

* Son of Dr William and Mrs Fanny Lawes. Frank was six years old when he arrived with his parents in November 1874. Frank Lawes died in 1895, twelve years before his father.

succeeded in locating his quarry but instead of making arrests, his party received a thorough trouncing, though without loss of life. When MacGregor returned, he was furious with Musgrave* for authorising the attempt in his absence, and realised the government would now have to act, whether he liked it or not. It had reached the stage where another expedition could hardly make matters worse, whatever the outcome. MacGregor organised a strong party under the leadership of Matthew Henry Moreton, his Private Secretary. Also to go in the party were William Armit (of the *Argus* expedition) and Andrew Charles English, Government Agent at Rigo, as well as a strong detachment of police. But true to Frank Lawes' prediction, the natives were difficult to arrest in their home territory. The majority of them simply left the area while the white party was there, and only a few minor prisoners were taken. The outcome of all these activities was that the official prohibition into the country north-east of Port Moresby was again firmly enforced.

Three years later, there was another major disturbance in the area, again caused by the intrusion of white travellers. In October 1896, an expedition left Port Moresby with the intention of passing through the district and crossing to Mount Scratchley (3,810 metres), about 50 kilometres to the north of Mount Victoria. MacGregor was unaware of these plans as this party took precautions to conceal their true destination, even going so far as to feint a move in the wrong direction.

The party, led by J. Anthony, left Port Moresby on 19th October 1896 by cutter, bound for Tupuselei, a coastal village

---

* Despite this disagreement between MacGregor and Musgrave, MacGregor was later one of the few people to offer assistance to Musgrave when he needed it. Musgrave, either as Deputy Special Commissioner or as Government Secretary, spent 23 years in New Guinea and served 5 governors. He left New Guinea on 30 June 1908, some time after but still in the wake of the 1906 Royal Commission into the operation of the New Guinea administration. MacGregor, during his time as Governor of Queensland (December 1909–July 1914), took Musgrave on as his private secretary. Musgrave, who did not receive a British New Guinea government pension and who was progressively ailing, worked in this position from 1909 until 1911 when he could no longer continue. Musgrave died on 6th June 1912. Musgrave's successor as Government Secretary in 1908 was Alexander Malcolm Campbell, who had been Resident Magistrate of the Eastern District.

about 15 kilometres to the south-east, ostensibly to capture birds and to do some prospecting. With Anthony went Francis A. Rochfort*, a miner from Queensland, and two Samoans, Jack and Willie. On 23rd October, they departed Tupuselei and cut back inland, ascending the coastal slopes of the Varirata Plateau. Their intention had been to recruit carriers as necessary from villages they passed through but the natives were not willing to cooperate, and their progress was slowed accordingly.

By 11th November they had reached Uberi Village and by 19th had attained Ginianumu, the village where Forbes had been turned back. The village was deserted so Anthony and his men formed camp within its precincts. Before long however, armed native warriors were seen to lurking in the scrub nearby. 'The native warriors did not seem inclined to take us on', recorded Rochfort, 'and on the morning of the 23rd a large number turned up, but they said they would only carry for us if we went back. We refused to retrace our steps, as we still hoped to induce them to take us forward towards the main range'.

The villagers were equally adamant the white party should not proceed. The next morning a small group of them returned to the village and finding the whites still encamped, attacked them and succeeded in literally putting a spear right through Willie before withdrawing. Rochfort summed up their predicament: 'After a review of our situation we plainly saw in case of an attack by any force that all must perish with barely a chance to defend ourselves if we remained in the village. We decided therefore to abandon it that night'. About two o'clock next morning, they stole from the camp and travelled a short way down the Nauro River where by doubling back on their track, they managed to elude their pursuers and to lay up for three days undetected. Most of their provisions had been left at the village in an attempt to divert the attention of the warriors away from the chase, the four men taking only as much as they could carry on their persons and still travel at a fast pace. As a

* Rochfort, originally from Northumbria in Britain, migrated to Australia with his brother in the 1860s. They invested a considerable fortune in pastoral property but lost this to drought. Francis Rochfort moved to New Guinea in 1896 prospecting for gold and spent the next 35 years seeking his fortune all over Papua. He died on Woodlark Island on 26th October 1931.

result, food ran short but Anthony decided nonetheless to go still further inland.

On 7th December they reached a point about 11 kilometres north of Nauro Village but here the rough country and shortage of food brought them to a halt. Fortunately for Willie, it was while camped here Rochfort was able to remove the piece of spear, which had broken off at both ends, from Willie's body. A postscript to Rochfort's account of the journey recorded: 'The length of spear extracted from Willie's body was about fourteen inches [about 36 centimetres]'. Amazingly, Willie survived.

At this camp, personal disagreements led to the break up of the group and Rochfort set off on his own back to the coast. He had no food with him and it was not until a week later he succeeded in shooting and eating a cockatoo. The next day, 15th December, weak with hunger, he met a police patrol, under the command of David Ballantine (Assistant Resident Magistrate for the Central Division) who had been sent out to search for him and the others, after word of the expedition's route had filtered through to Port Moresby from Sogeri. Anthony, Jack and Willie wandered about for another two weeks, proceeding no further inland, before returning safely to the coast. MacGregor was not pleased with Rochfort at the time, though he later recruited him into Government service.

Two more expeditions were to enter this area before the end of 1896. The first was another unauthorised venture, organised by the manager of Burns, Philp and Company, merchants of Port Moresby, and was an attempt to cross the ranges to Mount Scratchley but, as MacGregor later found, they 'never got far enough however, to be in any danger, and returned after a few weeks to Port [Moresby]'. The second expedition was an official one under the leadership of David Ballantine. His was a police party whose task it was to make peace with the warring tribes, an endeavour in which he was unsuccessful.

In the unsettled districts to the north-east of Port Moresby, the year 1896 had not brought about any improvement in relations with the inland tribes. If anything, the tribes there had been further stirred up by the clumsy intrusions by white explorers. But, also in this year, and offsetting the lack of progress in this region, was the exploration made elsewhere in

British New Guinea that was the most significant expedition in the country's short recorded history. This was carried out by MacGregor himself and resulted in the first successful crossing of British New Guinea. MacGregor in fact had embarked upon this journey even before Anthony's party had left Tupeselei.

As with his ascension of Mount Victoria seven years earlier, MacGregor chose to ignore the routes made during previous trans-Papua attempts and in fact, made the crossing in 'reverse', from north to south. He left Tamata Station on foot on 11th August 1896, accompanied by John Green and Andrew English, not then with intention of crossing to the south coast but merely to inspect the gold diggings and surrounding districts. Following the track cut by Simpson, MacGregor and his party reached Simpson's Store on 15th August, and by month's end had attained a feature known to the miners as the 'Look Out'. It was their furthest inland camp. To verify his navigational triangulations, MacGregor needed to climb higher and to this end decided to ascend Mount Scratchley (3,810 metres) which lay to the west. On 1st September, his party departed the Look Out to begin the ascent, cutting their own track as they went and by camp the next day, they had reached the 1500 metre level. Here, MacGregor was able to obtain his bearings to Mount Victoria and other features. He was also able to obtain a good view of the eastern portion of the Owen Stanley Range. He observed:

> Some half-score of miles [about 16 kilometres] east of Mt. Victoria, there is a depression in the Owen Stanley Range, the bottom of which appears to be a narrow glen, and at an altitude of probably 5,000 or 6,000 feet [about 1500 to 1800 metres]. One seemed to be able to see along this glen in a southerly or south-easterly direction for twelve to fifteen miles [19 to 24 kilometres]. The mountains on either side of it rise several thousand feet higher.

This is the first accurate description of The Gap, the fifteen kilometre-wide depression in the Owen Stanley Range through which the Kokoda Trail passes today. Though he was to change his opinion later, at the time, MacGregor was of the opinion 'it did not seem a very promising route to follow from the south coast ...'.

On 12th September, the party reached the summit of Mount Scratchley and following a review of the remaining supplies, MacGregor decided to push on to the south coast. He sent English on ahead to see if a track could be found from Mount Scratchley to the Owen Stanley complex proper without having to cross any deep valleys. English was successful in this, his efforts being remembered today in the name of English Peaks, twin summits of a mountain to the south of Mount Scratchley. He established camp at the base of this mountain and while waiting for MacGregor to join him with the bulk of the expedition, despatched several of the natives in his party to the south to look for possible routes. One of these scouts returned to English Peaks on 17th September, the same day as MacGregor marched in from the north. Sir William recorded:

> On the same day Romi, a native of the village of Saroa—in the Rigo district, the man sent out to cut the road where necessary as far as the Owen Stanley Range—returned to camp with a cut end of a sapling that had evidently been divided several years ago by a sharp instrument. This proved that he had cut onto my former track on Winter Height, and that the passage from Mt. Scratchley to the Owen Stanley Range was easy. This same man Romi, had partly cut the track on Winter Height in 1889, so that he was the first native of this colony to complete the traverse of the island.

By 22nd September, MacGregor had reached his old campsite on Winter Height. The following day, Green left to return to Tamata Station. He had orders for the captain of the *Merrie England*, the government steamer then lying in Mambare Bay, to meet MacGregor at the mouth of Galley Reach on the south coast. By 29th September, the village of Gosisi on the south-western slopes of Mount Knutsford had been entered where the inhabitants were found to be very different from the fight-loving tribes north-east of Port Moresby.

> It was extremely difficult [wrote MacGregor] to allay the fears and timidity of these people. Clearly they did not apprehend violence of any kind at our hands, for none of them carried arms of any description; and at least as many women as men, about half-a-score of each, visited our camp the first day.

The party travelled via Mount Musgrave, Mount Kowald and the Vanapa to reach Koni village on 12th October. Here Green, who had travelled on the *Merrie England* from the

Mambare, was waiting to greet them. The party reached the coast the next day and then travelled by boat to Port Moresby. After seventeen years, New Guinea had finally been crossed. A land route now existed to the Mambare goldfield and the northern coast. But it was a difficult track, as MacGregor realised:

> Were a permanent goldfield once established in the interior probably a much better road would be found for supplies than taking them over the tops of the highest mountains in the country. *

The deficiencies in this route were to become obvious only three months later. Indeed, the circumstances leading to this situation were already coming into being. By the end of 1896, 168 prospectors were working on Mambare fields, at and about Tamata Station. As the numbers of prospectors increased, so too did the attacks against them by the native inhabitants. Miners working in isolated areas fared the worst and much of Government Agent Green's time was spent in chasing after those responsible. These attacks however, always were mounted as the opportunity presented itself. Though Green achieved relative success by attending to each individual matter in turn, the fact attacks were occurring haphazardly and at random, and with apparent lack of coordination, the total magnitude of antagonism against the whites was not appreciated. This absence of intelligence, combined with MacGregor's initial poor view of his overland route, meant improvements to the communications between Port Moresby and Tamata Station were not of high priority. In January 1897 however, a more-or-less organised uprising against the miners was to precipitate a major alteration to this attitude.

---

* MacGregor was almost certainly the first European to make the crossing of the New Guinea island but he cannot claim to be the first man, Romi notwithstanding. His 1896 expedition was preceded by the ill-fated attempt of the Germans Otto Ehlers and Wilhelm Piering in 1895. They departed the northern coast from Samoahafen (now Salamaua) on 14th August with a party of forty-six persons total strength, to cross to the southern coast. They were the only white men in the group. Sixty-seven days later, on 21st October 1895, twenty-two survivors staggered into a village on the Papuan coast, suffering from severe malnutrition after having had to eat leaves and grass to stay alive. Both Europeans had perished, believed murdered by two of their carriers.

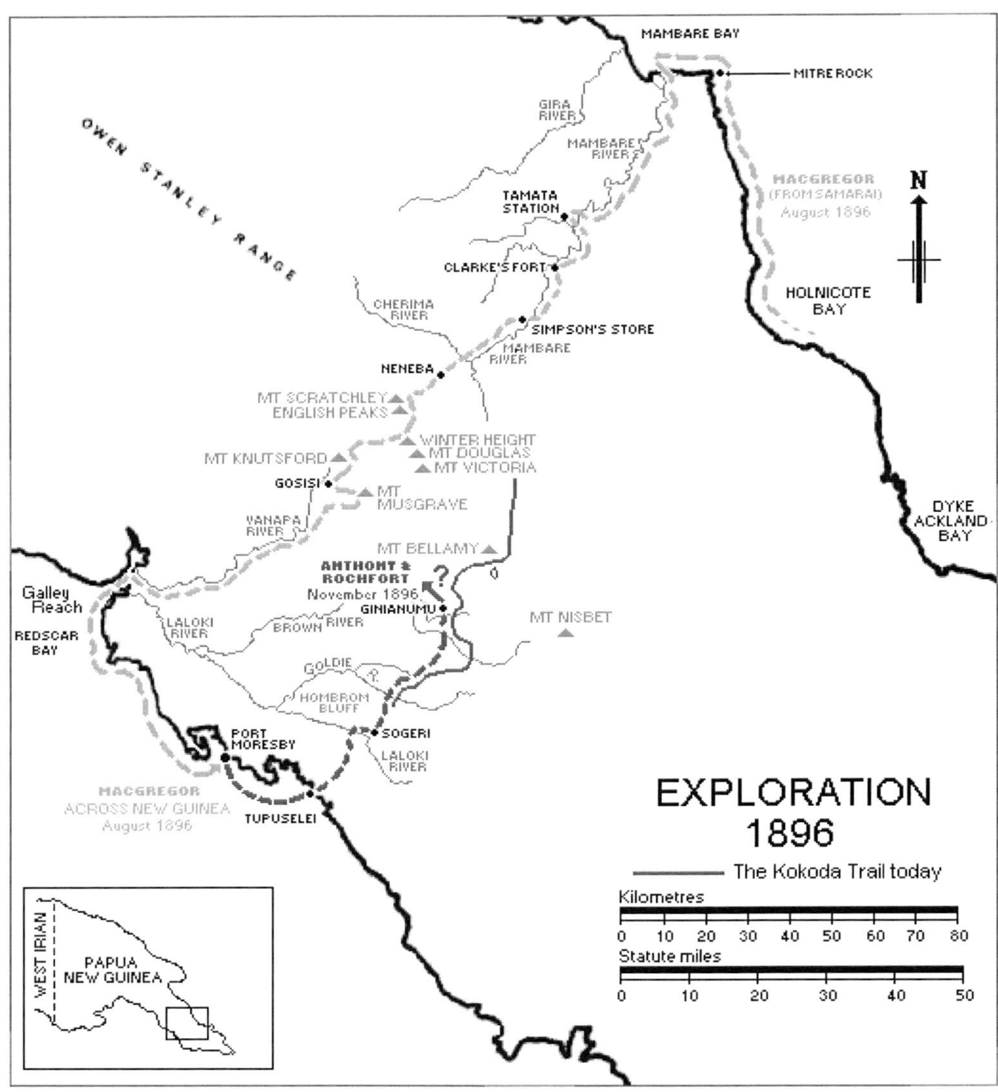

Summary of exploration 1886. *Author.*

5

The Tamata Station uprising and its consequences (1897)

It was the Government's policy at this time to return ex-prisoners to their home districts after they had served their time in goal. These ex-prisoners, having spent a period in the alien environment of the white man, were able to absorb an inkling of a completely different lifestyle to their own. They were exposed to many of the white man's ways which could only be enjoyed by the natives if they too, lived peacefully with their neighbours.

Ex-prisoners who returned to their homes were appointed as 'village constables'. Many of these appointees were regarded by their fellow villagers in much the same way as highly qualified professional people are regarded in modern society, not necessarily knowing everything about all things, but having extra experience that made it wise to listen to their advice. It was not a unique scheme, having been used by British administrators in other countries, but it was to prove very successful in British New Guinea, especially in the Mekeo and North-Eastern Districts. In a country without schools, ex-prisoners were the educated elite.*

* This practice continued into modern times. As an example, the Papua New Guinea *Post-Courier* of Monday 27th November 1972, included in its pages the following article:

Thus, it was not unusual for John Green, Assistant Magistrate and Government Agent for the Mambare, to ask that Dumai, one of the six prisoners captured following the attack on MacGregor at Clarke's Fort in 1895, be released into his charge. This was done and Dumai was taken on as a probationary constable at Tamata Station.

> From this appointment [wrote Charles Monckton] came later the tragedy of Tamata Station, for which many have been blamed, including and principally Green. It is not my wish to blame or excuse anybody, but in this matter no-one other than Green was in error ... He was given a difficult job, and it was therefore necessary that he should have a free hand in the selection of his men.

Green had found the original site of the Government Station chosen by MacGregor flooded during the wet season and had decided to shift it to higher ground. A new site was chosen five kilometres away and work was started on clearing the ground and erecting new buildings. Daily, Green would depart the old station to work at the new, always accompanied by an armed detachment of police. This practice commenced on the 6th January 1897 and continued for a week, so establishing a recognisable pattern of behaviour. On 13th January, Dumai, the new constable, approached Green and complained, ostensibly on behalf of the local villagers, Green's orders forbidding the carrying of arms on or about the station were unjust because he (Green) and the police were always armed. Green explained Government orders required them to be armed at all times, but as a mark of good faith and trust, he and his men would leave their weapons at the old station when they left to work at the new.

Next morning, with the police work party fallen in under Corporal Sedu, the senior non-commissioned officer on the

---

KILLERS LEAD TOURISTS ON PATROL

It's true—convicted killers do make the best guides in Biami country. [The] tour organiser ... said today that last week's British tourists had been taken aback when they found that six of their carriers in the Nomad area had 'done time' for murder.

'It was the only solution ... In that part of the country there are no schools. The only men able to work as interpreters in Pidgin or Motu are those who have been to prison. Travel—to Bomana [the large prison in Port Moresby] —is very educational'.

station, Green gave the order to ground arms. Amid dissenting mumbles, about two-thirds of the men did so but Corporal Sedu and some of the more experienced policemen retained their weapons. Green chided Sedu on his lack of courage and convinced him the local natives could be trusted. Eventually, though with great reluctance, Corporal Sedu lay down his Snider, the other dissidents slowly following his example. Thus a completely unarmed group left Tamata Station on the morning of 14th January, Green not realising he had made two crucial mistakes—firstly in deciding to disarm his party (though he himself still wore his revolver), and secondly in telling Dumai the previous evening he would do so. Dumai therefore had ample opportunity to set the trap that now awaited Green's work detail.

On reaching the work site, Green sent half his men under Corporal Sedu into the forest to gather timber, while he and the remainder of the detachment set to work on the partially completed buildings. Apparently, Green took off his revolver

Tamata Government Station, 1906.

PNG National Library.

and belt to work on some roof trusses and while aloft, a native scooped up the weapon and ran off with it. This was the signal for a general attack upon Green and the two policemen with him, who perished in the rain of spears directed at them.

Corporal Sedu, meanwhile, hearing the commotion, organised his party and returned to assist Green. They were hopelessly outnumbered and being unarmed, were slain with their officer. The attack on Green's party was not an isolated incident for there had been other attacks on white miners on the coast just prior to the main one upon Green, as well as a later move against the police remaining at the old Tamata settlement. MacGregor later reported 'all the tribes near the station were implicated'. When the uprising had settled, at least nine government staff had been killed, including four policemen, and many more wounded. Up to 40 local natives may have died too, and at least one white miner, a man named Fry, drowned while fleeing to the Mambare mouth. Monckton recounts another miner perished when he was stoned from a tree and clubbed to death by children.

Two miners reached Samarai by the 16th February where they told of the events to Government Agent Moreton. After immediately despatching news of this to MacGregor in Port Moresby, Moreton, with Alexander Elliot, the miner who had done much exploration in the area with Simpson and Clunas three years earlier, went to the Mambare in the government vessel *Siai* to determine what could be done. They found Tamata Station had been over-run and the natives were running riot, captured rifles being used against the *Siai* as it travelled up river. 'For these, however', wrote Monckton, 'they had already expended most of the ammunition, and were at best extremely bad shots'.

Moreton concluded, after undertaking a reconnaissance of the station and checking on three miners further inland, there was nothing he could do with his small force, so prudently retired to the *Siai* anchored downriver to await the arrival of MacGregor. However, the message he had sent to Port Moresby had been inadvertently delayed, and it was almost seven weeks before the Lieutenant-Governor arrived. He bought with him a large squad of police who scoured the areas about the river and

Tamata Government Station in 1906. The original 1895 station was on the Mambare River-Tamata Creek junction. The photographs at right and previous page show the new Tamata Creek station site upstream of the junction. This was chosen by John Green and was the place where Green and others were killed in January 1897.

Charles Monckton's observation that officers preferred to resign rather than accept a posting to Tamata Station is readily understood. Even the new site could not escape the oppressive landscape of dank mudflats and rotting vegetation, the dense gloom of the encroaching jungle, and the hordes of fever-bearing mosquitoes, flying-ants and sandflies.

PNG National Library.

into the mountains, but had little success. Despite MacGregor's later aggressive accounts of his visit, the poor showing of the government patrols did nothing to diminish the warring tribes' rising confidence. A fresh detachment of constabulary under a new Government Agent, Michael Shanahan, was installed, and the area returned to a tense peace. But the unrest on the northern goldfields was to continue for years, making Tamata Station a very unpopular posting, as Monckton observed:

> The Northern Division [encompassing Mambare and Kumusi goldfields, of which Tamata Station was the administrative centre] was destined for many years to prove the death of a long succession of officers, or at best, the grave of their reputations. Shanahan, Armit, Lynch, Park, and Close were to die; whilst several others were either dismissed or called upon to resign. Many officers in later years preferred to resign rather than be sent there.

The native uprising and the death of the Government Agent and others at Tamata in January 1897 drove home to MacGregor how inadequate his Government's resources were in dealing with trouble of this kind. This realisation, in fact, was the seed from which the Kokoda Trail came into existence. The straight line distance of the northern goldfields from Port Moresby was no more than 160 kilometres, yet there existed no passable road for administrative intercourse or indeed, for the general traveller. The only available route at this time was a sea voyage via Samarai at the eastern tip of the Possession on irregularly scheduled vessels. Perhaps in favourable conditions, and with an available steamship, a fast voyage could be done in fourteen or fifteen days, but this was still too long a delay if expedient Government action was necessary. MacGregor wanted a land route direct from Port Moresby, but ready access through the Uberi area to the north-east was still not feasible without risk to the white traveller. He decided therefore, his previous track across the island via the Vanapa River and Mount Scratchley should be improved. He was not enamoured of this choice since it meant a detour of almost 50 kilometres to the west before overland travel could start, but the logic of using the Vanapa track was obvious: passage was known to be possible, and the natives at least on the southern side of the Owen Stanleys were known to be friendly.

Actually, even before his April 1897 trip (the post-massacre visit) to Tamata, MacGregor had already started investigating the Vanapa route, sending Amadeo Giulianetti, Travelling Government Agent, there with instructions to develop the Vanapa track as far inland as he could. In fact, Giulianetti was sent out twice to do this, firstly in February 1897 with Francis Rochfort, and again five months later, after MacGregor had returned from the Mambare, but both times he was unable to produce results acceptable to MacGregor. In March of this year also, George Belford, one of the most experienced and resourceful New Guinea travellers of the day, lost his way on this track while on his way to the northern shore. This is significant because Belford had accompanied MacGregor when the first part of the track was originally cut to Mount Victoria and knew the area.

Corporal Sedu, the courageous senior non-commissioned officer of the Armed Native Constabulary at Tamata Station in January 1897.

Sedu was killed during the native uprising when he went, unarmed, to the assistance of the Government Agent, John Green, who was under armed attack. Sedu had ample opportunity to save himself but chose to go to Green's aid.

Ela Beach Public Library, Port Moresby (New Guinea Collection).

The fact remained this track was just too long and too physically demanding to be suitable for general pedestrian traffic. The difficulties experienced by the various travellers in the first half of 1897 merely confirmed to MacGregor his original appraisal had been correct. Though not immediately discounting the route, MacGregor did not have high hopes a better Vanapa track would eventuate. He began to re-think his initial view of the usefulness of the major depression (The Gap) he had seen in the ranges to the east of Mount Victoria, during his north-to-south crossing eight months earlier. If a route could be found to The Gap, and if this route avoided the unsettled areas to the north-east of Moresby Harbour, then perhaps more direct communications with the northern goldfields from Port Moresby were possible. With this in mind, and even before sending Giulianetti to the Vanapa for the second time in July 1897, MacGregor despatched a party under Francis Rochfort inland in an attempt to open a horse track to The Gap.

Rochfort left Port Moresby on 28th May 1897 on horse-back and after crossing the Laloki River struck north to pass to the east of Mount Lawes. Following a north-easterly course, he 'got on to some good travelling country', and on 14th June reached the Brown River. Generally following this river's course inland, Rochfort estimated he penetrated about 65 kilometres from the coast before he was forced to abandon his expedition because of sickness of members of his party and the loss of some of his horses. Though Rchfort did not attain his objective, MacGregor found his report encouraging. Rochfort's had been the deepest incursion into the district for ten years. As well, though he skirted the main unsettled areas, Rochfort's journey had been done without any trouble with the natives. 'We made a good track all the distance traversed by us', reported Rochfort, 'and it all could be made into a fair horse road'.

Meanwhile, Giulianetti, back on the Vanapa track for the second time, had tried a new course in his efforts to find an easier path, but as a result found himself lost. Giulianetti could keep himself out of trouble but following in his track was a party of prospectors led by George Wriford, at one time Commandant of Native Constabulary. Wriford was leading a group of prospectors who had heard of the finds on the McLaughlin and were attempting to cross overland to that stream and to the Mambare from Port Moresby. They too, found themselves lost but compounded their problems by making further wrong moves, eventually finding themselves too far to the west, and in the district of the Goromani people. Here they were attacked and eventually besieged. One of Wriford's native scouts escaped and was fortunate to stumble onto Giulianetti's party who were making their way back to the coast. Giulianetti immediately sent word of Wriford's predicament on ahead by runner to Port Moresby. MacGregor himself lead a strong police party to Wriford's relief, all of whose party were rescued without injury. With peace restored, MacGregor now took the opportunity to find out for himself the difficulties impeding Giulianetti and, accordingly, continued on up the Vanapa and over the ranges to the Mambare, going back along his old north-to-south track to make the first government crossing of the Owen Stanleys from south to north.

While MacGregor may have carried out the first *official* crossing, it does not seem as if he was the first white man to make the south-to-north journey to the Mambare. This was first done, as it appears, by at least two miners who reached the camp of John Schmitt on the MacLaughlin from the south coast, though there is some contention about the identity of this pair. Schmitt had been on the MacLaughlin since early October 1896, having travelled up from the Mambare through Tamata. Schmitt recorded in his diary the two men who came overland were called Kelly and Nettle, and they arrived on 2nd May 1897 after having spent two months on the journey. However, D.H. Osbourne, writing in the *Pacific Islands Monthly* of June 1941, believed the 'only' two men who got through to Schmitt's camp were Steve Wolff and one other whose name he had forgotten, and they arrived four months earlier, on 15th January 1897, the day after the massacre of Green and his staff. Schmitt made note of the Tamata killings in his diary (he found out four days after the event) but made no record of overland visitors in January. Osbourne, writing more than 40 years after the event, stated Wolff, who was later deported from Papua, had told him the story.

Time may have clouded the details and it is possible it is the same two men. Schmitt's record, made at the time, would seem preferable, yet it is also quite possible four men made the journey. Certainly, the times are different and the stories are not consistent in some details. Osbourne wrote by the time Wolff and his partner reached the MacLaughlin, 'their food was almost finished. Three white men [Schmitt, and his companions Ryan and Burns] were there but they could not spare any supplies'. Schmitt, on the other hand, recorded he 'got a little flour, tea and sugar' from the two men who had travelled overland. In any event, irrespective of which miner is recognised as having made the first south-north journey across Papua, it was MacGregor's crossing which was to prove of greater significance as it officially confirmed how difficult this route really was. (A comment in Schmitt's diary for the 14th May 1897 well illustrates this. Burns' health had been getting worse for months and he had decided to return overland to Port Moresby, via the Vanapa route. Schmitt wrote: 'Burns came back to-day. He was away 15 days trying to make Port Moresby. He was in a very bad state when he got here'). MacGregor's findings put paid to any further development of the Vanapa River path, and instead swung the emphasis firmly onto locating a route direct from Port Moresby. He recorded:

> It [the Vanapa track] is one that it would be unwise for any one to follow who merely wished to cross from the south coast to the Mambare watershed. For carriers it is difficult and exhausting in a high degree ...
>
> It becomes all the more important to persevere with a path from Port Moresby to cross the main range at the gap at the head of the Wowea Valley on the northern branch of the Brown River.

MacGregor knew from Rochfort's initial venture in May and June 1897 a track direct from Port Moresby was geographically possible but success would ultimately depend on the permanent pacification of the area's unruly tribes. He was unwilling to accept the moderated behaviour, as found by Rochfort, as evidence of a lasting change and decided to inspect the area himself, leaving on 2nd August 1897 in company with Resident Magistrate David Ballantine. MacGregor, in characteristic vein, put the object of his trip in pithier terms:

> The necessity ... of establishing the superiority of the Government over the fighting tribes of Hagari, Ebe, and Baura, and of ascertaining whether a road could be got over the Owen Stanley Range at the depression familiarly known as the 'Gap', now made such an inspection urgent.

They were to have only limited success. They reached Kagi (Hagari) by mid-August and remained there until 25th August when they moved camp to a position about 10 kilometres from The Gap. The Kagi people, identified by MacGregor as 'a fighting, aggressive community', could not be contacted and on this occasion obviously wanted nothing to do with the white men:

> They remained quite unsoftened by the presents we left for them ... [On 26th August] Mr Ballantine went about half way up to the gap—that is, to about three miles [about 5 kilometres] from it—whence he could see that a path to it was easily practicable, and almost certainly existed. He returned to camp on the evening of the 27th.

On 28th August, the party commenced their return to the coast, without establishing even working relations, let alone 'the superiority of the Government', as MacGregor had hoped. Yet he did not see the expedition as having failed, reporting 'it is only a question of time' before the hostile tribes were brought to a state of peace. He also wrote it was made evident

> a road could be got across the main range, through the 'gap' at an altitude not exceeding 7,000 feet [about 2100 metres]. The great question that remained was whether the bridle track cut by Mr Rochfort ... to the Brown River could be carried on to Hagari [Kagi] ...

In a later paragraph of the same report, he added 'the joining of the two roads has still to be effected. This will be tried until it is accomplished'.

It is interesting to note MacGregor and Ballantine's route inland did not follow the route MacGregor was then favouring, that is, Rochfort's track along the course of the Brown River. Instead, they went via Bomana, Sogeri, Uberi, Nauro (then Wamai), Baura, and on to the Kagi (then Hagari) area. In going this way, MacGregor and Ballantine had walked about half of the route taken by today's Kokoda Trail. Indeed, this is the earliest official use of the route of today's Kokoda Trail that can

Detail from an early geological map of New Guinea illustrates the extent of knowledge of the interior inland from Port Moresby up to 1892.

The country north-east of Port Moresby, which included the upper Laloki River, was known from the travels of the missionaries (since 1874) and the miners (since 1878).

The Vanapa River was known from MacGregor's 1889 journey to Mount Victoria but much less was known about the Brown River. The supposed course of the Brown River (shown as a heavy dashed line) was the basis for MacGregor's insistence that an overland track from Port Moresby should follow this stream's course back into the mountains.

Department of Resource Industries, Brisbane.

be established. But at the time, MacGregor did not see this track as a route in its own right but merely a convenient access into the mountains where a much better track would supposedly come from another direction (that is, from further to the west).

It is not difficult to see why MacGregor favoured the Brown River route instead of the more easterly track. At this time much of the river's course had yet to be accurately mapped and it was supposed it lay much more to the north of Port Moresby than it actually does, in the direction in which travel was desired and along country affording fair passage. Once on the Brown, all the traveller had to do was follow the stream back into the mountains. This would, it was supposed, automatically take the traveller in the right direction towards The Gap. The Brown River route also skirted, to large extent, the unsettled Ebe and Wamai (Uberi and Nauro) areas. On the other hand, the route via Bomana, Sogeri, Uberi and Nauro (the route of the Trail today) took the traveller into the mountains much earlier and required a detour of about 40 kilometres to the east before swinging back in the desired northerly direction. This route then was more physically demanding, was longer, increased the risk from aggressive tribes, and required the traveller to find much of his own way to The Gap.

Thus, even though Ballantine, Rochfort and even MacGregor himself were using the more easterly route at this time to go into the mountains, the apparent attractions of Brown River route meant the Kokoda Trail track was not considered by MacGregor as a serious contender for the overland route. Still, it is curious the Kokoda Trail route did not warrant more attention, given the Brown River route had to be constructed while it was found much of the more easterly route already existed. MacGregor recorded in his report

> from the time we left Port Moresby until we arrived at Hagari [Kagi] we used native tracks the whole way, and never had to cut any part of the road except for a few hundred yards near the Nauro [Brown] River.

Given the Kokoda Trail largely existed before the white man ever ventured into the mountains—albeit as short, disconnected native foot-pads—it is likely the route would have been inaugurated much earlier had not Morrison's foolishness one and a half decades earlier resulted in many explorers being denied access to the area.

MacGregor wasted no time in following up his conclusions. Only weeks later, on 25th September 1897, Ballantine and

Rochfort left Port Moresby on another expedition, their destination this time being The Gap itself. Again, the Kokoda Trail route of today, through Uberi and Kagi, was followed inland, their instructions including to seek a connection with the horse track cut by Rochfort on their return to the coast. They reached the village of Efogi on the 4th October, from where they attempted to continue towards The Gap but stiff native resistance forced their return to Efogi.

On the 9th October, Ballantine and Rochfort tried again to reach The Gap and although they were attacked again, crossed the Fagume River and establishing a fortified camp near Kagi village. Here, much skirmishing took place, and it was not until 17th October, after having been heavily reinforced, the party was able to move forward into the valley leading to The Gap. By climbing trees and having others in their way chopped down, Ballantine and Rochfort were able to see eastwards into The Gap. But this was as far as they were to get.

> Unluckily the mists began to rise ere we had finished our observations [recorded Rochfort] and, as our supply of food was nearly exhausted, there was nothing for it but to make our way back ... At noon we reluctantly turned our faces to the valley, and started of down the track.

They were due for further frustrations. Their progress, hampered by persistent native attacks, was further impeded by Rochfort falling ill to such a degree he could not walk. Ballantine therefore, sent him back with eight policemen via Uberi and Sogeri (that is, back the way they had come), while he went further to the west to try and locate the horse road near the Brown River. He got on to a tributary of the Brown, the Nauro River, but could not find the track, and eventually had to follow the course of the Goldie River into the Laloki Valley. He reached Port Moresby on the 6th November, a day before Rochfort. Though the link with the Brown River track had not been achieved, a vital piece of information had been obtained, which gave encouragement for the future. It had been noted the village nearest The Gap had been sited so as to repel an attack from the north.

> The foes then that they dreaded [Rochfort noted] could only come from across the main range ... The only conclusion I could come to is

> that there is communication between the tribes on either side, and by this track ... the way was rough, but a good track could easily be found and made.

MacGregor persisted with the view the Brown River route was best, even though problems with it began to appear. Since Ballantine and Rochfort had failed to satisfy his instructions, he decided to lead a party himself to the Brown 'to determine whether any further efforts should be made to extend a path by that route towards the main range'. He found it was already very difficult to find at places any trace of Rochfort's track cut the previous year but in spite of this, he was determined passage in this direction was desirable. For MacGregor, the Brown River provided the only feasible route inland:

> It seems to me to be clearly best to push the track along the Brown, never losing touch with the river. Undoubtedly, this will lead to the crossing of numerous steep and difficult ridges that abut on the river. But ... even if the labour involved is greater than by following another route, ... it is best to push the track along it [because] any progress made along the river cannot but be in the right direction.

Consequently, MacGregor authorised John MacDonald*, the Head Gaoler and Overseer of Works, to construct a road from Port Moresby to as far up the Brown River as he could. MacDonald, using prison labourers, had recently completed a roadway from Port Moresby to the Varirata Plateau, overcoming considerable engineering problems in doing so, and the results had much impressed MacGregor: 'If he only demonstrates the same skill and ability on the Brown track, it is sure to succeed unless the difficulties are much greater than they look'. MacDonald commenced work immediately and after three months had constructed a road

> about twenty feet [6 metres] wide; at very few places does it cross ground that would in ordinary weather be dangerously soft. It did

* Born in 1862 in Scotland, MacDonald, a shipwright, migrated to Australia in 1883 and settled in Brisbane. Through his service with the Queensland Maritime Defence Force, he obtained an appointment in 1893 as Warrant Officer-Gunner on the British New Guinea Government vessel *Merrie England*. He was appointed Head Gaoler and Overseer in 1897 and later became Superintendent of Works. He retired in 1923 to Port Moresby where he died on 11th August 1935.

not appear ... that very much more would be necessary to make it suitable for light wheeled traffic.

However, MacDonald had been following the Brown's south bank and had found difficulty in obeying his instructions to keep as close as possible to the river. Accordingly, he made a crossing of the stream at Karema (then Korima) and carried the road along the north bank for another 19 kilometres, but this took progress inland only 3 kilometres passed the 'old' road on the opposite bank. It was found the higher up river progress was made, the rougher the country and slower the work necessarily became. A point was reached where MacDonald estimated an extra three or four kilometres in a straight line would entail the cutting of a further ten kilometres of track and this, he reckoned, would take a year to accomplish. Work on the new road was therefore halted and he was directed to improve that portion of the track already made.

The Cherima River crossing in 1929.
University of Papua New Guinea.

Three members of the Armed Native Constabulary pause to be photographed on a rudimentary bridge at Cherima River crossing in early 1929.

MacGregor crossed the Cherima here on his trans-New Guinea crossing in August 1887 and rated this part of the route as 'difficult and exhausting in a high degree'.

Later, in the early 1900s, many miners travelling to the 'Yodda' from Tamata or Clarke's Fort avoided this route, preferring to take the longer track through the swamp country of the upper Opi and Kumusi Rivers. Near this site today is the small settlement of Karukaru.

University of Papua New Guinea.

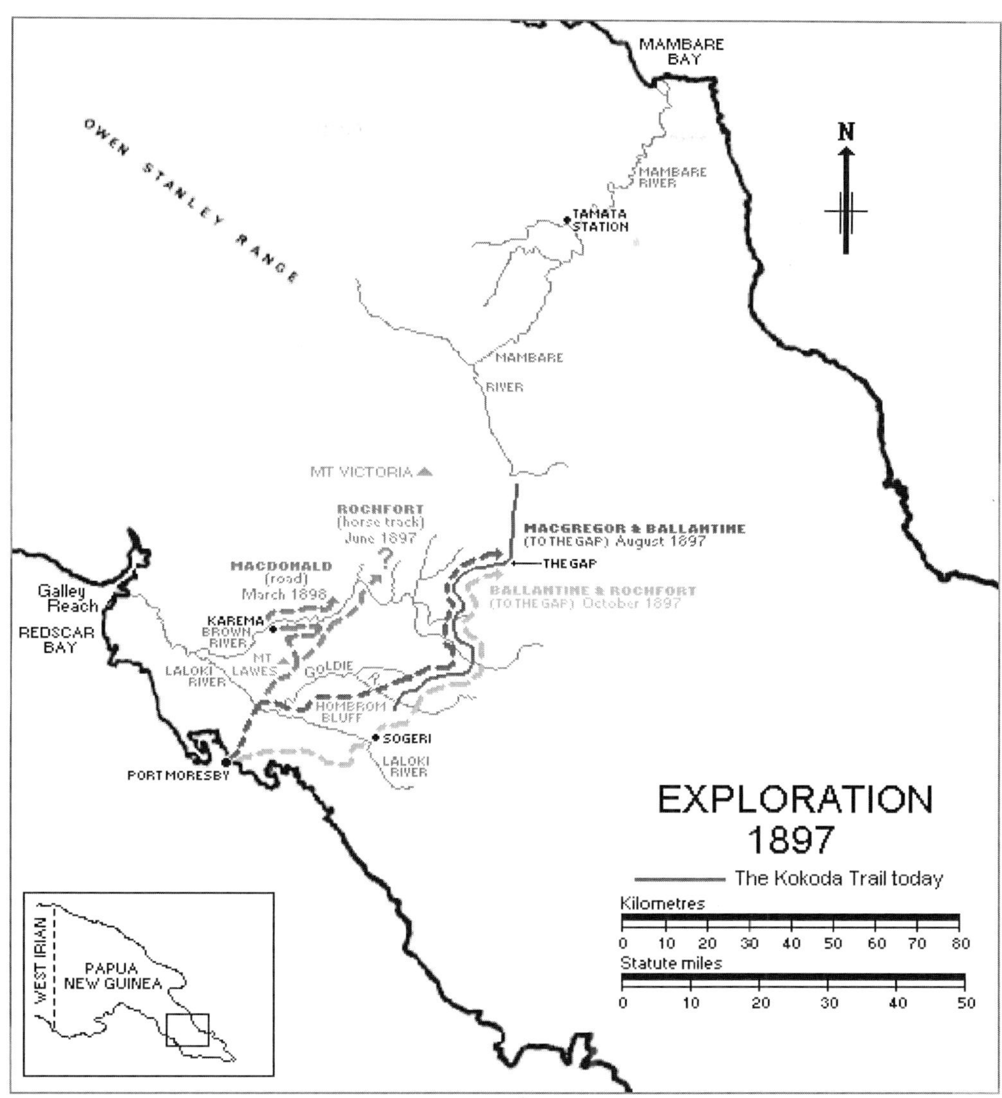

Summary of exploration 1887. *Author.*

6

Surveying the route (1898–1899)

The search for new routes on the south coast in the late 1890s was paralleled by similar development on the northern goldfields, though it was the desire for new diggings rather than administrative efficiency motivating most new exploration there. In the 18 months since Clarke's arrival in mid-1896, most of the mining activity had been confined to the Mambare and to the small creeks feeding it. However, by the end of 1897, new exploration was reaching ever further from the Mambare Valley and it was not long before a more promising area was discovered. A miner named Coleman cut through the dense scrub northwest from Tamata Station for about 30 kilometres into the basin of the Gira River where, from one gully alone, he extracted 56 kilograms of gold. Many Mambare prospectors transferred to the Gira Valley but though some individual finds were substantial to start with, the gullies from which the gold had been extracted were, as a mining report of the time observed, 'very shallow and narrow ... and soon worked out'. The Gira was never to have the popular appeal of some later gold fields in British New Guinea but it provided a fairly steady income for a fluctuating band of prospectors for several years.

Despite the apparent attractions of the Gira field, which was northwest of Tamata, the region in the opposite direction, to the southeast, also began to receive attention. This developed because of the difficulties of travelling along the course of the upper Mambare, upriver of the Cherima River junction. Since the earliest days on the Mambare, the areas inland of Tamata Station, in the region of Green, Fish, Clunas', Simpson's and McLaughlin's Creeks and the Cherima River, had always hosted some miners. In fact, this is where the original group of miners under Simpson established themselves in August 1896 following George Clarke's death and this group was soon followed, in a matter of weeks, by other groups and individuals, including Schmitt, Burns, Ryan, Davis and Nelsson. But the terrain once past the 'corner' of the Mambare, at the Cherima junction, presented such laborious and exhausting passage exploration had been considerably impeded in this direction. However, the lay of the land suggested the upper reaches of the Mambare could probably be entered from the other end of the (upper Mambare) valley. What was needed to reach this point, if the hardships of the Cherima were to be avoided, was a new track travelling in a south-easterly direction from Tamata or Clarke's Fort and which ran more or less parallel with the upper Mambare, transecting the upper Ope and Kumusi Rivers.

Three attempts were made to establish such a route and each of these, in their own way, had significant consequences for the development of the region. The first expedition, led by Alexander Clunas, departed Clarke's Fort in April 1898, striking east then south, to cross the upper Ope River and to enter into the valley of the Kumusi. By following the Kumusi inland, they reached the headwaters of the upper Mambare. Clunas travelled down the Mambare to as far as Yodda Creek, a tributary of the river, before re-tracing his steps. Clunas' journey was the most important of the three because it demonstrated there was a way into the upper Mambare valley from the eastern end. Importantly too, Clunas did the whole trip without any trouble from the local natives.

The next expedition, later in 1898, was not as fortunate. It consisted of George Arbuck, Bob Peel and George Griffith. Arbuck elected to travel directly from Tamata to join with Clunas' track from Clarke's Fort. However, Arbuck's group was ambushed inland of Bogi, on the Kumusi, even before they reached the Mambare and though they were able to extricate themselves without serious injury, they made the mistake of retreating back to Tamata rather than going on. This repeated the circumstances that developed with the tribes inland of Port Moresby. Not that the inhabitants of the upper Ope, Kumusi and Mambare river systems needed any encouragement; these were already a far more aggressive people than those on the south coast but Arbuck's actions confirmed the impression the white man was easy to repel and did nothing to deflate the confidence of the warriors. The blame probably cannot be wholly attributed to Arbuck's poor showing but for the next five years, all the natives of the region adopted an aggressive stand against any foreign traveller trying to get through to the Mambare.

In November 1899, the third group to enter the region, comprised of Matt Crowe, Sam McLelland, and Archibald Lyon Walker, followed Clunas' track into the head of the valley and reached a barricaded village where they attempted to buy food. The occupants of this village, which was later to be the site of the town of Kokoda, attacked the expedition killing some of the carriers. But rather than go back as Arbuck had done, Crowe's party proceeded further down the river testing the 'colours' as they went. Eventually, they travelled the whole length of the upper Mambare, emerging at the Cherima Crossing. They followed the Mambare back to Tamata, crossed over into the Gira Valley and traced the Gira down to its mouth. From here, they re-entered the Mambare and returned to Tamata Station. Their prospecting had shown the potential of the upper Mambare valley and they sought and were granted reward claims for their efforts.

The publicity surrounding the outcome of the third expedition triggered a new rush, Though the track pioneered by Clunas was far from being an easy route, there were many, particularly those still working tired (lower) Mambare claims, who were willing to try it, given the promise of the new Yodda field*. The old track along the river, from Clarke's Fort via the

* The upper Mambare valley was referred to as the 'Yodda' Valley when it was first opened to gold miners and the 'Yodda Goldfield' was officially established on 31st July 1900. A second proclamation, for a larger field with the same name, and including the original tract, was made on 3rd June 1908. The schedule accompanying the latter proclamation described areas adjacent to nearly the whole length of the Mambare, from its mouth to Kokoda. Despite this, in practice the term was popularly used to describe only the

McLaughlin and Cherima, quickly fell out of favour with the miners. It was reported at the end of 1899 miners wishing to work even the McLaughlin preferred to take the longer, circuitous route from Tamata via the Ope and Kumusi Rivers, rather than travel along the Mambare via Clarke's Fort. Thus, the Yodda goldfield came to be.

It was unfortunate Clunas' new track was preferred and not the alternative through the Cherima Crossing, as the people of the Ope River in particular were found to be 'truculent and aggressive' and took pernicious delight in attacking prospecting parties moving through their area. On the other hand, the situation on the Mambare, from Cherima junction to Tamata Station, had changed for the better. 'The [lower Mambare] people have at last taken heart of grace', an official dispatch noted, 'and their confidence in the promises of the Government to befriend them is now fixed'. Paradoxically, this harmony was a cause of unrest among the Ope villagers, the same report noting their conduct was 'due in a very large measure to the state of isolation in which they have been cast by the pacification of the Mambare people'.

Although the threat of violent death may have lessened for those living and working about Tamata, it was still far from being a healthy place to live. There were many deaths from malaria and one report of the time put the annual death rate among white miners as high as thirty percent. William Simpson died of 'fever' in December 1897, as did Michael Shanahan, the officer appointed by MacGregor to replace John Green, in August the following year. Shanahan was succeeded by his assistant Captain Archibald William Butterworth who served for only 26 days before being relieved for duty elsewhere by Henry

upper Mambare River (from the Cherima River to source) and citations referring to the 'Yodda' should be read with this in mind. The terms 'Yodda Valley' or 'Yodda River' do not seem to have ever been officially promulgated though they appear often in official reports. There is a small stream in the area, the Yodda Creek, which flows north-east to meet the Mambare about half way between Kokoda and the Cherima junction. The early mining area included this creek and it is supposed this is where the term originally came from. From about the 1930s, a settlement called 'Yodda', which was situated on this stream, appeared on maps of the area though this town is not shown on modern maps. The township of Kokoda is situated on Madi Creek.

Hamilton Stuart-Russell on 1st September 1898. Stuart-Russell's occupancy was also to be a short one for on 3rd January 1899, he was replaced by William Armit (of the *Argus* expedition of 1883). Armit's assistant was the former miner Alexander Elliot, now in the Government service.

There were also changes at higher levels, not the least being that of the Lieutenant-Governor. MacGregor had been promoted to Governor of Lagos and left British New Guinea in November 1898. Succeeding him was Francis Winter, Chief Judicial Officer

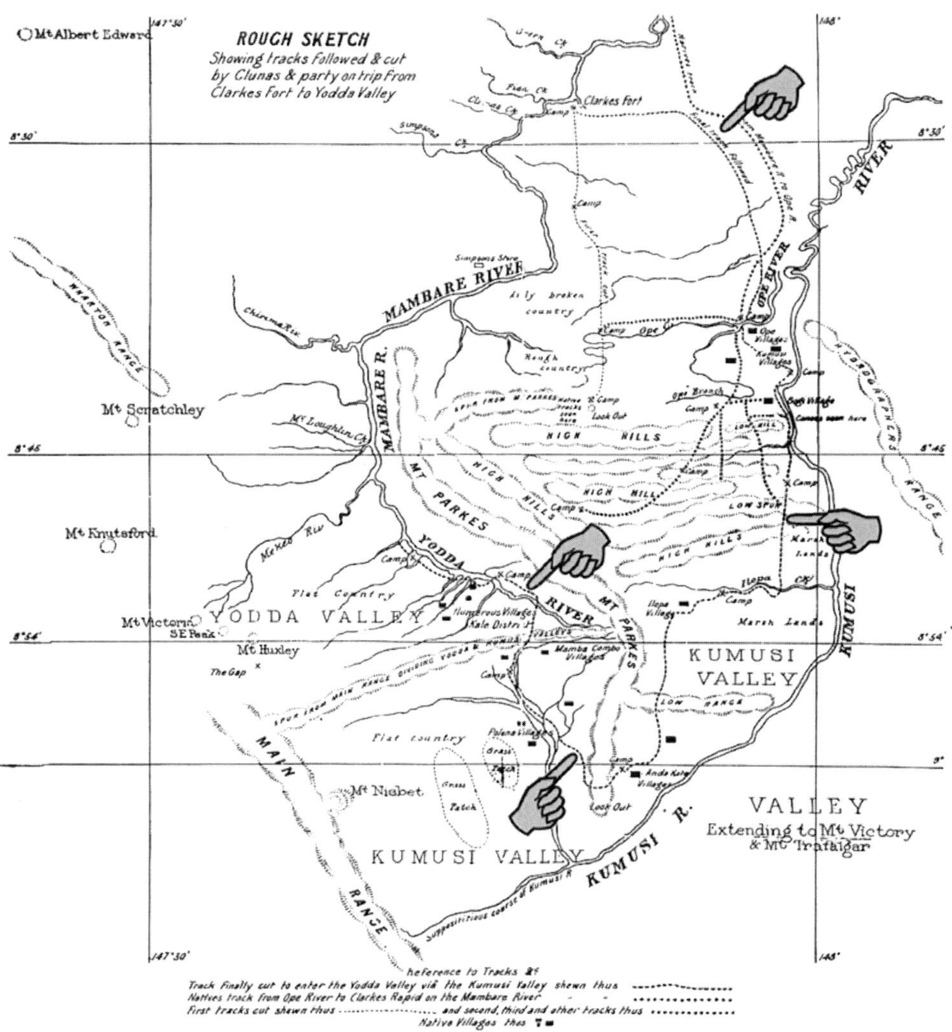

of the Colony, who was appointed Acting Administrator pending the arrival of the new Lieutenant-Governor, George Ruthven Le Hunte in March 1899. The change worthy of note however, is Stuart-Russell's. From Tamata, he travelled to Port Moresby where he was to resume the duties of his substantive position of Government Surveyor. Stuart-Russell's first task under Le Hunte was to conduct a proper investigation into a route from Port Moresby to the northern goldfields. He was, in effect, to survey the Kokoda Trail.

At the outset, Le Hunte, the new Lieutenant-Governor, was as keen as MacGregor to have a track going directly from Port Moresby to the northern goldfields. Within weeks of his arrival in March 1899, he had appreciated the advantages such a link would provide, commenting it was 'of urgent importance' communication should be opened with the interior and the northern coast 'by way of the main range'. And, for the first few months at least he was in the country, Le Hunte continued with MacGregor's view the Brown River route was the one to which development activity should be directed. Consequently, he instructed the Government Surveyor, Stuart-Russell, to travel via MacDonald's Brown River road and the Brown River valley to The Gap,

> examining and surveying [the country passed through, and] extending ... investigations a reasonable distance beyond The Gap, with a view to ascertaining the conditions under which the road could be extended towards the Mambare, or some other suitable terminus ... [At this time, the town of Kokoda did not exist].

Exploration of the miner Clunas in 1897 and 1898.

Early mining on the Mambare River upstream of the Cherima River junction had indicated good prospects in the upper reaches but the track along the Mambare, through Clarke's Fort and Simpson's Store, across the Cherima and on to the 'Yodda' was too arduous.

Though longer, Clunas' track from Clarke's Fort, shown here as 'Final track followed' (indicated), offered easier going and was the breakthrough that led to rapid influx of miners into the upper Mambare basin and ultimately to the founding of the settlement at Kokoda.

PNG National Library.

As Stuart-Russell's proposed track would take him through the still officially hostile district about Kagi, another party was sent out to pacify, or attempt to pacify, the unruly tribes before the surveyor reached the area. To this end, David Ballantine was sent inland with instructions to join Stuart-Russell's group after his task was completed. This was to ensure the strongest possible force was available to the surveyor when he entered the unknown country to the north of The Gap. Though The Gap was the common destination, Ballantine, as with his previous journey inland with Rochfort, again favoured the route through Uberi now taken by much of today's Kokoda Trail. His group departed Port Moresby on 24th April 1899, the day before Stuart-Russell.

Stuart-Russell's party included John MacDonald, eleven police, sixteen prisoners and warders, three horseboys, and thirteen horses and mules under the charge of Robert Hunter, brother of George (of the Kemp Welch expedition of July 1887). The party spent three days crossing a flooded Laloki River and it was not until 30th April the camp at Karema on the Brown was reached. Turning to the north-east, they followed MacDonald's 'old' road, reaching its terminus on the seventh day. Here the party rested. Stuart-Russell recorded:

> Mr. MacDonald and myself went on, in order to open up a track for our party when ready to start, and ascertain, if possible, something about the movements of the other party. Returned on the fourth day, and met the police who had accompanied Mr. Ballantine. I then found that the gentleman had returned to Port Moresby.

The route taken by David Ballantine in 1899. Ballantine's task was to smooth the way for Stuart-Russell's surveying party approaching by the Brown River route, by making friends with hostile native tribes.

The track out to Ballantine's '[camp] 8' approximates about a third of today's Kokoda Trail.

University of Queensland.

It was unfortunate the two parties had not made contact as planned because Stuart-Russell had been counting on the services of Ballantine's carriers as they were difficult to employ at this time. In addition, Ballantine had taken back with him the only available interpreter for the Hagari and nearby Serigima districts. The Serigima, neighbours of the Hagari, lived in the area of The Gap. There was one consolation however: Ballantine had succeeded in his efforts with the Hagari people though he had found the Serigima were in a state of unrest. Despite the original plans going astray, the surveyor pushed on, departing his Brown River camp on 24th May.

> Progress was slow [recorded Stuart-Russell] as the rain, which had been pretty constant all along, showed no signs of abating, and several men were on the sick list; also the track had to be cut all the way.

On 4th June, the expedition reached the village of Omali, but the going was found too difficult, and they retraced their steps to the previous night's camp. From here a better route was found, and on 7th June, after having peacefully passed through the Hagari locality, Stuart-Russell and his men reached The Gap. Here he waited for fresh supplies.

Meanwhile, back in Port Moresby, Le Hunte had been concerned by Ballantine's failure to meet Stuart-Russell as he was aware the strength of the surveyor's party alone was insufficient for entry into unknown territory. He had also

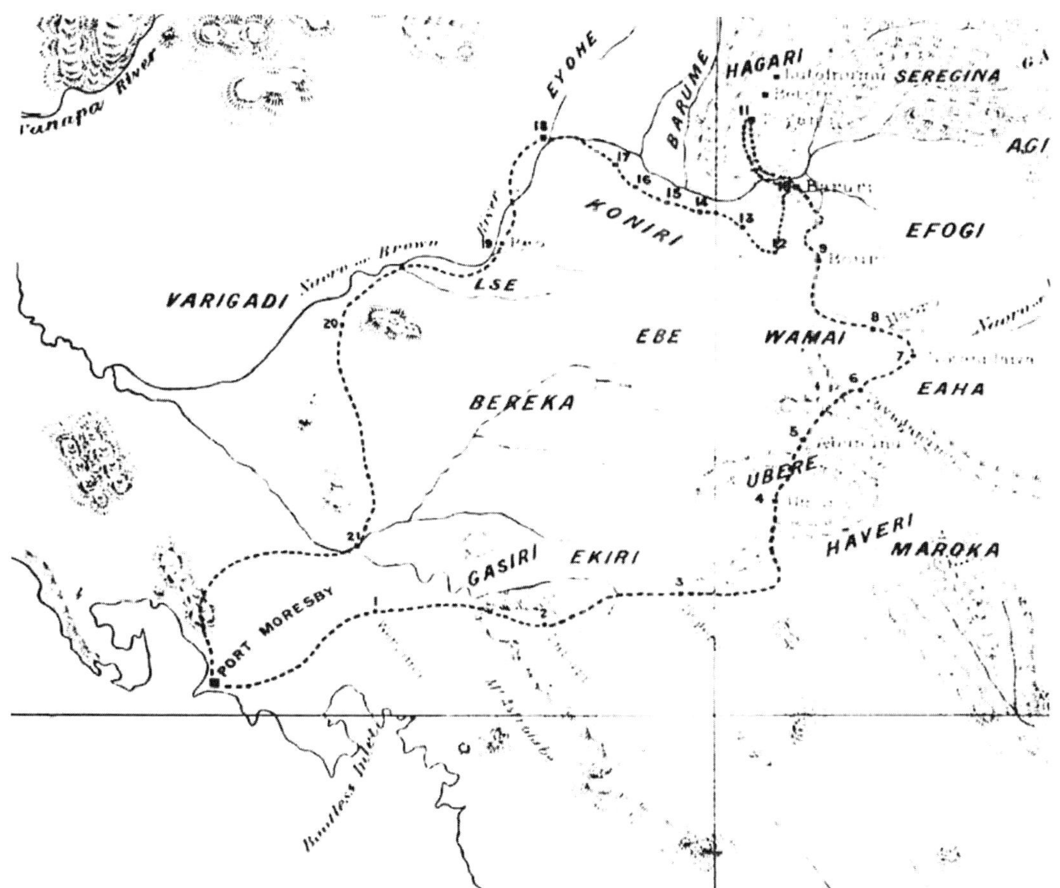

realised the cost of the expedition would be more than had been estimated so decided to instruct Stuart-Russell not to proceed past The Gap. Orders to this effect and a relief party under Charles Monckton were immediately sent inland, on 22nd June, and Monckton with the impetus of urgency, initially made good time along Stuart-Russell's track until he was unexpectedly delayed some distance up the Brown River. A punt he had been using to carry stores was swamped and all supplies on board lost, Monckton himself narrowly escaping being drowned. He had to wait for over a week for replacement of the lost items from Port Moresby.

Unaware of Monckton's misfortune, and after waiting for three weeks, Stuart-Russell was impatient to get going and had decided to push on, despite not receiving his reinforcements and fresh supplies. Fortunately, Monckton had sent on an advance carrier team with some supplies and MacDonald, following behind Stuart-Russell with a detachment of the survey party, had met this group on the track. The combined parties arrived at The Gap just as the surveyor was leaving.

> Just then MacDonald arrived ... I learned that Mr Monckton was on the way with ample supplies and five or six extra police. This was the 29th June, and, as Mr Monckton it appeared, left Port Moresby on or about the 23rd I judged he must be well on his way. However, I would not wait his arrival, but sent him a letter requesting him to station a couple of police with the two I intended to leave a few miles further on, then to build a store and await my return.

The following day (30th June 1899), Stuart-Russell continued his journey northwards, passing for the first time (by a white man) through The Gap, to a point about 15 kilometres further on. Here he established a fortified storehouse and installed two policemen there.

> All the superfluous baggage was left here [he recorded]. The party now consisted of Mr MacDonald and myself, two picked men of the armed constabulary ... and three warders— two of whom could shoot fairly well. Altogether, five rifles and two shotguns ...

Stuart-Russell realised he was taking a risk in not waiting for Monckton's relief expedition and expected a hostile reception to greet their small party. He needed have had no fear of the first group of natives contacted 'who throughout were most friendly and hospitable'. The natives conducted the party to their principal village of Eora (then Iuoro) where they were presented with food and drink.

> The old chief, Iovo, tried hard to dissuade us from going on to the Yodda Valley [recorded Stuart-Russell] declaring we would all be killed. However, when he found we were resolved to go on, he personally escorted us some distance.

On 2nd July 1899, the party reached the upper reaches of the Mambare near its junction with Eora Creek, thus proving conclusively passage across the country via The Gap was possible. Almost immediately, they came across two natives fishing on the bank. This pair greeted the travellers cordially enough but left after signalling to Stuart-Russell to go no further. Half an hour later, the two men returned accompanied by forty or fifty men,

> preceded fully 100 yards [about 90 metres] by their chief. Waving aloft a taro plant, he rushed right up to us—an instance of confidence that I have never seen before so boldly displayed, and at once dispelled any doubts I may have had as to our friendly reception.

So convinced was Stuart-Russell of the natives' peaceful intentions, he moved his camp the following morning to a hill near their village. During the afternoon however, 'a change set in', as he put it, and after a rifle was snatched up and an unsuccessful attempt was made to discharge it, the surveyor realised he was in a precarious situation.

> Men came pouring in, from all quarters, armed to the teeth [he later wrote]; the discharge of that rifle would have been the signal for a general attack, in which we would have had a very slender chance.

Consequently, Stuart-Russell commenced his withdrawal, at first without conflict but while crossing the Mambare, the party was attacked.

> Looking back as far as I could see was a forest of spears and clubs ... Though they came on again and again with the usual bravery of all natives belonging to that district, they were repulsed every time with loss, and eventually drew off, not a man in my party having been injured.

Meanwhile, Monckton, still pushing inland towards The Gap, had reached the point near Omali where Stuart-Russell had re-traced his steps. Here Monckton lost the surveyor's track but an amusing incident arose out of his predicament. Stuart-Russell had dismissed this route because it took the road along a sharp, narrow spur—a razor-back ridge—and had back-tracked until he found an offshoot of the crest down which he continued his journey. Monckton however, had missed this and had followed Stuart-Russell's original axe-blazes up to the knife-edged spur. Monckton, admitting to a fear of heights but believing this was the path leading him to Stuart-Russell, gritted his teeth and determinedly set out to cross the ridge, despite his being, as he put it, 'half-paralysed with funk'.

> Then, afraid to look down* [he wrote] I walked as far as I could, with the cold sweat of fear streaming from me; then I sat, straddled that fearsome spur with my legs, and slowly—leap-frog fashion—began to work my way across thirty feet [about 9 metres] of the worst part, the stones and dirt I dislodged falling so far that their impact sent up no sound. Half-way across, my thin cotton breeches began to tear badly with the stones; as I went, I suddenly felt if ten thousand red-hot pincers were tearing at the portion of my anatomy exposed by the torn garments; I stood the agony for a second, then—unable to bear it any longer—leapt to my feet, and ran like a tight-rope walker across that narrow crumbling ridge. Reaching safety and a wider part of the spur, I sat down and tore a score of bull-dog ants from my skin; I had worked my way clean over a nest of the malignant little beasts.

With his dynamism activated, it did not take long for Monckton, despite having to find his own way, to reach Stuart-Russel's camp at The Gap. He recorded:

> At last our journey ended. One afternoon we marched into a large clearing, in which stood a log hut, surrounded by a ring of natives camped at a safe distance from Russell's men in the hut, but closely investing it; it was the last post Russell had placed [as far as Monckton knew], before disappearing across to the Yodda. We soon swept away the surrounding natives, who had been patiently waiting until the men in the hut were starved into the open.
>
> As the rattle of our rifle fire died away, in marched Russell from the other side ... . Russell had been having a very tough time: he had by degrees broken up his force, leaving them in log huts to guard his line of communication ... When I came up, he was falling back upon a weak camp surrounded by hordes of savages; his stores were exhausted, and most of his ammunition spent. Replenished with fresh police, stores and ammunition, I left him, taking with me all the sick and exhausted carriers and worn-out police back to Port Moresby. Russell remained for a week to complete some survey work.

Stuart-Russell returned to Port Moresby on 30th July to review his findings and to finalise his report. He found 'much remains yet to be done' but considered 'a cross country road to

---

* Razor-back ridges are narrow ridges which rise very steeply on either side to produce a ridge top, typically of about 200 millimetres or so in width. They can be hundreds of metres high. In the area discussed by Monckton, the majority of the ridges have only sparse vegetation. To fall off a razor-back ridge is akin to falling from a cliff.

the N.E. coast via the Gap is practical'. While he was unsure of the best route such a road should take out from Port Moresby, he at least had an opinion on where it should *not* go. His report finally killed of any possibility of MacGregor's long-favoured Brown River route being officially adopted:

> The existing track via Korima [on the Brown River] is unsuitable. It unnecessarily increases the distance by fully twenty miles [32 kilometres], necessitating the crossing of the Laloki at a very awkward place.

The siting of MacDonald's road was also viewed unfavourably because it crossed low-lying land that became swamp during the wet season and would therefore be 'very costly' to maintain. Stuart-Russell personally felt it was best to enter the high country as soon as possible after leaving the coast, and included two alternate routes in his report for consideration and further examination, one of these incorporating the route across the Sogeri Plateau and through Uberi regularly taken by Ballantine. The approach to The Gap also caused him some concern. 'The rainfall is abnormal', he found, 'and the road will have to be corduroyed or metalled'. In spite of these difficulties, Stuart-Russell was confident a passable route could eventually be put through. He concluded his report by stating:

> Assuming that the construction of the road is commenced at both ends with fifty men in each party ... it will take about two years to complete the work. The cost will probably be about £10,000.

Though Le Hunte was pleased with the outcome of the expedition, it was likely the high estimate to complete the project was the reason why an order to commence work was not immediately issued. Indeed, the fact the finances of the Colony were already well over-committed was the reason why Le Hunte had wished Stuart-Russell to go no further than The Gap. Yet, he did attempt to push the project through:

> My economical purposes, though well intentioned, were therefore ineffective, and I cannot honestly say I am sorry for it [Le Hunte wrote of Stuart-Russell's entry into the country north of The Gap]. The fact of a surveying party remaining in the mountains and passing through the interior in friendly relations with the natives from whom we anticipated obstruction, if not actual hostilities, will have a most excellent effect, and I shall rely on a liberal appreciation of this when I apply for the approval of the expenditure which has

> been incurred in this important work of development of the country and extension of the authority of the Government.*

However, finance for a continuation of the project was not forthcoming and without separate ear-marked funds, it would have been impossible for the Administration of the day to go ahead on its own. (The entire public works budget for 1898/99 was only £100). Le Hunte asked for £500 for the 1899/1900 period solely for 'Roads to the Interior and Goldfields' and received nothing allocated solely for this purpose; but in the event, the Colony spent £558/6/9 on roads in the 1899/1900 period, most of this going to the north coast gold fields area, with none being available for work on the overland route. The total revenue from all sources for the entire Colony for the year ended 30th June 1900 amounted to only £13,834, while expenditure for the same period totalled over £21,000. (The revenue for the Colony was still below £20,000 three years later). As a result, Stuart-Russell's recommendations for an overland route were not taken-up and the project was officially shelved.

---

* There was an amusing consequence of Stuart-Russell's journey that gives an insight into how pleased Le Hunte was at the results achieved by the surveyor. Le Hunte had been annoyed that circumstances had conspired to prevent his instructions to Stuart-Russell not to proceed past The Gap being acted upon. He felt that the surveyor took unnecessary and unwarranted risks in leaving before Monckton arrived, and that had he waited, he would have received his instructions to go no further.

> Russell, however [wrote Monckton], being a keen hydrographer, had, at the imminent risk of his own and his men's lives, descended upon the opposite side, and got into difficulties; the magnificent work he did saved him from censure or blame; but as a matter of fact he richly deserved the sack for attempting it. Russell afterwards showed me a letter from Sir George Le Hunte which began, 'You dear disobedient person, I should be very angry with you, but instead, I can only feel pleased'. I made but one remark to Russell, and that was, 'You thank your stars you are dealing with Sir George instead of Sir William MacGregor; for if you had disobeyed him, you would have had something to remember!'.

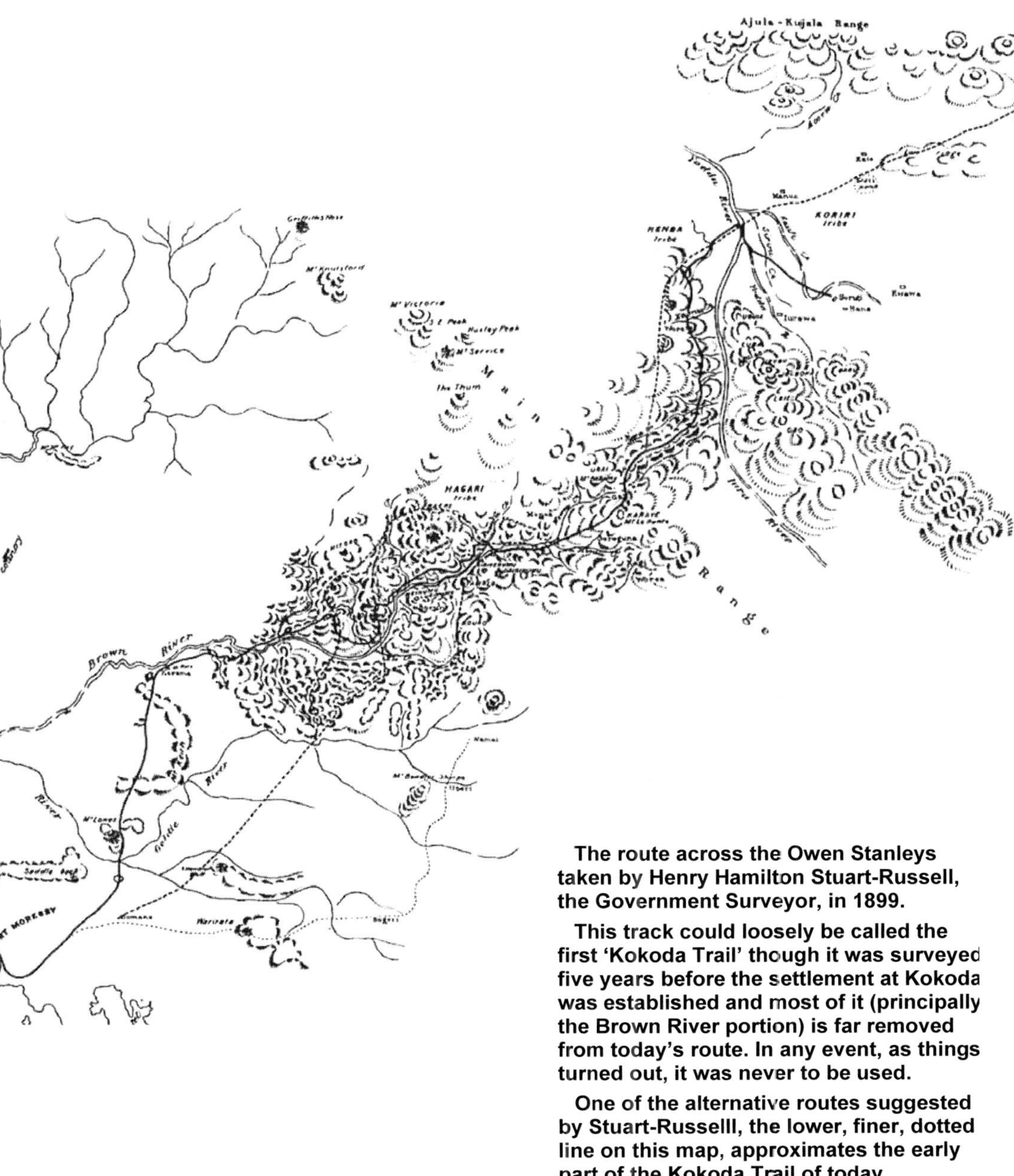

The route across the Owen Stanleys taken by Henry Hamilton Stuart-Russell, the Government Surveyor, in 1899.

This track could loosely be called the first 'Kokoda Trail' though it was surveyed five years before the settlement at Kokoda was established and most of it (principally the Brown River portion) is far removed from today's route. In any event, as things turned out, it was never to be used.

One of the alternative routes suggested by Stuart-Russelll, the lower, finer, dotted line on this map, approximates the early part of the Kokoda Trail of today.

University of Queensland.

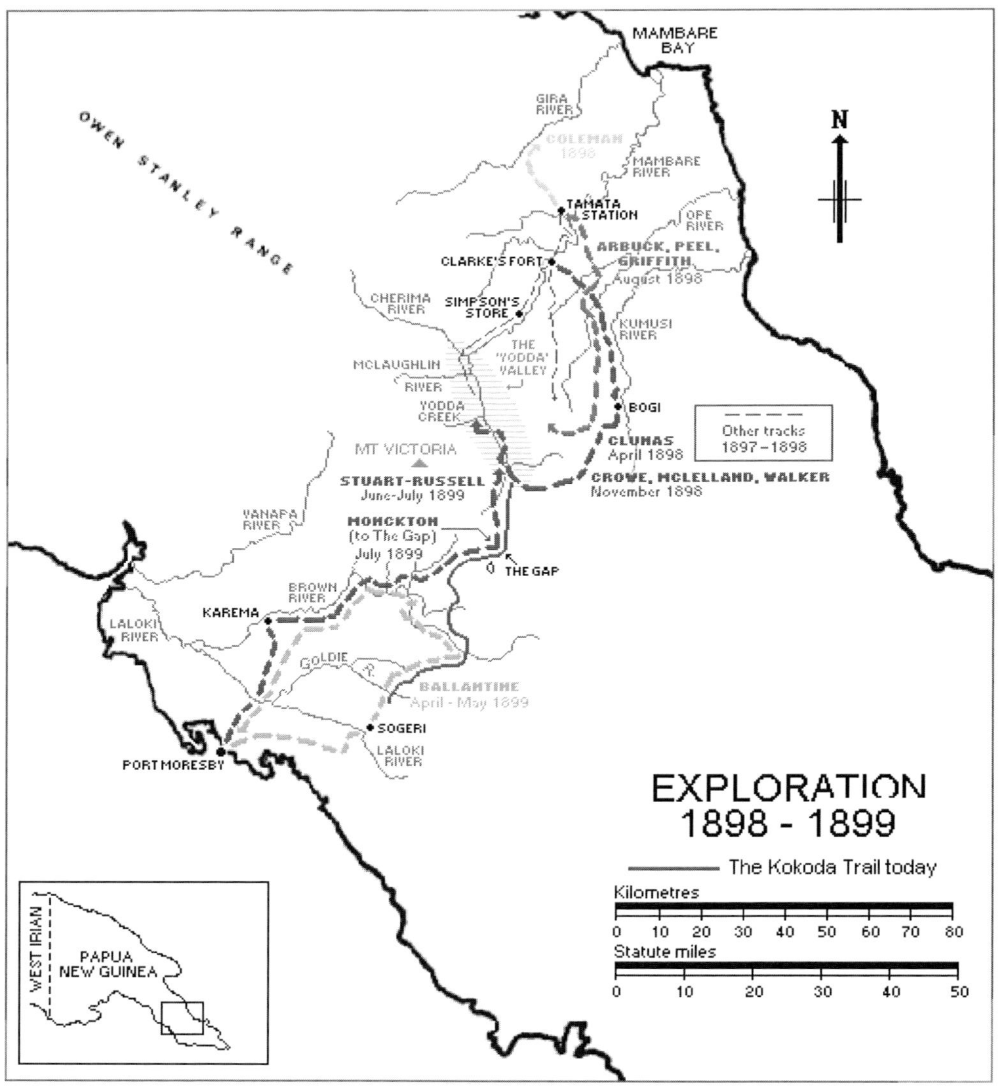

Summary of exploration 1898–1899. *Author.*

Part 2

Heyday

1900-1939

High's the road to Port Moresby, and rough,
Yodda Valley lies west in a trough,
Aye, digger, 'tis quite enough,
The sixty long miles to Kokoda.

From 'Via Kokoda' by 'Decemvir',
Papuan Courier, 13th January 1928

7

The northern goldfields (1900–1905)

As the 19th century drew to a close, there were persistent indications the alluvial gold was becoming more difficult to obtain and a decline in gold production on many of the northern goldfields was imminent. Francis Winter, following an inspection of the north coast mining areas in his capacity as Acting Administrator in January 1899, reported 'some miners appear to have done well enough; some have not made a living. We brought away three destitute men'.

This was fairly typical on the older diggings. The new Yodda (upper Mambare) field, the track to which was pioneered by Clunas in April 1898, was the only locality on the Mambare affording any encouragement to the prospectors and many left their old sites to try their luck there. The prospects were so promising on the Yodda, which was proclaimed as a goldfield on 31st July 1900, Resident Magistrate Armit was moved to comment it was 'the best goldfield ever opened in New Guinea'. In the eleven months following the proclamation, during which the total number of miners and indentured labourers peaked at 715, almost 280 kilograms of gold were extracted, or an average of almost two and half kilograms of gold for each white miner there.

Alluvial mining on the Yodda goldfield, c. 1900. By the end of 1909, most of these claims had been 'washed out'.

University of Papua New Guinea.

But it was a very difficult field to work on. At the beginning of 1900, when the first resident miners moved in following Matt Crowe's expedition, all food to the Yodda field had to be shipped from Samarai, brought up the Mambare to Tamata by boat, then carried in from Tamata via Clarke's Fort by native carriers. This route followed the track established by Clunas in 1898. The distance between Tamata and the main Yodda camp at the time was 210 kilometres. This distance meant the bulk of a carrier's load of food was consumed by the carrier himself, resulting in the cost of the too few supplies that were delivered being grossly expensive. To alleviate this, Armit decided to bypass Clarke's Fort and establish a shorter route direct from Tamata Station, a route originally shown to be feasible by Arbuck in November 1898. Armit's track, put in during the first three months of 1900, terminated in the region of the Koko people on the northern slopes of Mount Bellamy, less than seven kilometres from The Gap.

Armit's new route was a significant accomplishment but the merit of his work was overshadowed by controversy. As noted earlier, the native inhabitants of the Ope, Kumusi and upper Mambare rivers were of aggressive disposition, a fact well appreciated by Armit. He had been the only white man in his expedition of 77 persons which passed through country occupied by people who were, as Armit found, 'well-to-do, numerous, treacherous, arrogant, truculent, and bitterly hostile'. Accordingly, he adopted an attitude of 'aggressive' defence to ensure he always had the upper-hand in dealing with any warring tribes, never allowing his party to be put at a disadvantage. During the three month expedition, his party was responsible for shooting dead a total of 54 actual or potential native attackers without loss to the expedition. Needless to say, this was not acceptable to the government executive in Port Moresby. Le Hunte was appalled to hear of Armit's actions, and sent him a stern official memorandum, which concluded:

> I do not ... underestimate the difficulties of such work as you have so well performed, and which I am satisfied will have good and permanent results, but I think you may not be aware how very serious a thing it is in my view to have to take human life, or I am certain you would not have spoken of it in your official report as if it was, when justifiable, of but little moment.
>
> I shall be glad to have the fuller particulars I have asked for as soon as possible, for the information of the Governor of Queensland and the Secretary of State.

It is indeed a serious act to take a human life. However, if one takes Armit's position, it is perhaps possible to at least understand his actions if not condone them. The only white man among primitive people, with grossly inadequate resources to satisfy the Port Moresby government's expectations, and knowing from experience it is impossible to reason with somebody in the process of throwing a spear, he did what he felt was necessary and unavoidable.

On top of this, Armit was suffering from malaria for the whole trip. One particular incident too, while camped at Papangi on the upper Kumusi River on 17th February, may have had much to do with Armit's frame of mind. His men had chanced upon the remains of a cannibal feast, and Armit's report of the incident, written the evening of the same day, shows the extent of the strain he was under.

> At 4 p.m. Constable Ade marched into camp, followed by six of my carriers carrying five human legs and the fore-quarter of a girl about twelve years of age ... They were all crying bitterly, the tears rolling down their cheeks, and showing signs of deep emotion. They deposited these gruesome trophies at my tent door ... I felt completely nonplussed. I did not know what to think, and gave up the attempt for a time. I felt sick, although inured to every sort of horror; this, after my recent illness, quite unnerved me. ... The girl's left side and arm and hand presented a heartrending spectacle as it lay on the ground; the arm extended, the pretty, shapely, little brown hand resting on the ground. ... The whole incident was horrible beyond description.

It was of course Le Hunte's duty as governor to quickly condemn Armit's apparently outrageous behaviour and demand a full account. Nevertheless, the fact remained the indigenous people of the area from the Mambare River to the Kumusi River were far more aggressive than those on the south coast and it was necessary for Armit, if only for personal survival, to take an opposing stance of equal intensity. This differed to great degree from the approach taken to tribes about Port Moresby, with which Le Hunte was most familiar. As well, Armit's reports were written as events occurred and tended to suggest a coarseness of sensibilities when read later out of context, particularly in the relative tranquillity of Port Moresby. Of the several government officers who were to serve in the region in the early years of the district, only those who took a similar hard line to Armit were to have any real success in developing and pacifying the area. Though a trite rationalisation, there is considerable truth in saying the area was 'warrior' country and government officers needed to display those qualities admired by the warriors of the region to gain their respect.

In any event, despite his efforts during the expedition, even as he returned to Tamata on 1st April, Armit realised his new track was not suitable because the hostile areas it crossed made it too risky for unaccompanied strangers to enter. As well, his track was still too long and crossed much swampy ground totally unsuitable for a general purpose route. Armit reported of his journey:

> When on my way out, and again when returning to Tamata, I had to wade a distance of 13 miles [21 kilometres], waist deep, and in very cold water—a very unpleasant experience, as in many places no road could be detected, and I had to cut my way in search of the track.

In March 1900, as Armit returned to Tamata, Clunas and partner W.M. Clark established a retail store at Bogi, the limit of navigation on the Kumusi River, 97 kilometres from the coast. This was the incentive Armit needed to abandon his new track and put into action a personal plan he had been considering for some time: a track which would bypass Tamata entirely and proceed directly to the Yodda field from the north coast. In June 1900, he reported

> ... the development of the [Yodda] goldfield has been ruthlessly strangled by the exorbitantly high price of provisions, ... [and] men are working there in a state of semi-starvation, and battling with virulent fevers and exposed to terrible privations, and it is this very knowledge with the superaddition of the fact that, in spite of all these disadvantages, the miners cling tenaciously to the ground, which leads me to the conclusion that, given a mule track from Holcinote Bay [on the north coast] ... the Yodda Gold Field would, in a very short time, give lucrative employment to several thousand miners.

In a report on his Tamata–Yodda route, he opined it would be 'very improbable' his new route would ever be utilised to any great extent by miners. He pointed out

> ... the traffic to the Yodda Gold Field has already been diverted from Tamata to the Kumusi River, a very difficult waterway to navigate, owing to the rapidity of the current ... a waterway I trust I shall shortly be in a position to supplement by cutting a good mule track from Holnicote Bay across the long slope of Mt. Lamington ... This road will reduce the distance to the field by at least 90 miles [145 kilometres], and the substitution of mules must, I think, reduce the cost of provisions *pro tanto*. ... We can, therefore, assume that, for the present at least, the initial starting point for land carriage will be at Gobi [Bogi] landing, where Messrs. Clunas and Clark have established a store.

He reinforced his argument by summarising as follows:

> From Tamata to the [Yodda] field the distance is 130 miles [210 kilometres].
>
> From Kumusi mouth to [the Yodda] field, 160 miles [257 kilometres].
>
> With a mule track from Gona, in Holnicote Bay, about 73 miles [117 kilometres].

But he did not under-estimate the difficulties posed by the natives and he took pains to reiterate the inclinations of the local people:

> They are certainly not destitute of courage, but, on the other hand, they are treacherous, truculent, aggressive, cruel and cunning. It will prove a task of some magnitude to keep these tribes in check ... They are cannibals from a sheer love of human flesh, and hunt each other simply to gratify their carnivorous desires. They fight treacherously and lie abominably. ... From the little that I saw of the people inhabiting the trans-Kumusi, I came to the conclusion that there will be trouble there whenever I start to cut a mule track across the long slope [of Mount Lamington].

Following his return to Tamata in April 1900, Armit established a new Government post at Bogi, installing Alexander Elliott in charge. This appointment allowed Armit some freedom from his other duties and in June 1900 personally began the task of cutting the new track from Gona, assisted only by unskilled native labourers. This was across terrain completely unknown to and uninhabited by Europeans. However, despite some minor skirmishes, the anticipated serious trouble did not eventuate though there were difficulties of another kind. In the damp, steamy conditions of the Gona swamplands, the task

Armit had set himself offered only gruelling, unremitting, debilitating labour, and after eight weeks, Armit physically could not continue. However, after a short break in Australia in August 1900 to recuperate from his exertions and recurring malaria, he returned to the task and had nearly finished the project by December. But his failing health, exacerbated by the physical exhaustion of his work and given no real chance to improve, forced him once again to stop work on the Gona road. Suffering chronically from malaria, Armit's conditioned worsened at Christmas 1900, and on 3rd January 1901, he suddenly collapsed and died at Tamata Station.*

Government carriers negotiating the Kumusi River in minor flood, c. 1900.

PNG National Library.

Succeeding Armit as Resident Magistrate for the Northern Division was Archibald Lyon Walker. Walker, who had previously been Chief Clerk of the Government Secretary's Office in Port Moresby, was an ex-miner who, with Crowe and McLelland, had been one of the pioneers of the track into the Yodda valley in November 1899. Nevertheless, he had no easy baptism to government field work. He was based at Tamata and found dealing with the regions about Armit's new track to be demanding work, if only for the distances he had to travel from his base. One of his early reports indicated:

> Beyond Bogi to the head of the Kumusi and the Yodda Valley [a people called the 'Orokaivas' occupied this region], I am sorry to say the people seem to be most determinedly antagonistic to the Government and the white mining population that is continually passing through their country.

On the day Armit died, two white miners, Thomas Campion and John King and three of their carriers, were murdered on their way to the Yodda by a group of Orokaiva people. With twelve policemen from Tamata Station, Alec Elliot (based at Bogi), along with William McLelland (of the original Mambare group under Simpson, who had entered the area 13 months

* The reports of Armit's cited in these pages are taken from official records. Armit was a journalist by profession and was a prolific keeper of diaries. After his death, these went to his son Lionel Armit, then living in Samarai but who later moved to Port Moresby, and who was also in the Papuan government service. All of William Armit's diaries were destroyed in February 1942 during an air raid on Port Moresby. Copies were never taken of the diaries and it is to be regretted that such a valuable record of one of the original white pioneers of the country has been irretrievably lost.

earlier with Walker and Matt Crowe, and who had been with Campion and King when they were attacked), attempted to apprehend those responsible. A spirited fight erupted during which King's actual murderer and 28 of his supporters were killed. Coming only 12 months after Armit's expedition into the same area, Le Hunte was furious at first to learn of these further deaths. However, when he and Walker toured the region in April 1901, and he saw the fighting spirit of the Orokaivas, he began to better understand the difficulties his staff faced.

Walker, a young man of tolerant and understanding disposition, was himself dismayed at the turn of events. Even with his previous experience of the area, he was astounded at the unrelenting determination of the natives not to be friendly and was distressed circumstances had eventuated as they had. Walker realised the natives' point of view had to be recognised if a lasting peace was ever to be established:

> Crime amongst the natives in a community such as this, with a host of intruders constantly coming against them, whose motives they do not understand, has not yet been reduced to the limit it assumes in an ordinary civilised society.

Walker persevered, undertaking a course of action not uncommon in British New Guinea at the time. He organised three patrols to enter the various districts of others suspected to have taken part in the attack on Campion and King, and each patrol summarily took one prisoner each. These prisoners were incarcerated in the gaol at Tamata Station.

> These natives have been kindly treated [reported Walker] and on their return home they should have a good influence upon their respective tribes, and be a means of initiating a better state of things amongst these unsophisticated people.

Some relief for the staff of the undermanned Northern Division had brought about when a new division, the North-Eastern, was created on 8th April 1900. The purpose of this was to better control the parts of the Northern and Eastern Divisions (headquarters of the latter being at Samarai) which were far distant from the government stations and which could not receive proper attention. Charles Monckton was appointed the Resident Magistrate of the North-Eastern Division and was installed at the new Government Station established at Cape Nelson. The Northern Division had also received an addition to its staff with the appointment of Richard de Moleyns in February 1901 to Bogi Station to assist Elliott.

By the end of 1901, in spite of a wide-ranging patrol programme, Walker had made little headway in pacifying the villagers of the Upper Ope and Kumusi districts. The most troublesome area was on the Bogi to Yodda section of Armit's track, where the warriors made it, in Walker's understated terms, 'somewhat unsafe for travellers'. To counter this, he established another Government Post at Papangi (also known then as Papaki) in early 1902. The intention of this was to protect the western flank of the Bogi–Yodda track from roving Ope River warriors. From this time, there began a slow change for the better in the attitude of the previously hostile groups, and a more optimistic outlook for the district became evident almost immediately in official reports. Papangi was ideally located, being midway along the road to the Yodda field. De Moleyns, from Bogi, was placed in its charge.

> The establishment of this post led to beneficial results [reported Le Hunte in the Annual Report that year]. It deterred the natives from attacking travellers, and it gave the Magistrate in charge of it [de Moleyns] time and opportunity to get into communication with them. After a while many of the natives, finding that the

Charles Arthur Whitmore Monckton, Resident Magistrate, explorer and founder of the town of Kokoda. Much of the route of today's road from Buna to Kokoda was developed by Monckton.

After leaving Papua in 1907, Monckton went to New Zealand but on the outbreak of the 1914-18 war, he enlisted in the army and served in Europe. Monckton died in England on 1st March 1936.

PNG National Library.

Government did not wish to harm them, became more or less friendly.

On 20th June 1902, Walker succumbed to an attack of the lethal Tamata 'fever' and was succeeded by R. Hislop*. Because of the improving relations with the natives, Hislop found the task of overseeing the goldfields easier than earlier Resident Magistrates. Elliot had eased the difficulties of access to the Yodda field with the cutting of a new track direct to Papangi from the coast. But despite these improvements, life on the Yodda field was still far from pleasant. Sickness, high prices, and a dearth of native assistants were continuing impediments to economical mining and a gradual drift of miners away from the field began. The Gira field too, north-west of Tamata Station, was having one of its periodic resurgences of popularity, and by June 1902, only seventy white miners remained on the Yodda.

On 1st September 1903, Hislop went on leave of absence (during which he resigned) and Monckton of the neighbouring North-Eastern Division was put in charge of Hislop's area in addition to his own. This was not unusual in the light of the chronic staff shortages then prevailing in British New Guinea, though it gave Monckton a huge area to look after. Monckton was not well liked by the executive of the Government, mainly for his frequent use of force to establish 'peace', but he was efficient, energetic and courageous, and his general competency was grudgingly recognised in Port Moresby. Monckton's first action was to set about completing a series of cross-patrols between his two Divisions.

In April 1904, de Moleyns reported from Papangi a change in the attitude of the Koko hill tribes at the head of the Yodda Valley to the miners encamped there suggested serious trouble was brewing. The unrest came from the same people who had attacked Matt Crowe's exploring party in 1899. Monckton acted upon de Moleyns' warning at once, shifting de Moleyns and his staff from Papangi, and Elliott from Bogi into the Koko region.

* Immediately before his arrival at Tamata, Hislop had been acting in charge of the Mekeo District on the south coast following the death of the substantive Resident Magistrate, Amadeo Giulianetti. Giulianetti, it will be recalled, was employed by MacGregor to develop the Vanapa Track across the ranges in 1897. He was accidentally shot dead by a Mekeo native on 4th November 1901.

Initially, this post was intended to be only a temporary one. However, its location was so successful in leading to more effective administration, and so better sited from a health point of view, being over 300 metres above sea level, Monckton decided to make the move a permanent one. Accordingly, in June 1904, and without reference to Port Moresby (or, as Monckton put it, 'I did not enter into a long correspondence with Headquarters on the subject'), he closed down both Papangi and Bogi Stations, and transferred all remaining Government staff and equipment to the new settlement. Thus, the township of Kokoda came into being.

(Monckton was certainly instrumental in the establishment of the Kokoda settlement. However, there is a subtle implication in his *Some Experiences of a New Guinea Resident Magistrate* it was he and he alone who recognised the importance of Kokoda's location. This is not the case. The value of the site was first recorded by William Armit in 1900, four years earlier. In a report outlining a scheme to counter the perceived menace of the people in the area, Armit recommended [in recommendations numbered 3 and 4] as follows:

> 3. Headquarters station at Koko, mining warden, twenty-two constables, gaol, one warder.
>
> 4. Proclamation of township of 4,000 acres [about 1600 hectares] (or less) near Koko to be included in the goldfield.

It is not known whether Monckton was aware of Armit's specific recommendations—however, though Armit's recommendations were not acted upon by the government in Port Moresby, it is likely the desirability of the Kokoda site was common knowledge among Northern Division staff. That Monckton was privy to this knowledge would be consistent with, and explain to some extent, his refusal to confer with Port Moresby when his turn to act came).

The establishment of Kokoda Station was the catalyst for the subsequent developments on and about the Yodda goldfield. The improvement in the attitude of the native population, commencing around 1901 during Walker's time and slowly gaining momentum since, picked up noticeably, the native population quickly coming to accept the new white settlement in their midst. It was not to be a temporary undertaking on the natives' part either. Monckton's (admittedly self-serving) report in August 1905, over a year later, indicated

> since the establishment of the station, a most satisfactory state of affairs in regard to the lives and property of the mining population on the gold-field has been brought about; not a single case of robbery at a camp has taken place, before so rife, nor has an instance of assault or attempt to murder occurred. The value of the abolition of Bogi and Papangi stations, and the transference of their combined staffs to Kokoda, is thus clearly demonstrated.

But Kokoda was an isolated post and in the same report, Monckton highlighted their special situation:

> The station is situated some 13 miles [about 21 kilometres] from Mt. Victoria, and 70 [113 kilometres] from the coast; it is the farthest inland Government station in British New Guinea. ... Kokoda has from the first laboured under peculiar difficulties, for it must be remembered that nearly every ounce of food consumed by Armed Native Constabulary, prisoners, and officers, together with building material, ammunition, and the hundred and one requisites necessary for a large Government post had to be carried in on the backs of carriers for six days' journey from the coast.

As noted, the economics of the transport of supplies into the region had been recognised right at the start of the Yodda goldfield as a serious impediment to development. Since 1900, there had been several attempts to find a road direct from the coast, rather than through Tamata Junction or Clarke's Fort or from points on the Ope or Kumusi Rivers. Despite the efforts of others, Armit's 1900 route from Gona had not changed much in three years and, unsuitable as it was, remained the only direct link with the sea. The alternative, by boat and canoe via the Kumusi River to Bogi, and then overland to the Yodda, was slightly less expensive but carried its own set of dangers and difficulties. The terminus of any route into the area was the 'Yodda field' or 'Yodda Valley'. These terms were, in a sense, vaguely defined. But with the establishment of Kokoda Station in 1904 providing an official and specific place to which the track would be directed, to a certain extent a fresh imperative came to be recognised, leading to the refocussing of efforts to find, once and for all, the most economical supply route from the northern coast.

Earlier, in July 1903, Monckton (then in charge of the North-Eastern Division only) and the Acting Administrator Christopher Stansfield Robinson (who had succeeded Le Hunte in June 1903) had attempted to put through a track from Ketakerua Bay in Dyke Acland Bay, about 67 kilometres south-east of Holnicote Bay, to Papangi on the Kumusi. They

abandoned this route after finding 'a road across the country traversed was quite impracticable'. Monckton kept well to the north of this rough terrain on his next attempt. In September 1903, when he also had charge of the Northern Division, he had his officers put in a considerable amount of time in cutting a new track from Buna, in Holnicote Bay about twelve kilometres

Crossing the Kumusi River was a hazardous undertaking when the river was in flood. Here, a hemp hawswer has been utilised to provide a measure of safety while crossing over on a log jam. This photograph was taken in about 1906.

Later, a wire hawser was installed and then in April 1907, Assistant Resident Magistrate Francis Naylor and a miner named Gunton erected the first 'wire rope' bridge. The crossing and the nearby settlement which developed was later to become known as Wiarope.

***PNG** National Library.*

down the coast from Gona. The route Monckton took connected with and was roughly that of Armit's for much of the way, but generally improved and re-routed where desirable. This was to become the basis of the present road from Buna to Kokoda. Following Kokoda's establishment in June 1904, the intensified work rate resulted in a new portion of road being put in over the main branch of the Kumusi. Previously, this crossing had been avoided by travelling on a longer track further to the east, where narrower streams only had to be negotiated. To assist in this project, Monckton obtained the services of the Government Surveyor, Ernest Septimus Tooth for several months.

In June 1904, the Acting Administrator, Captain Francis Rickman Barton*, visited the northern goldfields to inspect the diggings and to examine the track put in by Monckton and Tooth. He was very pleased at the physical and social progress made in the region, recording in the Annual Report for 1903/04:

> A considerable proportion of the time of the Divisional Officers was given to the making of the new road to the Yodda Valley Gold-field from Buna Bay. The greater part of this road was cut by the rawest of wild savages—local tribes who, up till very recently, refused to submit to, or even parley with, the Government. By exercising tact and forbearance Mr. Monckton and his officers succeeded in winning the complete confidence of these wild people, and they eventually came in shoals to assist in felling the hugely high and dense scrub through which the road passes. Without their help the road would have cost considerably more, and it is even doubtful whether in that case it could have been made at all.

In the same report, Monckton gives some details of the work done:

---

* Previously holding positions of private secretary to Le Hunte, Commandant of the Armed Native Constabulary, and Resident Magistrate of the Central Division, the well-connected Barton lobbied for and obtained appointment as Acting Administrator on the suspension of the previous incumbent Christopher Robinson. Robinson, the son of a New Zealand doctor, was suspended from office following the scandal in March 1904 at Goaribari Island where a party under his command allegedly shot fifty natives. He had been attempting to secure the return of the remains of Oliver Tomkins who, along with James Chalmers, was murdered and eaten by the Goaribari people at Dopima in April 1901. Shortly after his suspension, on 20th June 1904, Robinson committed suicide in Port Moresby. Barton, on the other hand, enjoyed a long life. After the 1906 Royal Commission, Barton returned to London where, in 1908, he was appointed to the Ministry of Zanzibar. He retired in 1913 and died in Devonshire on 4th October 1947.

Government carriers crossing one of the Kumusi River's feeder streams, c. 1900.

University of Papua New Guinea.

> Fifty-one miles [82 kilometres] of road from Buna Bay towards the Yodda Valley Gold-field have been cut, and a major portion of the bridges required put in—sixteen miles [26 kilometres] remain to be done. A wire hawser, with iron traveller, has been placed across the Kumusi River by which passengers and loads up to 1 ton [about 1 tonne] can be crossed with safety.

These improvements produced instant benefits and though the road was still not completed, porterage charges dropped by £1 for each 23 kilogram load. The last 26 kilometres of the Buna to Kokoda road was completed in June 1905 by Raynor Laming Bellamy, who had been Assistant Resident Magistrate at Kokoda since September 1904.

Six months before the final stretch of the Buna–Kokoda road work was completed by Bellamy, a route reaching directly from Port Moresby on the south coast to Kokoda was established. This new route was substantially the same as the track now known as the Kokoda Trail. Compared with the extended difficulties of the time in developing the route from the north coast, the instituting of the Trail seemed almost a minor event. This sense of anticlimax may be due in part to post-war hindsight. Nevertheless, given the twenty years of unrest of the native inhabitants of the Port Moresby hinterland, and the ten years of effort by MacGregor, and later Le-Hunte, to establish an overland route from Port Moresby, the reporting of the new track's inauguration was a curiously subdued one in the Annual Report for 1904/05, where prominence was given to north coast activities.

The Kokoda Trail had its immediate genesis during Barton's inspection of Kokoda in June 1904, when he had met with local miners to hear their suggestions on development of the Yodda field. The original idea of the overland communication route from Port Moresby was raised, it being pointed out the new township of Kokoda was only about 10 kilometres north of The Gap. Official correspondence took about six weeks to travel the 900 kilometres from Port Moresby to Buna by ship, and by porter to Kokoda, whereas it would take a week or less if sent overland. Barton agreed with the idea and on his return to Port Moresby in November, organised an official expedition. On 10th December 1904, an inland expedition departed Port Moresby for The Gap, travelling by way of Bomana, Sogeri, Uberi, Nauro, Menari and Kagi.

Carriers of a government patrol crossing the Mambare River near Kokoda by a rough log bridge.

This photograph was taken in 1912.

PNG National Library.

> The main object of the journey [Barton recorded later] was to test the feasibility of establishing an overland mail service between Port Moresby and Kokoda. ... Considering the fact that none of the tribes between Sogeri and the Gap had been visited for five years, it was satisfactory to find them trustful and at ease. No difficulty whatever was experienced in obtaining carriers ...

Captain Barton himself took charge, with David Ballantine, now Treasurer for the Colony, and Guy Owen Manning, Barton's Private Secretary accompanying him. A message was sent overland by runner to Kokoda (via the Trail) to tell Henry Lysaght Griffin*, the Senior Assistant Resident Magistrate of the

* Henry Griffin was an officer of the Papuan government service who, like Monckton, was tough and competent, and inclined to independent action. These qualities did not endear him to the Port Moresby government but were essential to governing, and surviving in, the remote and dangerous Northern Division of the early 1900s. On the Yodda and other northern goldfields, the personal capabilities of Griffin and Monckton were appreciated and respected by the miners. Writing in the December 1942 *Pacific Islands Monthly*, ex-miner Nixon Westwood recalled that 'Monckton and Griffen [sic] were two men who could use language to make even the most hardened gold-miner stand to attention, and Matt Crowe had a lot of affection for both of them'.

Northern Division, the expedition was on its way. (Griffin had been placed in charge while Monckton was on leave). Griffin's instructions were to meet Barton's party at The Gap on Christmas Day 1904. The native policemen and carriers with both parties were incredulous such an arrangement was possible. In fact, those with Griffin refused at first to believe an agreement could be struck with somebody who was absent, and were convinced he had concocted the story as an excuse for taking them away from their comfortable billets and into the cold, wet mountains. Their disbelief turned to astonishment when the rendezvous was effected on the 22nd December, three days earlier than planned. It was an occasion for celebration and ceremony, as Griffin noted:

> ... we opened a bottle of champagne that Captain Barton had brought for the purpose, and drank it—but out of enamelled iron mugs. ... Then Manning drew up a paper narrating the circumstances, and after it had been signed by everybody, we put it into the now empty bottle, corked the latter well, and solemnly buried it, raising a small heap of stones over the place.

This journey by Barton's party provides the earliest evidence of the course of the Kokoda Trail being officially recognised as a legitimate route in its own right. Other cross-country routes to the northern goldfields, in particular MacGregor's Brown River road, were now abandoned. From this time, this route became the sole overland link between Government offices in Port Moresby and the Yodda settlements. In addition to the communication link, Barton noted other desirable benefits would accrue to its use, particularly because it would bring 'several inland tribes into constant and friendly touch with the Government and with each other'. Accordingly, mail delivery using this route was officially found to be feasible and a mail service viable. In fact, the mail service, which was to be a fortnightly one, was inaugurated with Barton's expedition, for it itself had carried mail for the northern goldfields. But, as the service became established, it was to become unlike any other mail run in the world. Griffin explains how it worked:

> Two policemen from each end took the post bag, the journey taking from four to six days, according to the weather. The two police waited two or three days after delivering same, and then returned with the mail in reply. It was a pretty stiff journey and, in wet

weather, having to cross several rivers in flood, not without a spice of danger and considerable discomfit.

The establishment of the mail route also had another, unexpected, result, as Griffin reported in the Resident Magistrate's report for 1904/05, only six months later:

> Kokoda will, for the future, owing to its regular and rapid communication with Port Moresby, pending the establishment of a coastal station, be the headquarters of the Resident Magistrate for the Division in place of Tamata.

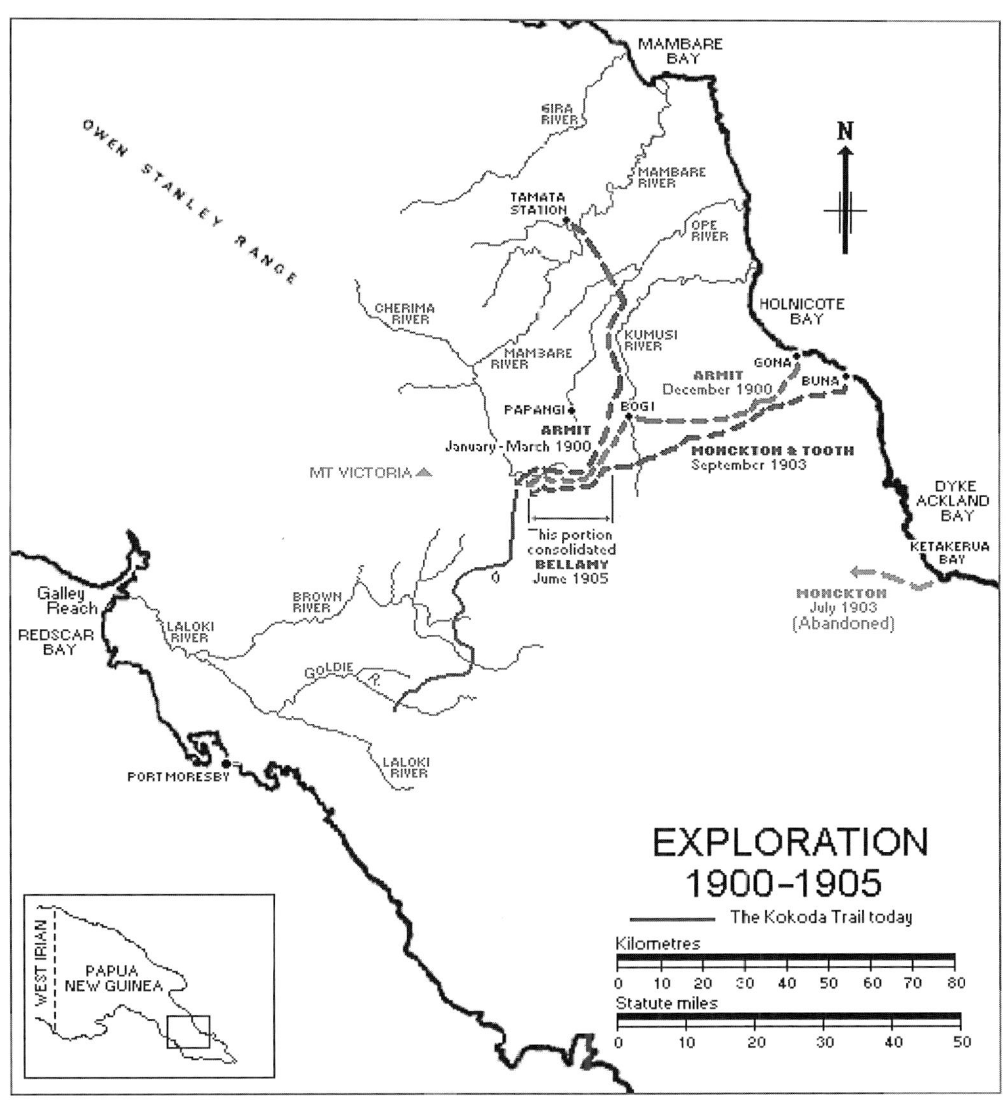

Summary of exploration 1900–1905. *Author.*

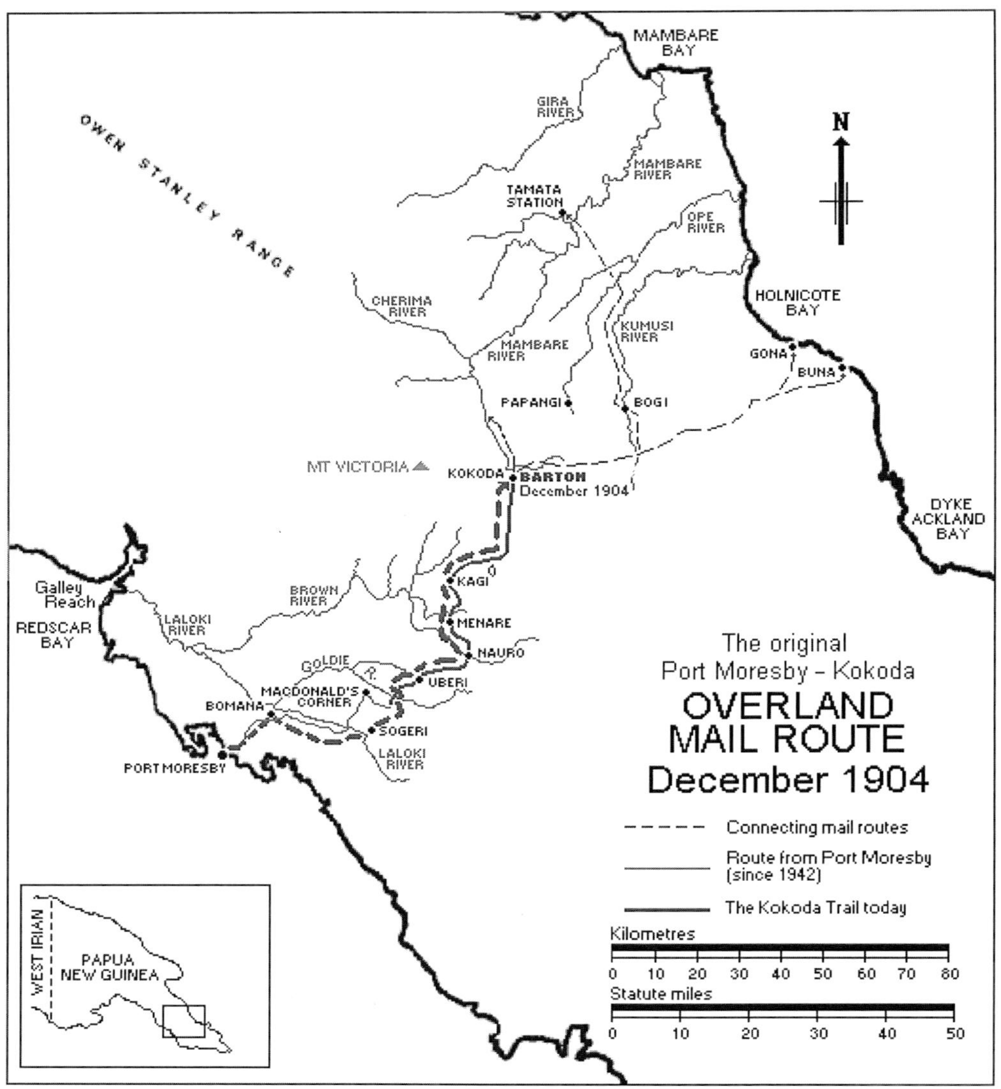

The Port Moresby–Kokoda overland mail route. *Author.*

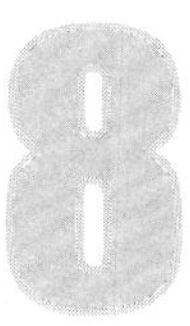

The Buna-Yodda Track (1905-1910)

Even though conditions remained harsh on the northern goldfields (the harsh conditions not the least being government red tape; for example, 17 claims were resumed in September 1905 for non-payment of rent and for not complying with labour conditions), with the advent of a regular communication with Port Moresby, and with increasing pacification of unruly tribes removing most of the major difficulties and risks, the Government's efforts in the Northern Division slowly started to show results. Activity on Yodda claims began to pick up and by the end of 1905, over fifty miners were again working the rivers and creeks about Kokoda. But it was recognised this was still well short of the earlier population and it was the continuing high cost of living and difficult conditions keeping many white settlers away.

The northern goldfields were very unhealthy places too, particularly for native labourers, amongst whom the death rate in 1903 was over 20 percent. The high mortality was due to incessant cold, high humidity and poor food and living conditions labourers, typically from warmer coastal regions, had to contend with. The health situation of labourers became so grave the government eventually introduced a regulation forbidding the recruiting of carriers or labourers with a chest measurement less than 32 inches (about 81 centimetres). There was no doctor permanently based at Kokoda (not until 1908) and the onus was on the Resident Magistrate and his staff to ensure the indentured labourers were fairly treated. An item in the Executive Council minutes for the meeting of 7th December 1905 (by which time the official death rate was about 18 percent) notes six of a particular group of 64 native labourers had died in less than six months. The Tamata and Kokoda Magistrates were ordered to cancel the work agreements of the remaining 58 'in the event of any further exceptional mortality among them'. Even rudimentary arrangements of this nature had quite startling results, dropping the mortality rate from 18 percent to 6.25 percent in two years. In 1907, the maximum load a native porter was permitted to carry was fixed at 50 pounds (about 23 kilograms).

For the white miners however, while relatively swift administrative communication had now been made possible via the overland mail route to the south, this did not reduce the cost of provisions, all of which had to be portered in from the north coast. Accordingly, the emphasis now swung to the improvement of the northern portion of the overland route established by Monckton and Tooth, and later consolidated by Bellamy. A determined effort was made to have a permanent way established along the track from Buna Bay, about 10 kilometres from Gona, to the Yodda. The idea was to introduce pack mules, which enabled cheaper transport of supplies. To this end, the first 'Superintendent of Roads', J.T. Seymour, was employed to oversee the work. It was a thankless task, as a Government report of the time noted:

> Owing to the sudden and frequent spates to which creeks are subject it is work of never ending toil to keep the road in even moderately good repair, and it is ... owing to this drawback that no mules have as yet been put on the road. It is intended that for the future a Road-overseer shall be permanently employed in this work.

In January 1907, Alfred Edward Oelrichs, Senior Assistant Resident Magistrate at Ioma (previously Tamata Station), was transferred to Buna Bay to open a new Government Station there. This post was created partly as a result of the overland mail route being established, specifically 'for the receipt and despatch of mails for the Yodda Valley, [regular deliveries of ship-borne mail from Samarai along the northern coast were being established at this time] and the receipt and despatch of Government stores for Kokoda Station'. A storehouse, '25 feet by 12 feet [7.6 by 3.7 metres], with 8 feet [2.4 metres] verandah in front ... all hardwood, and covered with corrugated iron, on piles about 3 ft. 6in. [about 1 metre] clear of [the] ground', was erected to house Government stores, and a stone jetty was constructed to facilitate the unloading of supply vessels. Clunas and Clarke, and the brothers Whitten who also had earlier opened a store at Bogi on the Kumusi, shifted their establishments to the new township. With the upgrading of the Buna–Kokoda road, it now by-passed Bogi entirely and, increasingly, miners who would previously have travelled up the Kumusi to Bogi now travelled by land. For the local population too, the rapid expansion of Buna Station was providential. Monckton reported in July 1907 'small groups of natives and families, remnants of once powerful tribes, have migrated there and placed themselves under the protection of the village constables'.

The character of the area from the coast to the Yodda fields had now undergone major changes, and was continuing to evolve, from what it had been in 1900. Monckton reported in his 1906/07 report carriers could now go unmolested along the entire length of the road. Tribes living along the way had taken to bartering taro and other vegetables with passing carriers in return for tobacco and glass bottles. But for Government staff, the mail service had brought not a little extra work. Francis Henry Naylor, the Assistant Resident Magistrate at Kokoda, reported on 30th July 1907

> the work of the district has suffered ... The duties, judicial, mining, postal, ... consequent on Kokoda being the station for the Yodda gold-field, and also resulting from the presence there of a large number of indentured labourers and carriers, as well as the fact that the overland mail for Port Moresby is received and despatched at this point, prevents the officer from leaving the station for any length of time to attend to other matters in the district. ... The work on the [Buna to Yodda] road has been of a very spasmodic nature. On such occasions as I could get away for a day or two, I have left the station to fix up bridges, &c., in the vicinity, and at other times I have sent the police to do such work, but in the absence of supervision, their work is of little value.

Kumusi River bridge at Wiarope, 1914, with woven cane decking.

The bridge was 202 feet (about 62 metres) long.

PNG National Library.

Despite his full schedule, Naylor found time to institute a welcome improvement on the route to the coast. The Kumusi had originally been spanned by a wire hawser in 1903 by Monckton to facilitate the transfer of stores, though travellers were still required to ford the stream. However, in April 1907, Naylor and a miner named Gunton, erected the first 'wire rope' foot bridge across the Kumusi. The crossing and later nearby settlement became known, through a *tok pisin* corruption of 'wire rope', as Wiarope (pronounced WHY-a-ROPEY).

For the road itself however, Naylor stressed the magnitude of the task could not be satisfied by the part-time attention of government officers. Professional help was needed if they were ever to make headway and 'a proper and systematic attempt to "make" the road is very necessary, as is also the provision for keeping it in repair'. The Director of Public Works in Port Moresby, Miles Staniforth Cater Smith, agreed though he was limited in the resources he had available. He reported in August 1907 on the work then being undertaken or was planned:

> ... the road is being roughly graded, and culverts and bridges erected to make it possible to substitute pack mules for the porterage system at present in vogue. When this is completed, and

pack mules obtained, a very great reduction in working expenses on this gold-field should be effected.

But the road was never to be developed enough for mules to be used. The alluvial gold, the basis of all industry in the area, was quickly running out. In 1904/05, and again in 1905/06, the prospectors on the Yodda had taken over 170 kilograms of gold. The return for the year to June 1907, when the mining population reached sixty-one, was down almost a fifth, to 142 kilograms, and for the 1907/08 period, 102 kilograms. The effect this decline had on the future of the Buna-Yodda road is revealed in the Annual Report for 1907/08:

> Considerable difference of opinion exists as to the permanence of the Yodda Gold-field, some declaring that it is worked out, and others maintaining, with equal confidence, that only the surface has been scratched, and that a field of unparalleled richness still remains to be discovered. Upon the solution of this question depends to some extent the amount of expenditure which should be incurred upon the road from Buna ...

Because of the doubts surrounding the field's future, the idea of mule transport on the Yodda road began to be seen as less viable from this time. Instead, it was decided to stay with the carrier lines for the present and to upgrade conditions for them. There were about 200 carriers employed along the way at any one time. It was intended to install proper rest houses for them at intervals of 16 or 17 kilometres, this being established as the maximum distance a loaded carrier would be required to travel in one day. The maximum load to be carried was also fixed, at 50 lbs (about 23 kilograms). The rest houses were to accommodate 100 carriers at a time, and were buildings of considerable size. A Public Works report for the 1908/09 period outlined the main features of the proposed shelters:

> The length of each rest-house will be 93 feet [28 metres] and the width 25 feet [8 metres], and the roofs will be of corrugated iron. Two sleeping platforms, 6ft. 6in. [2 metres] width, run the whole length of the building. These are separated by a passage 4 feet [about 1 metre] in width. Provision is also made for a large fireplace in each for cooking.

But the gold yield of the Yodda continued to fall, principally because the continuing high cost of provisions forced out the prospectors who were already there, or kept new prospectors away. By September 1908, only thirty-eight miners worked on the Yodda, and in the next nine months, this dropped still further, to twenty-four. The Yodda goldfield was dying just as the difficulties of transport and the impediments posed by hostile natives had largely been surmounted. The Director of Mines, reported in 1909

> the Gira, Aikora and Yodda Gold-fields on the mainland all tell the same tale—a gradually diminishing gold yield, and fewer miners and indentured labourers. This result can hardly be otherwise, as these fields have now been worked for a number of years and, in the absence of new finds, the richest 'wash' must inevitably become washed out.

But the most severe blow to the northern goldfields, and especially to the Yodda and the track to Buna, was yet to fall. In fact, the Government itself hastened the end. There had been growing official concern at the declining yields on all the alluvial fields in the country. A government-sponsored prospecting party under the experienced Yodda miner, Matt Crowe,* with Jim and Frank Pryke, had been fitted out in early 1909 to search for new fields, principally to the largely unknown area to the west and north-west of Port Moresby. Crowe's subsequent discovery resulted in the proclamation of a new mining area on 13th December 1909, on the Lakekumu (then Williams) River in the Gulf of Papua. The proclamation had an immediate effect on the Yodda's population, as the Mining Warden's report of the time noted:

> On the 25th December, 1909, news came overland to some of the residents on the field that payable gold had been found by the prospectors on the Williams River, and immediately a general exodus of the miners of this field started, and inside one week there were only about six men left on the Yodda, and at the end of January, 1910, two men only remained, while a little later one of these also departed, leaving one miner on the Yodda Gold-field.

Though four miners had returned by June 1910, the Lakekumu rush signalled the end of the Yodda as a major field. In January 1919, a decade later, the number of miners had again

* The *Pacific Islands Monthly* of 16 September 1930 attributes Crowe as the originator of a saying which became part of the colonial folklore in Papua New Guinea and which was current up to at least the early 1970s. When asked if there was any gold in the country, he replied: "There's gold everywhere—but an awful lot of Papua is mixed up with it'.

slumped to one, and the gold production for the entire 1918/1919 year was only 1.6 kilograms.

Besides the departure of most of the miners, there were three other significant consequences of the Lakekumu find. A rumour the Government was going to abandon the Kokoda region gave rise to widespread uneasiness among the native people, and the government moved quickly to allay these fears. The significance of this was it reinforced to the Government their presence was desired by the native people and necessary for their common protection. Even without gold production, it was clear the potential of other attributes of the region, particularly agricultural land, could probably be exploited to the advantage of both the white investor and black farmer. Indeed, it was in the aftermath of the Lakekumu rush the first experiments with rubber seedlings were made at Kokoda.

The field's desertion also affected the upgrading of the Buna/Yodda road. Maintenance work stopped immediately and the erection of the five rest houses, for which tenders had already been called, and the proposed construction of four additional suspension bridges, were held in abeyance until direction from Port Moresby was received. Despite the desire for development to continue in the area, the Government still had to conserve their limited funds. Without the interior goldfield, there was now no need for the large teams of carriers used hitherto, and therefore a much reduced need for major road works and carrier rest houses was indicated. With some reluctance, the administration called a temporary halt to all works on the Buna to Yodda road: 'It is not advisable [the 1909/10 Annual Report recorded] to spend any very large sum of money on this road ... until the future of the Yodda Gold-field is more assured.

The third result of the Lakekumu rush was that, in March 1910, Kokoda's prominence in the Northern Division officially ended. Alfred Edward Oelrichs, the then Resident Magistrate, reported

> the head station of the Division was transferred from Kokoda to Buna. Now that practically all the miners have left the Yodda, the change is undoubtedly beneficial, as really all the native population of the Division are in the Buna District.

The Wiarope Bridge across the Kumusi River about 1930. During the wet season, the swollen Kumusi could be up to 150 metres wide. At such times, the traveller could do little but wait until the torrent subsided, since it was impossible to cross safely. As shown here, an attempt was made to raise the bridge well above flood level and for all its crude technicalities, the structure presented quite a magnificent sight. (See also following photograph).

University of Papua New Guinea.

A typical native suspension bridge, of the same construction used for the Wiarope Bridge across the Kumusi River shown in the previous photograph.

A degree of fatalistic resolve was required to use these structures on a regular basis, particularly if you were a heavily-laden porter. G. M. Rio, a labour recruiter who worked in the Mambare area, gives an insight into what it was like to use these bridges:

> **I had to lead the procession on to them, not because I wanted to, but because it was the accepted thing for a white man to do, and the carriers needed that example to encourage them to follow along. When they were more than usually timid, and hesitated, there was nothing for it but to stop in the middle of the contraption and taunt them, asking politely sarcastic, if they were Mambare or Orikaivas [fighting tribes about Kokoda], or just Port Moresby girls in a family way. That usually worked it.**

Author.

9

Developing the southern end (1899–1914)

Despite the apparent ease in which the overland mail route was established by Barton in December 1904, some sections of the track from the south were to prove very difficult to establish. The first part of the overland route, from Port Moresby to the northern edge of the Sogeri Plateau, where the Owen Stanleys proper started, had always presented a more difficult prospect to early settlers than had the northern end. The terrain presented road construction problems which were, in places, insurmountable to the inadequately equipped public works department of the time.

On top of this, it will be recalled due to Morrison, development of routes in and through this area had been delayed considerably by the government bans prohibiting travel through the region. The ban was originally imposed by Scratchley in 1884, and continued until about 1896 when MacGregor authorised several government expeditions to enter the region in connection with the development of the Brown River horse-route. Though these, and later, expeditions had some successes with pacification of the aggressive tribes, the government was never truly convinced a lasting peace had been established. It was not until May 1899, after one and a half decades of continuing intermittent trouble from the area, the breakthrough finally came. It was Le Hunte's pleasant task to report the niggling sore of Morrison's legacy to the country had finally been put to rest:

> Several of the chiefs from inland between the Astrolabe [Varirata Plateau] and the Main Range came to see me, and the chief of the tribe close to "The Gap" who had opposed Mr Russell last year [the Serigima], sent word that he wished to make friends. I sent him a present, and his neighbour said that he would bring him down with him next time. I look on this as a most satisfactory indication of the gradual quiet spread of the Government influence, and I think Mr. Ballantine, to whom much of it is due, is not exaggerating when he said that he believed one could now go unarmed the whole way to "The Gap".

Since Forbes had set up his station in 1885, there had always been some white settlement on the Sogeri highlands. The earlier settlers lived in constant wariness of the Uberi people who lived in the (then) prohibited area to the immediate north. The Sogeri Plateau and adjacent Varirata Plateau, particularly the latter, were favoured by early residents as holiday destinations, as the cooler atmosphere provided a refreshing break from the energy-sapping heat of Port Moresby. In the 1901/02 Annual Report, Dr Craigen, the Chief Medical Officer, officially recommended it, pointing out 'a period of residence on the Astrolabe (Varirata Plateau) has a good effect, especially in the case of children'.

As early as 1895, a track from Port Moresby had existed, later improved and consolidated by John MacDonald in 1897, to run to the east of the town and south of the Laloki Valley, to the summit of the Varirata Plateau. (At this time the Brown River route, which went almost directly north from Port Moresby and which crossed the Laloki lower down-river, was still much in favour as the commencement of the overland track). The Varirata track was the first more or less permanent route onto the Sogeri Plateau though it had many shortcomings. MacGregor, who was pleased with any advancement achieved in the Colony, praised MacDonald for his enterprise but was not entirely happy with the route:

> By the existing path horses can, though not without some risk and difficulty, be taken over this mountain; but a body of prisoners have lately been sent to improve the road at the difficult places, especially near the top of the mountain. It was my intention to examine the track to see where a better bridle-path could be obtained ... but a stormy night prevented anything from being done.

MacGregor was not the only one to find fault with the road either. Though MacDonald's prisoner road-gangs continued to work on the track, by October 1898 they had still not attained a sufficient standard to evince much praise from Francis Winter, MacGregor's replacement: 'I am disposed to think that an easier, if more circuitous road could be constructed from the coast to Warirata [Varirata]'.

Yet, despite the extent of the task, MacDonald persevered. By early 1899, Burns, Philp and Company had established an experimental coffee plantation of 324 hectares on the plateau, as had David Ballantine on the adjacent Sogeri Plateau. The Government had acquired over 5,000 hectares on these uplands from the native owners, to be leased out for these purposes. In June 1899, Le Hunte accepted an invitation from Walter Henry Gors, the Burns Philp manager, to visit their estate on Varirata. Le Hunte was taken with the improvements MacDonald had made on the track out from Port Moresby, though he too, like MacGregor and Winter before him, still seemed to have some reservations about the route:

> We rode the whole way there along an excellent road ... The road up the face of the spur which leads to the estate, and which had been very well constructed by Mr MacDonald, Overseer of Works, is in good order, but will require a little attention, clearing, side-drains, &c., before the next wet season.

Given the rough terrain and the unskilled workers at his disposal, the efforts of a resolute MacDonald over many years undoubtedly deserved praise. The truth was however, the Varirata route upon which he was expending much time and effort was not suitable for general traffic travelling into the plateau areas north-east of Port Moresby, mainly because of the steep gradients to be negotiated. It was at this time as well the government began to officially recognise the deficiencies of the Brown River route. Le Hunte had inspected this track in April 1899 and was far from enthused:

> We found the road cut last year much overgrown, and Mr. MacDonald and his prisoners had to recut it in many places. ... I cannot say I was favourably impressed with the scheme of the road ... [as the beginning of the overland route]

After MacGregor left, promotion of the Brown River horse-road dissipated and despite the problems of the Varirata track, it became by default the means of entering the mountains for the small population on the Sogeri and Varirata tablelands. This on its own would not have warranted the expense of developing a better route but it was hoped the coffee and rubber now being grown on the plateaux would produce export income. It was this desire which eventually prompted the search for better access than provided by the Varirata track.

Actually, suggestions were being made about alternate tracks up to two years earlier. Francis Winter had examined the Laloki Valley proper, some kilometres north of the Varirata track in October 1898 and had pointed out then 'a good road could be made as far as this valley without much labour'. The difficulty of this area though, and why the Varirata track avoided it, was the head of the Laloki Valley, which contains the 90 metre Rouna Falls, was a *cul de sac*, ending in sheer cliffs over which horses could not be taken. This is why the Laloki Valley route took so long to be adopted, even though, as Winter intimated, it would have been relatively easy to build a road over the floor of the valley, up to at least the cliffs at Rouna Falls.

By 1899, white settlement was well established in the Laloki Valley. A market gardener called Richard Edward Weaver cultivated 103 hectares of vegetable gardens on the rich river flats about 16 kilometres from Port Moresby. A condition of Weaver's lease, which cost him 2/6 per acre (about 60 cents per hectare), was he have 10 acres (4 hectares) of Arabian coffee under cultivation by November 1899. He also planted coconuts, oranges and limes. Weaver had varying success with the exotic crops but the vegetables thrived and he was able to supply the town once a week with fresh produce, establishing for himself, as Joseph Albert Blaney, the Resident Magistrate for the Central Division observed at the time, 'a fairly profitable business'. Weaver also built up good trade in shooting and selling *maganis* (small wallabies). In the days before refrigerators, he could not keep up with the demand for fresh meat.* A small settlement

* Weaver death in March 1906 provides a curious historical footnote. It was at first thought a crocodile had taken Weaver as his clothes and boots were found on the bank of the Laloki. William Bruce, at that time Commandant of

had also been established by Willie Lifu at Bomana. The Laloki Valley was also popular for weekend shooting trips for Port Moresby residents and it had many minor tracks traversing it.

In this way, the terrain of the whole of the valley below Rouna Falls and south of the river became well known. The land across the river, between the north bank and the steeper southern slopes of Hombrom Bluff, did not offer generally as easier going. Traders in search of the patches of sandalwood examined this region thoroughly until the discovery of a large stand further down-river, near Galley Reach, drew their interest away.

Late in 1899, MacDonald was directed to turn his attentions to the construction of a road up the Laloki Valley, and the speed at which the new route was created bore witness to the accuracy of Winter's initial appraisal. On the 5th January 1900, Le Hunte inspected this route and was very pleased at the result:

> I went with Captain Barton ... to see the new road towards the back of the Astrolabe Range and the Sogeri country, [that is, to the north of, and roughly parallel with, the Varirata track and north of the Varirata buttress itself] on which Mr MacDonald has been engaged with a gang of prisoners for some months. We found him camped a short way beyond the Rona [Rouna] Falls at the head of the Laloki Valley. About 18 miles [about 29 kilometres] of good riding road has been made; a considerable amount of blasting had to be done along the valley, and the road taken zigzag over some spurs; it is not practicable for a cart road beyond the falls.

At this time, the 'road' to Rouna Falls was little more than a dry-weather horse or mule track though it received regular maintenance to prevent it becoming overgrown. As early as 1902, it was referred to in a Public Works Department report as

---

the Armed Constabulary, was in charge of the investigation into Weaver's disappearance and initially accepted the circumstantial evidence. However, according to Henry Dexter writing in the *Pacific Islands Monthly* of 24th September 1935, some days later, Bruce's wife recounted a dream in which she visualised Weaver being clubbed to death. She was so insistent about the clarity of her dream that Bruce was prompted to send his 'shooting boy' Wasagi to the villages undercover and Wasagi managed to overhear a conversation in which a man named Hariki boasted of the murder. The investigation was reopened and Weaver's body was subsequently discovered in a shallow grave, beaten to death as Mrs Bruce had dreamed. Hariki was later hanged for the crime.

the 'Sogeri Road', but it was not for some years additional work was commenced to make it truly suitable for wheeled transport. Though the Sogeri Road (more accurately, this should have been called the *Rouna* Road because that's where it stopped), along with the Buna–Kokoda and Ioma–Gira roads, were identified for a number of years as the major routes to which development funds should ideally be directed, the demands of the latter two routes meant the Port Moresby road often missed out. This was convincingly illustrated in the Annual Reports for 1903/04 and 1904/05 where it was reported, with only the virtually-free labour of John MacDonald's prisoner road-gangs, 'the Warirata and Sogeri roads have been repaired and put in good condition for mounted travellers and pack animals', while, some months later, it was reported, over the preceding twelve months, 'a sum of over £1,000 in making and repairing the Buna–Yodda road has been expended ...'.

But the northern trunk routes were not to have their own way indefinitely. The early years of the twentieth century saw a growing dissatisfaction with the lack of development in the Central Division (the large area of Papua bordered by the south coast of which Port Moresby was the focus). The Government was anxious to encourage development of primary industries, particularly agricultural pursuits, centred on the town. The large tracts of land taken up by the Government on the Sogeri highlands were reserved for this purpose. By August 1905, after the plantations had been established for over four years, B.W. Bramell, the Resident Magistrate for the Central Division, was able to report 'the coffee plantations at Sogeri and Warirata [Varirata] are thriving'. It was more this local success, rather than any specific desire to improve the early stages of the track to Kokoda, which triggered a swing, albeit minor at first, towards increased development funding for the Port Moresby-Sogeri road:

> During the year [reported Barton of the 1905/06 period] an amount of £1,250 was expended in improving roads in the Territory. A dray road is being constructed from Port Moresby towards the Astrolabe tableland, where there is good agricultural land available for settlement. At the end of June [1906] about 3 miles [about 5 kilometres] of road was made. It is probable that this road will be

continued, as funds admit, for a distance of about 20 miles [32 kilometres].

But a much more energetic push for development of this route came only six months later and for an entirely different reason. John MacDonald, in late 1905, had discovered copper in the region of the track to the Sogeri Plateau and had reported this to the authorities. This caused a rush of feasibility studies over the following twelve months, eventuating in the proclamation of the Astrolabe Mineral Field on 21st December 1906. The proclaimed field covered a huge area of 259,000 hectares though the country containing the proved copper-bearing lodes did not exceed 8,000 hectares. By July 1907, there were three major mines in operation: the Hector (on the site of the original discovery) and Gordon mines on the Laloki, about 20 kilometres from Port Moresby, and one a few kilometres further up the valley controlled by the Astrolabe Copper Syndicate, near the junction of Sapphire Creek with the Laloki.

NEXT PAGE:

Remains of the copper miners' ore processing buildings near Sapphire Creek in 1987. These buildings date from the mid-1920s. *Author*.

Buildings of the copper miners near Port Moresby in 1916. The establishment of the copper mining industry followed John MacDonald's discovery of the metal in 1905, and led to the accelerated construction of the road from Port Moresby to Sapphire Creek in the Laloki Valley. *University of Papua New Guinea.*

The establishment of these industries put an entirely different face on the importance of the Sogeri Road. The tenor of the Public Works reports underwent an almost immediate change, the 1906/07 Annual Report noting an unmetalled cart-road (an unsealed road for wheeled traffic) was 'being pushed out as rapidly as possible to the locality of the mines'.

Other mineral exploration from Port Moresby, principally for gold, had also been undertaken in the early 1900s, though on a less frenetic basis than in other mining areas and with less success. One venture was carried out in early 1906 by George Belford who, in company with a miner named A'Beckett, made a prospecting trip right up the Brown River to its head, near Menari. Like the prospectors on the Brown, Laloki and Goldie Rivers twenty-eight years earlier, they found though the gold was present, there was 'not sufficient inducement for them to remain'.

The early 20th century saw significant changes occurring to and within the government executive of the country, and in some respects, this was advantageous to the development of the Sogeri road. The appointment of Le Hunte in 1899 as Lieutenant-Governor was the last to be made by the British Colonial Office for in 1901, responsibility for the Colony was ceded to the Government of newly-federated Australia. Australia did not formally accept their new acquisition (which was subsequently renamed the Territory of Papua) until September 1906. The intervening half decade became a period of uncertainty and speculation for officers of the New Guinea administration as to the country's, and their, future. Policy direction was lacking and an uncomfortable feeling of impermanence pervaded government circles in Port Moresby. The consequent strain had to tell somewhere. By mid 1906, the senior echelon of government officers had split into two bitterly opposed factions and after serious allegations had been levelled at Acting Administrator Barton, he was obliged to seek a Commission of Inquiry into the workings of his administration. A major outcome of the inquiry was Barton was replaced by another Acting Administrator, John Hubert Plunkett Murray, who had been Chief Judicial Officer of the Colony since 16th September 1904. Murray, who was to rule the country for the next thirty-

Sir (John) Hubert Plunkett Murray, Lieutenant-Governor of the Territory of Papua from December 1908 to February 1940.

Murray remained in Papua for 34 years and was much admired by the native people. He made a promise to them that he would never leave the country and, after his death at Samarai on 27th February 1940, was buried in Hanuabada cemetery in Port Moresby.

PNG National Library.

four years, was confirmed as Lieutenant-Governor in December 1908, the first Australian to hold the office permanently.

In the latter part of 1906, the previously-hostile tribes of Efogi and Kagi made a return to their old ways. Three carriers returning along the mail route to the south coast from the northern goldfields were ambushed and killed. To prevent 'the more passionate instincts of the people' redeveloping into the open hostilities of 20 years earlier, a strong patrol of 12 armed police was sent inland immediately. This patrol stayed in the mountains and continually patrolled the unsettled areas during May and June 1907 until tempers had settled down. But two months later, another two returning carriers were murdered, the Kagi people again being involved. Another two month police patrol under William Cunningham Bruce was undertaken, 10 of the tribesmen responsible being arrested and sent for trial. These police patrols were seen to be so effective (there was no regular government presence between Sogeri and Kokoda at this time) plans were made to establish a new government station 'somewhere between Uberi and Kagi'. Implementation of the plans was initially delayed because of man-power shortages but the scheme was eventually dropped altogether after the rush to the Lakekumu River field at the end of 1909. This robbed the Yodda field, and the mail route, of much of its earlier importance* and greatly reduced the numbers of travellers going overland. Nevertheless, at the time these incidents highlighted the necessity for a higher government profile along the mail route, a requirement in turn implying better roads into the area were needed.

Murray seized upon this fact. He had realised at the outset the lack of development finance in the new country would force

* The extent of the official swing away from Yodda district and the mail route from Port Moresby can be appreciated from the fact that no new civil government station was established anywhere in the Central District between 1911 and 1946. In mid 1946, a new post was opened at Nauro on the Kokoda Trail to assist the people of surrounding areas in post-war rehabilitation but this was closed early in 1947. The only 'new' station to be opened on the old mail route was in 1957 at Sogeri where a permanent post under the Department of District Administration was opened to replace the 'temporary' camp used by Port Moresby-based Patrol Officers. This continued until 1965, only 10 years before PNG became independent, at which time it became the local police station.

the Government to select, from competing claims for funding, those projects producing greatest benefit for the country. Murray earlier, as Chief Judicial Officer, had had some experience of other areas of the country, including experience of the overland track to Kokoda. In fact, Murray, along with John MacDonald, had originally been members of Barton's December 1904 expedition which had established the overland mail route. Both had left Port Moresby with Barton and the others but on reaching Uberi, Murray had fallen ill to such a degree he could not continue necessitating, with MacDonald's assistance, his return to the town.

A major problem for Murray in wanting to develop the road to the Sogeri Plateau was that the Laloki Valley ended in sheer cliffs at Rouna. His rudimentary public works department simply did not have the engineering skills or capacity to put a road over this barrier.

This photo of Rouna Falls was taken in 1957.

Author.

Although as governor he now had wider responsibilities, Murray did not forget the practical demands and requirements of field (or as they were known in pre-War Papua, 'outside') operations. In his first Annual Report in 1906/07, he firmly established 'no expenditure can be justified that is not necessary to the development of the Territory'. He then stated the three major existing trunk routes were, in his view, the only 'justifiable' projects and would therefore go ahead before all others:

> Financial considerations have compelled the Government to confine their attention only to such public works as are absolutely necessary, that is to say, to the three roads to the Yodda, the Gira and the Astrolabe [Sogeri and Varirata Plateaux]

Murray had so set his mind on the development of the major routes, particularly the Sogeri road, that on 19th December 1907, he was able to secure an Australian Federal Government grant of £5,000 specifically to be applied to road works. The grant also included the secondment of an 'engineer for road construction', James Henderson, who arrived in Port Moresby on 23rd March 1908. Before Henderson's arrival, the road to Sogeri consisted of about 28 kilometres of 'cart track' out from Port Moresby to as far as the junction of the Laloki River and Sapphire Creek, with MacDonald's mule track continuing on to Rouna. Henderson's first assignment was to extend this road to the Sogeri tablelands and he kept MacDonald and a gang of native workers continuously occupied for months in laying out his new route.

Henderson had decided the steep slopes at the head of the valley at Rouna Falls, which had defeated all efforts by John MacDonald to traverse with anything other than a mule track, were best avoided altogether. He opted to cross over the Laloki further down the valley (a half kilometre or so upstream of the Sapphire Creek junction). From here, he would ascend the steep southern slopes of Hombrom (then Hombro*n*) Bluff to the Sogeri tableland. Once on to the high country, comparatively easy connection with existing tracks there would be possible. To cross the river, it was proposed to construct the country's first vehicular bridge, the longest span of which was to be over 15 metres. This was an enormous task for the Government of the day to attempt. The Public Works Department report for 1908/09 described the bridge:

> Its total length will be 160 feet [49 metres], exclusive of approaches, with a width of 15 feet [4.5 metres], and will cross the river in four spans. In the absence of a saw-mill, an immense amount of work has been entailed in sapping and squaring by hand the bed logs, corbels, and girders; and two or three months have been occupied in drawing these dressed logs a distance of several miles to the site of the bridge.

The bridge was completed in early April 1910 at a cost of £725/5/11, allowing the cart road to be taken across the river to the base of Hombrom Bluff. Though he had hoped to carry the vehicular way to the top of the Bluff, the best Henderson could accomplish up the steep slope was 'a good horse road', which cost £363/9/4 to construct. By June 1910, the Government had established a plant nursery on the top of Hombrom Bluff where the track emerged and had had a cottage built for its curator. Murray was delighted with the new road. He pointed out in the 1909/10 Annual Report it would now take Port Moresby residents only five hours to travel to Sogeri, where previously it had required an overnight stop.

With the road through Sapphire Creek to Rouna being seen as an important 'highway', with the copper mines in full operation, and with the opening of the new bridge, the government had high hopes for the Sapphire Creek area. A small settlement called Gagebegai had developed at the junction of the Rouna road and Henderson's new track and, in anticipation of further growth, the Executive Council reserved 259 hectares in September 1912 as the site for a new town. Planning for this does not seem to have progressed beyond reserving the land and it does not appear as if it was ever formally proclaimed a township.

The government was fortunate the Hombrom Bluff track and the Laloki River bridge were completed for harder times for both north and south coast roads were imminent. These were to last for the best part of a decade, though it affected the northern areas and the Yodda in particular, already hard hit and despite government efforts to rejuvenate the field, to a greater degree. Much of the Government's attention had been drawn to the Western Division on the south coast, where first, in December 1909, gold on the Lakekumu had been discovered. The

The southern edge of Hombrom Bluff showing the type of terrain early road builders were faced with.

The approximate location of Henderson's 'good horse road' is indicated. Henderson considered it was easier to ascend here than trying to get over the cliffs at Rouna (out of picture at the lower right).

The Laloki River is at lower left.

Noel Shacklady.

Lakekumu did not develop into the *el dorado* the government had been hoping for and, like the Yodda, was an extremely unhealthy region, with 258 indentured labourers succumbing to an epidemic of dysentery in the first 6 months. The poor long-term promise of the Lakekumu was a great disappointment to the Government, as it originally had high hopes for this field, as Murray reported in 1912:

> It must be admitted that the Lakekumu, though it has produced 17,500 ounces [2,411 kilograms] of gold, has not proved a second Yodda, as it was once hoped would be the case.

But other minerals looked promising, if only briefly. Two prospectors, Garnett Thomas and Lewis Lett, had discivered oil in the Gulf Of Papua in August 1911, and coal had been discovered, originally in 1908 by Mackay and Little, and confirmed by Little in 1910. With all this potential wealth to be

The bridge across the Laloki River in 1910.

This was Papua's first vehicular bridge. It carried the road from Port Moresby up to the base of Hombrom Bluff where it linked with the mule track up the southern slopes of the Bluff and onto the Sogeri Plateau.

The policemen carrying the overland mail between Port Moresby and Kokoda used this bridge from 1910 until at least 1923.

In 1942, Australian Army Headquarters staff used the bridge to reach their headquarters established under the jungle canopy adjacent to a small lake part way up Hombrom's southern scree slope. This site became known as 'Blamey's Retreat' and after the war was officially designated a botanical garden, the idea being to build upon the many species of plants established by the soldiers during their stay.

There is little evidence today of the mule track where it crossed the grasslands between the bridge and the Bluff. However, parts of the track that ran under the jungle canopy on Hombrom Bluff could still be seen in a remarkable state of preservation as late as 1973.

University of Queensland.

had, it is no wonder the Yodda, an old alluvial goldfield suffering declining returns for years, slipped from official favour for a time. Yet further investigation prompted the Government to re-think its position. The coal was found to be of immature quality suitable only for low energy requirements such as cooking, while serious questions about the commercial viability of the oil deposits were raised. (Oil was still being searched for in the area 50 years later).

> It is proposed ... [stated Murray in the 1912 Annual Report] to attempt to revive the glories of the Yodda by sinking a shaft through the false bottom; the success of this undertaking, though by no means certain, is likely enough, and will surely cause a return of the mining population from the Lakekumu. In fact, such a movement is likely to take place in any event, for there is still good gold on the Northern Field, which was abandoned in the rush to the Gulf.

But Murray's hopes never eventuated. In the following year, no more than a single miner returned to the Yodda, only to depart a few months later to try his luck in German New Guinea, leaving the mining population on the Yodda at five. The results of the exploratory shaft also did not meet expectations. The two miners who were awarded the Government contract to 'sink 70 feet' (about 21 metres) 'sunk to within a few feet of their contract, and then knocked off work, owing to the large boulders they encountered, and the great influx of water'. Alfred Edward Oelrichs, as Mining Warden for the field, summarised the problems in his report for 1912/13:

> The fact that the trial failed, does not say that the wash is not there, but whether, even if the gold were found, it would be there in sufficient quantities to warrant the large expenditure it would take to place the necessary machinery on the ground, to keep the shafts clear of water, is a very debatable question.

By July 1914, there was still only five men on the Yodda field, and still prospecting by the inefficient alluvial method. There was a lingering belief however, by miners and Government alike, much gold remained. But to extract it, and to extend the life of the field, a more sophisticated means of mining needed to be employed. Two difficulties were tending to keep the individual prospector of old away. The first was the Yodda was still the most expensive field on which to buy supplies. The second was major equipment purchases, if this were now what was needed, were generally beyond the financial capacity of the miner working alone. The Yodda was really no longer a field for the small prospector and this perspective became increasingly evident as time went on. Wilfred Norman Beaver, as Mining Warden for the Division in 1914, personally believed 'hydraulic sluicing' (dredging) was the answer. mining inspectors from Australia who undertook a Government review of the field later that year supported this view.

But even if it now was the era of large mining corporations able to meet large capital outlays, there remained many difficulties to surmount. The major problem was how to shift the heavy mining equipment into the region. Beaver pointed out the problem of transport was 'a very serious one, and it is by no means easy to shift heavy machinery over 70 miles [113 kilometres] of track'. Indeed, in the previous year, the first five kilometres of track out from Buna had been completely washed away by flood waters, all bridges and culverts within this stretch completely disappearing. It seemed it was just not the type of country over which one could transport heavy loads.

Yet, despite the considerable engineering problems, somebody did concoct an ingenious scheme in 1914 to move heavy equipment across the soft and boggy ground between Buna and Kokoda, and this scheme actually worked, after a fashion. The equipment was owned by a consortium consisting of Ernest Oates (who had previously kept Whitten Brothers' store at Buna), Stuart MacLean and W.M. ('Hoppy') Clark, and was destined for use on a dredging claim the consortium owned on the Yodda field. The heavy equipment had been moved inland for about 17 kilometres, near Soputa, when news of the outbreak of the First World War was received. Two of the men immediately left to enlist, by the overland track through Kokoda to Port Moresby, and this brought the venture to a halt. The equipment gradually became overgrown and lay rusting silently until it was rediscovered by Australian soldiers during the Second World War. Like a riddle posed by some huge block of stone left in a Mayan jungle, many was the passing soldier who puzzled at how this large metal hulk came to be sitting in the middle of the New Guinea bush, and how such a heavy load could have been transported over the unstable ground of the Buna swamplands.

All that remains in 1987 of the 1910 bridge across the Laloki River.

This crossing remained in use up to 1948 when the central pylon (missing from this photograph), which was built atop a huge boulder, was undermined and displaced by flood waters, causing the bridge to fall apart. This pylon, though still in place in the early 1970s albeit greatly askew, has now been completely washed away, leaving only the two outer pylons and the end abutments.

The destruction of the bridge meant that the post-WW2 plans for a botanical garden were not realised and the gardens no longer exist.

The X marks the approximate position from where the photograph of the 1910 bridge (see previous photograph) was taken.

Author.

How was it done? The consortium used a portable railway track about a mile (1600 metres) in length, lifting the track after the load had passed, and re-laying it in front of the engine. The rail track would have had to be re-laid at least 10 times to reach Soputa, and it would have required another *sixty* similar sessions to have reached Kokoda, as well as the construction of a strong bridge over the Kumusi. None of the railway lines was in evidence in 1942 though this is not unexpected. In a region plagued by borer infestation of timber, there must have been many uses found for the strong steel rails in the 28 years since the consortium abandoned the equipment. The traction engine too, had disappeared. Curiously, the idea of a railway does not seem to have been ever tried again, even in the years before air transport became the preferred means of shifting mining equipment.

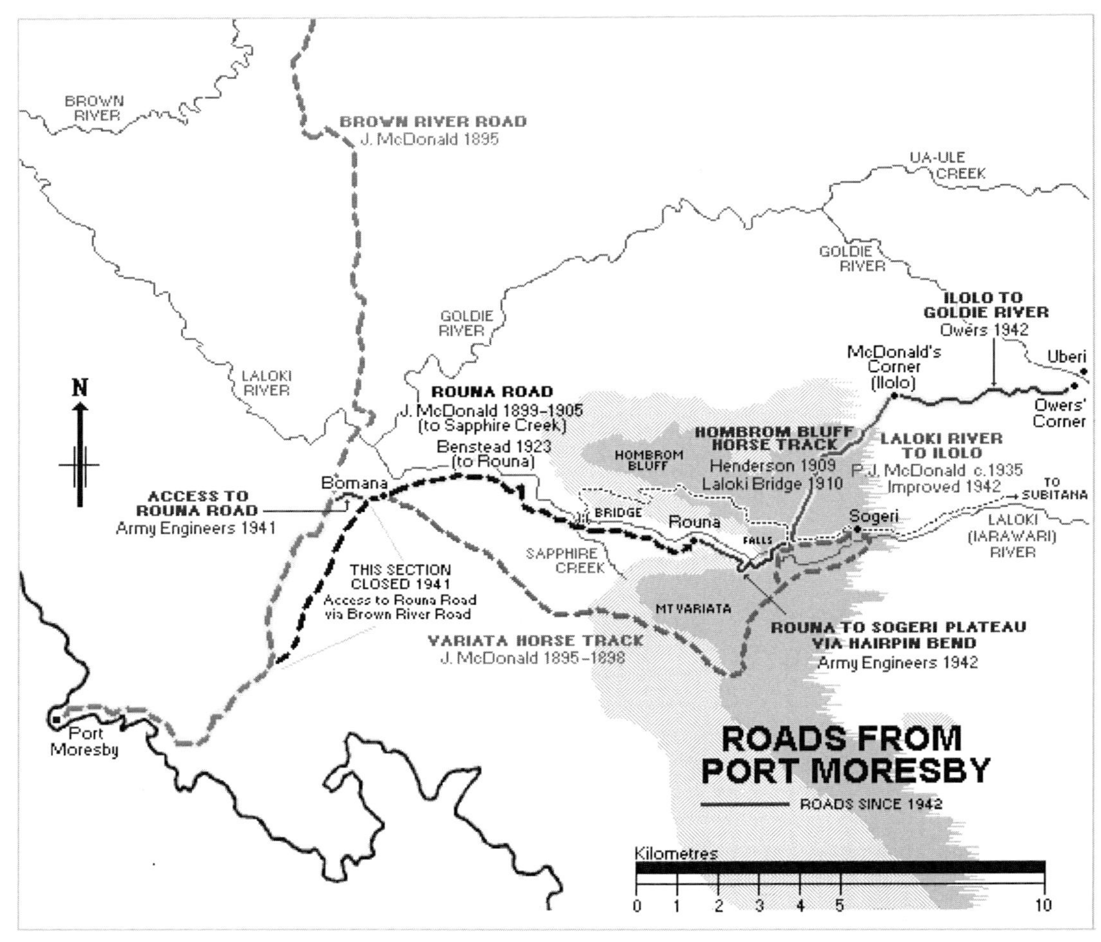

Roads from Port Moresby. *Author.*

10

On the track (1906-1938)

While the changes at the two ends of the overland route were taking place, the foot track itself also saw much activity following Barton's 1904 inauguration of the postal service. The track was used not only by the official mail carriers, but by many others. One expedition to use the route in the early 1900s was the one undertaken by two members of Barton's Royal Commission, Colonel Kenneth Mackay and Charles Edward Herbert, a Supreme Court Judge from New South Wales. Considering Mackay had a 'gammy' leg, as he put it, they made a quick journey, departing Kokoda on 23rd October 1906 and arriving in Port Moresby on 5th November. Colonel Mackay wrote a book in which he gives a good account of his crossing. In this, he makes a rare reference to unofficial mail carriers.

> [At Iorobaiwa] a native passed us bearing mail from Port Moresby to Buna Bay, or rather he would carry it to the next village, where another man would repeat the performance. So by uncertain stages it would go over the mountains and on down the level lands until in the fullness of time, the letters would reach their destinations, always supposing some post boy did not grow weary, or get killed and eaten. Official mails are, however, always carried by two police, who do the whole journey to and from Kokoda in marvellous time travelling both day and night.

Judge Herbert (left) and Resident Magistrate Charles Monckton at Kokoda Government Station in October 1906.
PNG National Library.

The unofficial mail service referred to by Mackay actually pre-dated the official service, being initiated by storekeepers serving north coast settlements to deliver mail and parcels between the Kumusi mouth, Bogi, the Yodda settlements and Tamata, the Gira and Aikora fields and other places in the region. Even consignments of gold were despatched by this method back to the storekeepers for safe-keeping. In about April 1905, some months after the establishment of the overland route, one of these concerns, operated by the Whitten Brothers firm which was based in Samarai, obtained a £50 government subsidy to operate a ship-borne mail service to Cape Nelson and Buna. The Whitten Brothers company engaged runners to take the mail from these places to points inland, particularly Kokoda, and as new stores were established on the goldfields near Kokoda, the private runner service for commercial correspondence was extended overland to Port Moresby. Another private mail service operating on a more or less regular basis was later established by the Anglican Mission between their bases at Gona, Sangara, Isivita and Kokoda.

Colonel Mackay also was impressed with the capacity of his native porters to carry their burdens over such rough country and offered an unwittingly prophetic observation of the carriers with his party, given what native carriers endured 36 years later on the Kokoda Trail. 'I doubt', he wrote, 'if the depths of endurance possible to the best Papuan carriers have ever been plumbed ...'. Charles Monckton accompanied Mackay and Judge Herbert from Kokoda to as far as Sogeri. At Sogeri, he turned about and walked back to Kokoda. In doing so, Monckton become the first person to make the first recorded double crossing of the Track in the one journey.

Monckton was also to claim another 'first' shortly after this, when he blazed a new route across the island. Murray, who was noted for his reticence in handing out praise, later called this journey 'a really notable achievement'. Monckton departed Kokoda in November 1906 under orders from Port Moresby to find a better route to the upper Waria River. Having done this however, he just kept going west, and then south. Of this, Murray noted Monckton 'appears to have crossed the main range somewhere near Mount Chapman and, coming upon the

Colonel Mackay, Charles Monckton and Judge Herbert on the Kokoda Trail in October 1906.

Mackay and Herbert's first hand experience of the difficulties of overland travel contributed significantly to the conclusions of the 1906 Royal Commission, of which they were members. Amongst the Commission's findings was a recommendation proposing that substantial increases in funding for internal communications in Papua be implemented.

PNG National Library.

upper waters of the Lakekumu, to have followed that river to the Papuan Gulf'. Once on the coast, Monckton boated back to Port Moresby. He was received in the town rather coldly for it was contended he had exceeded his instructions in crossing New Guinea, as well he had. Unfortunately, the fact he had explored much new country was completely ignored. He was not debriefed or asked for a report on his crossing; he was told simply to return to Kokoda. And so he did, by the mail route. But this last piece of red tape was the final straw for Monckton, an impulsive but capable man the government of the day could ill afford to lose. After tidying up his affairs, he left the country on 12th April 1907, never to return. Thus, no substantial record of this truly admirable feat of determination, endurance and enterprise was ever written, much to the regret of Murray. 'A detailed account would have been of great value to subsequent explorers', he wrote in 1912, 'and it is to be regretted that full particulars are not available'.

The official Government mail carriers were the most regular users of the overland track. Strictly speaking, when originally established, the mail service was intended only for official communications. Letters from the public were accepted without any formal guarantees and because of the dangers the mail carriers faced, the Government 'reserved the right to refuse to carry or deliver registered letters or any particular letters or mail matter ...'. In spite of the risks and the terrain to be covered, the delivery times achieved were quite efficient. Mail from Port Moresby took from four to seven days to reach Kokoda, then another four or five days to reach Buna Bay or Ioma. From Ioma it took a further two or three days to the goldfields—altogether about two weeks. This was considerably better than the previous average for ship-borne mail of forty to fifty days.

By July 1907, the service was well established. But, as Francis Naylor, the Assistant Resident Magistrate at Kokoda noted in the Kokoda Post Office report, the additional work entailed by this aspect of the already over-worked station officer's duties was not entirely welcome:

> The duties connected with this branch of the station occupy a good deal of time of the officer in charge. During the year 89 mails were received and 79 mails despatched. On their arrival here, the mails

> for the goldfield are sorted, and sent away to the Yodda without delay. Outward mails are despatched at least once every fortnight on a regular mail day, as well as on occasions as there is an opportunity of forwarding them.

Port Moresby and Buna were the extremities of the mail service and Kokoda was a mail exchange for both places. Policemen on mail duty and sometimes private runners, linked Kokoda with Port Moresby, Buna Bay and Ioma settlements, and from the latter, mail was forwarded to the Gira and other smaller fields. In the 1906/07 period, some '180 letters, 21 registered, 10 packets and 47 newspapers' were sent on to Ioma from Kokoda. In the same period, Ioma despatched 17 'mails' to Kokoda for forwarding to Port Moresby. On the 1st October 1907, an official Post Office was opened at Buna, providing for the recording of mail movements there. Buna also received occasional inwards mails from Samarai by ship for forwarding to Kokoda, Ioma and even Port Moresby so this too, added to the clerical burden of the Resident Magistrate and his assistants. In the 1907/08 period, 254 'mails' were received and 273 despatched within the Division. Resident Magistrate Griffin testily reported for this period 'a large amount of the District Officer's time is occupied with the mails arriving at the different stations'.

On the 19th April 1909 (8 months before the Lakekumu rush), the Northern Division, which, from Monckton's time, had encompassed the original Northern Division plus the original North-Eastern Division, was divided into three new divisions. The North-Eastern Division reverted to its original name and size, and the old Northern Division was divided into the Kumusi and the Mambare Divisions. The Kumusi Division looked after the Yodda field and had its headquarters at Kokoda. The Mambare Division, which included all other northern goldfields was to be administered from Ioma. Unfortunately for those officers at Kokoda, the time-consuming mail duties at Kokoda had not altered with the divisional restructuring. Wilfred Beaver, the Resident Magistrate at Kokoda in June 1909 pointed out 'no inconsiderable portion' of their time was taken up with handling the 164 mails in and 176 mails out for the period. In the following 12 months there was to be no let up with mail activity reaching an all-time high of 376 'mail' movements for the Division.

But with the Lakekumu gold rush, and with the shift of the Kumusi Division's headquarters to Buna in March 1910, the heavy postal duties at Kokoda came to an end. Though the overland mail through Kokoda continued to run, the shift of headquarters to a coastal station allowed the inauguration of a monthly steamship service to Buna from Port Moresby via Samarai, the *S.S. Mindoro* being a regular caller. This, along with the fact there were only four miners on the Yodda field in July 1912, meant a very large drop in the mail handled through Kokoda.

The total of 1,428 letters in the 1911/12 period (the recording of postal activity in terms of 'mails' had now been discontinued) was only one-quarter of the 4,887 letters for the previous 12 months. Both Clunas & Clarke's and the Whitten Brothers' retail stores on the Yodda had been closed, and storekeepers in Samarai, who had previously recruited indentured labourers for the white miners on the field, now 'put all their energy into obtaining recruits for plantations and Lakekumu Gold-field, apparently forgetting their old love, the Northern Division, which kept them in existence for many years'.

The decline in activity on the Yodda led to a reduction in the amount of mail sent overland, though this did not seem to have a lasting impact on the frequency of the service. Nevertheless, it could be expected the lessening of the need would have made the constables on postal duty happy, even if it only meant a lighter burden. There still was considerable threat to their lives from some of the tribes living along the track, though the country through which it passed was officially classified as 'safe'. Indeed, only some eight years had elapsed since it had been reported 'deserters from the northern goldfields were found penned up in coops in inland villages, to be carefully fattened for an approaching feast'. Since then, in 1911, two mail carriers were murdered near Efogi and two years later another went missing and was never found.

Yet even if a state of true peace existed, the mail carriers still had the arduous physical task of crossing the main range. This was (and is) an area where it rains every day of the year, an uncomfortable reality which, aside from ensuring clothes, possessions, and body were continuously soaked, made the going underfoot extremely tiring. The high mountains too, were cold. The novelist Beatrice Grimshaw,* who came to Papua in 1907 and settled at Rouna in 1910, wrote of overhearing 'the complaints of the native mail carriers coming down from the Kokoda track ... of the bitter chill and frost at the eight thousand foot [2400 metres] gap ...'. If all these hardships were not enough—the cold, the never-ending rain, the ill-formed path, the endless succession of sodden ridges—all these had to be negotiated with the additional burden of the mail bag.

The actual weight of the mail carried in a delivery is difficult to determine from official reports giving only the number of 'mails' in and out. Griffin, Monckton's successor, recorded in the Kokoda Post Office report for 1907/08, when 120 mails were received and 152 despatched, 'these mails consist of from one to six bags, including heavy parcels and papers'. It is not known if there was an official maximum weight. Indentured carriers on the Buna to Yodda road were restricted to a load of no more than 50 lbs (about 23 kilograms) and were required to do 10 to 12 miles (16 to 19 kilometres) a day over comparatively flat terrain. The mail carriers regularly did the 80 mile (about 130 kilometres) from Port Moresby to Kokoda in 5 days (16 miles or 26 kilometres a day) over rougher country, so it does not seem they were required to carry as heavy a load. As well, the policemen on postal duty never travelled alone, the smallest party being of two men, and therefore could apportion the load between them.

Possibly the best indication of the load carried by the official mail bearers is given by Walter Richard Humphries, in a book published in 1923. Humphries served in many areas of the country as a Patrol Officer and Resident Magistrate.† He had just

* In January 1933, Beatrice Grimshaw and her brother Ramsay purchased the Laloki Tobacco Plantation on the Laloki River from the film actor Errol Flynn, when Flynn left the country to go to Hollywood to make his first picture.

† Humphries became one of the longest serving Government officers ever to work in New Guinea, serving as an officer in Australian New Guinea Administrative Unit during the Second World War, and in the post-war

walked over the ranges from Kokoda and was just entering the outskirts of Port Moresby when he came upon a man sitting on a log, filling his pipe.

> Rising from his seat [Humphries wrote] he salutes. He is a policeman—heavily laden.
>
> 'What name? (What is it? who are you? where are you going?) is my greeting in the pidgin-English which these men understand.
>
> 'Kokoda', he replies; and the mailbag tells me the rest. He is the outgoing mailman. I note his load; rifle, ammunition, bayonet, pouch, sling-bag, swag-bag, swollen with spare uniform and blanket, a parcel of biscuits, a parcel of rice, two tins of meat, a coconut, and finally the mailbag. A pretty good load, you will say, for a man to carry on such a road? Yes, a pretty good load; but it were foolish to decrease it. There is an eight days' journey before him, and there is no food on the road. On the coastal portion he will travel by night; on the highlands by day. The worst stage of the journey is from Kagi to Kokoda, and there, should it be raining, the cold is cruel.

It is interesting even with the Lakekumu rush, with the move of headquarters from Kokoda to Buna, with the fading fortunes of the goldfield, and with the introduction of the coastal mail service from Samarai to Buna and the Mambare, the frequency of the overland service still remained fairly constant for many years. When established in December 1904, the service was a fortnightly one. Between April 1909 and February 1910, the overland mail was running once every 18 days on average, with the greatest time between trips being 28 days and the shortest, 7 days. Between January and December 1911, a year after the majority had left the Yodda field for the Lakekumu, the average time between trips was 15 days, with the longest and shortest periods being 28 days and 13 days. In 1912, the average time between trips was 16 days, with longest and shortest periods being 36 days and 12 days.

In 1913, the overland service from Port Moresby was tied to the schedule of the mail steamer from Australia, the service running 3 days after arrival of the ship at Port Moresby. This

---

Administration as Director of Native Labour. Humphries was killed on 21st January 1951 at Higatura in the Northern Division when the Mount Lamington volcano exploded.

Two mail carriers on the Kokoda Trail in the heyday of the track's use as an overland mail route between Port Moresby and the northern goldfields.

Mail was carried in this fashion on the Kokoda Trail until October 1949 and up to February 1958 on other overland mail routes in Papua New Guinea.

This photograph was taken in 1906.

PNG National Library.

meant the service ran about once a month. In November 1915, a return was made to a fixed schedule with departures being made on the same date of each month. This continued up until December 1922 when, for six months, the frequency was increased to one trip every 3 weeks, though a fixed four week interval was resumed in July 1923. In August 1925, a return was made to a schedule based on the arrival of the monthly mail boat at Port Moresby,* the overland mail now leaving two days after the arrival of the ship. This continued up until July 1930, when, once again, deliveries were scheduled on a fixed 4-weekly interval.

But this was the last moment of glory for the overland mail service. Increasingly, reliance was being placed on ship-borne deliveries by private operators under contract to the Government. A regular service along the south coast delivered mail from Port Moresby for northern destinations to Samarai where it was collected and delivered by the monthly north-east coast service. Mail from Australia was delivered directly to Samarai by the *M.V. Macdhui*† and other ships and the timetable of the north-east coast service was tied to the arrival times of these vessels. At about this time too, all Government activities were being constrained by the effects of the Great Depression. On top of this again, more directly, there was an increasing use of aeroplanes by private operators in Papua for internal communications.

---

* The arrival of a ship carrying mail from 'down south' (Australia) was always of some occasion for Port Moresby residents (and, to some extent, continued to be so until the 1950s). To enable addressees to collect their mail at the earliest opportunity, the Postmaster instituted the arrangement whereby 'immediately all inward mails are sorted at the Port Moresby Post Office, the M flag will be flown from the masthead by day, and a red light by night'.

† The *Macdhui*, launched in Glasgow, Scotland on 23 December 1930, was one of number of ships used by Burns Philp on the Australia-New Guinea run. The *Macdhui* (4,561 tons, 15 knots) went into service in February 1931, joining the *Morinda* (2,025 tons, 11 knots) and the *Montoro* (4,057 tons, 13 knots). Earlier, the *Marsina*, the *Mataram*, the *Mirani* and *Malabar* and the *Mindoro* had also plied New Guinea waters.

The *Macdhui* still lies in Moresby Harbour. It was run aground on a reef off Tatana Island after being bombed by the Japanese on 17th and 18th June 1942 with the loss of 15 lives. After the war, the *Macdhui*'s sister ship, the *Bulolo* took over the Pacific islands run for many years.

The last time the carriage of mail by foot was mentioned in the official Annual Report appears in the report for 1928/29, though the overland mail service to Kokoda was still being advertised in the Government *Gazette* in July 1930, 12 months later. At this time, the policemen carrying the mail left Port Moresby post office 'about 20th of each month'. Yet, though the service was slipping from official prominence, it was not disbanded, despite the fact it had to face further direct competition. In 1932, the construction of an airfield at Kokoda was commenced by Mack Rich, the innovative officer in charge at the time. This was a significant advancement in Papua, and particularly for the strip of country between Port Moresby and the northern coast, one of the oldest of the pioneering areas. The mild regret felt at the passing of a unique era in the country's history was put into words by Murray at the airstrip's opening:

> I have been visiting Kokoda, of course on foot, ever since 1907; and I walked there again this year. But this will, I think, be the last time, for the station is now linked to Port Moresby by an aeroplane service. ... it is with mingled feelings that I realise that the "foot slogging" of the past is at an end, and that in future I may fly instead of walking to Kokoda.

It may have seemed once the Kokoda airstrip was completed (the first plane, piloted by Frank Drayton and Orme Denny, landed on 28 September 1932), there would be little advantage to the postal service in continuing pedestrian deliveries. Even in the slowest of early aeroplanes, the journey from Port Moresby to Kokoda could be done in 40 minutes. However, the frequency and timing of flights was driven by the imperatives of the private mining companies. There was no regular air service to any Papuan destination and while mail was loaded upon aeroplanes whenever the opportunity and cargo space permitted, a scheduled airmail service was not implemented. Indeed, up until the outbreak of the Pacific War, the Kokoda airstrip and the one at Ioma (previously Tamata), which was first used (by Orme Denny again) on 30 August 1935, were considered at first only to be emergency airstrips on the more important Port Moresby–Wau route.

The result of this was the overland mail service to Kokoda and other inland stations in the Northern District never closed. The service may have been sporadic and no longer run to a

MAIL NOTICE.

The General Post Office,
Port Moresby, 26th March, 1909.

IT is hereby notified for general information that Mails for Letters only, will be despatched overland from Port Moresby to the undermentioned places, and to Port Moresby from the undermentioned places by police escort on the dates specified, namely:-

KOKODA *via* GAGEBEGAI (Sapphire Creek) and SOGERI ;

YULE ISLAND *via* Fairfax Harbour and KANOSIA ;

RIGO *via* TUPUSELEIA :-

1909. April 14th, May 2nd and 19th, June 16th and 23rd, July 11th and 28th, August 14th, September 1st and 18th, October 6th and 23rd, November 10th and 27th, December 15th.

1910. January 2nd and 19th, February 6th and 23rd.

Letters for TUPUSELEIA will be left at the house of the Village Constable, and for GAGEBEGAI at the Astrolabe Copper Mine, to be called for in each case, but no letters will be sent to these two places unless the addressees request the Postal authorities (in writing) to do so.

The postage on the letters will be at the ordinary current rates, but no letter will be despatched unless the necessary stamps are affixed. Postage at double rates will be charged to the addressees of letters without stamps handed to the escort at the places where there are no post offices.

H.W. CHAMPION,
Chief Postmaster.

MAIL NOTICE.

The General Post Office,
Port Moresby, 3oth July, 1909.

IT is hereby notified, for general information, that the mail services to Yule Island and Rigo, as advertised in Gazette No.7, of the 7th April last, have been discontinued. The service to Kokoda will continue.

H.W.Champion,
Chief Postmaster.

Various notices for the overland mail appeared in Government *Gazettes* for more than 20 years seeking to provide a regular delivery service. The last of these notices appeared in July 1930.

Ela Beach Public Library, Port Moresby (New Guinea Collection).

NOTICE.

TIME TABLE FOR OVERLAND MAIL.

PORT MORESBY TO KOKODA.

LETTERS to be at Post Office on previous day not later than 3 p.m.

YEAR 1911.
Date of Departure :

3rd	January	4th	July
17th	January	18th	July
31st	January	1st	August
14th	February	15th	August
28th	February	29th	August
14th	March	12th	September
11th	April	10th	October
25th	April	24th	October
9th	May	7th	November
23rd	May	21st	November
6th	June	5th	December
20th	June	10th	December

LEO E. GORS,
Acting Chief Postmaster.

The General Post Office,
Port Moresby, 3rd Jan., 1911.

NOTICE.

TIME TABLE FOR MONTHLY OVERLAND MAIL.

PORT MORESBY TO KOKODA.

YEAR 1913.

DATE OF DEPARTURE :

Three days after the arrival of the Dutch steamers from the South.

Letters to be at Post Office on the previous day not later than 3 p.m.

H. W. CHAMPION,
Chief Postmaster.

The General Post Office,
Port Moresby, 22nd April, 1913.

NOTICE

TIME TABLE FOR MONTHLY OVERLAND MAIL - PORT MORESBY TO KOKODA.

Year 1915.

DATE OF DEPARTURE :

The Overland Mail will leave Port Moresby on the 7th day of each month until further notice.

Letters to be at the Post Office on the previous day not later than 3 p.m.

R.W.T. KENDRICK,
Acting Chief Postmaster.

General Post Office,
Port Moresby, 12th October, 1915.

The first aeroplane to land at Kokoda airstrip, 28 September 1932. This photograph was taken by the Resident Magistrate of the time, Mack Rich. *University of Queensland.*

published schedule, but was, nevertheless, intact. A year after the Kokoda strip was opened, the Port Moresby–Kokoda track was still 'regularly patrolled', according to an observation of Evelyn Cheesman, an English entomologist, who visited Papua in late 1933. The late Bert Kienzle, who did not move to Kokoda until 1934, recalled receiving mail from Port Moresby by overland delivery. Similarly, the late Fred Turner of Port Moresby remembered mail being delivered overland on more than one occasion 'before the war, about the middle of the 1930s', though he had the feeling it was not a regular delivery.

No story of the Papuan overland mail service would be complete without mention of an extraordinary incident which took place towards the end of the 1920s. This concerned the murder of a policeman carrying the mail, not by hostile villagers but by the other policeman, his travelling companion. Unfortunately, the killing of one native by another was not particularly unusual in 1920s Papua. The incident may well have disappeared from the historical record had it not been for the later tragic circumstances befalling the central character.

In September 1929, two constables of the Armed Constabulary, Karo Araua (also reported as Ka*l*o) and Bili set off from Port Moresby with the mail. Before they reached Kokoda however, they had a violent argument—supposedly over whose turn it was to carry the mailbag—and, in the heat of the moment, Karo shot Bili dead. Karo did not try to cover up his awful deed—he saw no crime in what he had done. He continued to Kokod the same day to deliver the mail and where he calmly told the Assistant Resident Magistrate what had happened. Karo was subsequently tried and sentenced to five years in Port Moresby's Koki Bay prison for this crime. After completing the sentence, Karo was again arrested in December 1935 for the theft of £129 from a safe, of which £116 was eventually recovered. For stealing the outstanding £13, Karo was sentenced to 10 years imprisonment, double the period he received for killing Bili.

One night during his second sentence, Karo slit the throats of a prison warder and his family. This was not part of an escape attempt for he returned to his cell after the murders. At the following trials in the Court of Petty Sessions and the Central Court, Karo asserted, and it was generally believed, he had been strongly influenced by another prisoner Goava Oa, a murderer serving a life sentence, whose glib tongue and worldly ways by far had the better of the unsophisticated Karo. Nevertheless, Goava was found not to be legally implicated and it was left to Karo alone to feel the full weight of the law. He was sentenced to death and was hanged at Koki at 8 am on 8th August 1938 by Acting Resident Magistrate Sydney Howard Chance.*

* Even the execution did not go off as smoothly as the authorities would have hoped and there were some repercussions that bordered on the bizarre. The court hearings too, were not without controversy—for example, Goava was represented by his own legal counsel, Karo was not—and were of some significance in the development of the legal and social status of Papuans. For a comprehensive account of this tragic affair, see Amirah Inglis' *Karo - the life and fate of a Papuan.*

Carriers for a government patrol resting on the Kokoda Trail near Nauro in 1913, with the *bosboi* (foreman) standing on a 'patrol box'.

PNG National Library.

11

The Port Moresby–Sogeri road (1912-1937)

As noted earlier, the second decade of the twentieth century began with successful exploration for gold, oil and coal in the Gulf of Papua, north west of Port Moresby. This region included many areas where a white man had never trod, and because it was largely unknown, it seemed to hint of massive mineral deposits waiting to be discovered. The supposed potential of these new areas contrasted markedly with the old worn-out goldfields to the north and with the districts adjacent to the mail route, which were now officially considered to be fully under government control and 'safe for travellers'.

The seeming disinterest in the older settled areas arose from a calculated change in government policy. Previously, the government had moved into a new district only after, and because, miners, missionaries or others had first settled there. The new policy was to reverse this sequence and it was now intended to establish government stations in new areas before any settlers had arrived. The intention of the scheme was to extend government control over the entire Territory, literally, thereby attracting settlers. Murray summed up the basis of the new policy in the Annual Report of 1912/13:

> The object of extending Government influence is, primarily, to put an end to cannibalism, head-hunting, and other horrors, the existence of which is, it is felt, a disgrace to an Australian Territory.

Accordingly, the more primitive areas of the country attracted the most attention.

> The western part of the Territory [wrote Murray] presents the greatest problem, perhaps only because it is so little known. The present intention is to put one or two stations on the Fly and Strickland [Rivers], and a police camp at a distance up the Kikori River; probably the information supplied by the officers stationed at these points will enable us to decide whether other sites would be preferable.

Along with the consequences of the new policy, and on top of the falling gold production and declining population, came soon afterwards a further blow to the fortunes of the country—the First World War. This particularly affected road works at both ends of the track through Kokoda. Fifteen percent of the country's non-native population left to enlist for military service in Europe. By June 1916, the white population of the entire Territory was down to only 992 persons. The government service was particularly hard hit with the three northern Divisions being left with only nine officers between them. 'So many Government officers have enlisted', wrote Murray a year later, 'that it has become very doubtful whether it will be possible to spare any more. About fifty have gone already; that is, about half of the whole service'. Enlistments* included many of the prospectors as well. On the Yodda diggings, the number of white miners did not exceed three for two and a half years.

The demands of war production in Australia meant costs rose considerably in Papua. Expenditure on capital works had to be ruthlessly curtailed and all but the 'most necessary' public works were postponed. The Buna to Yodda track was left to receive only sporadic attention from the Resident Magistrate as time allowed, though the Port Moresby to Sapphire Creek road was one of only two routes considered important enough on which to keep up maintenance. (The other was along the Kemp

* Enlistments included Miles Staniforth Cater Smith, who joined in March 1916, Charles Theodore Wurth, who enlisted in December 1915, and Wilfred Beaver. Beaver, who served at Kokoda as Resident Magistrate, Postmaster and Warden for Goldfields from 1909 to 1914, was a Lieutenant in the 60th Battalion. He left New Guinea in November 1915 and was killed in action in France on 26th September 1917.

Welch River). The straitened circumstances however, meant only the barest essentials were possible, as Murray reported for the 1916/17 period:

> There is no intention of making these roads fit for motor traffic in the wet season; it will be sufficient for our purpose if they carry motors in the dry season and are open to horse traffic all the year round.

The Port Moresby road and the Kemp Welch road were favoured because they served inland plantation areas: about 800 hectares of rubber at Sogeri and about the same area of rubber and coconuts on the Kemp Welch. The Port Moresby road, out as far as Sapphire Creek at least, also serviced the copper mines (which had struggled along over the years with some success), and was becoming increasingly well-travelled. A Public Works report of December 1916 recorded some 615 tonnes, mainly copper ore, had been carried over it in the previous 12 months. But it began to be seen as a distinct disadvantage not to have vehicular access to the Sogeri highlands. In 1917, several attempts were mounted in earnest within the Laloki Valley to find 'a route along which a road might be constructed, which in time might be made fit to carry motors'. To help in defraying the expense, negotiations were also commenced with the Laloki copper miners. Murray arranged 'that they share the cost necessary to provide a road good enough to carry their heavy traction engines to be employed in transporting copper ore from the mine to Port Moresby'. (The Laloki Mine, nearest to Port Moresby, had earlier ordered a steam tractor and trailers to cart the ore to Port Moresby, 31 kilometres distant).

But a proper road right through to Sogeri was the ultimate aim. Murray appreciated Henderson's 1910 track up the side of Hombrom Bluff, which rose 457 metres in just over 3 kilometres, 'though passable for pack animals, could never be made suitable for vehicles or for motor traffic'. Yet, in 1917, a 'proper' road was not an easy thing to attempt. The road engineer at the time, a man named Janson,

> tried in various directions to find a route from the end of the existing road at Sapphire Creek up to the high country of the Sogeri District, and reported every route as impracticable.

Perhaps the frustration was too much for Janson for he resigned in November 1917 and left the country. Staff shortages of the time meant he was not replaced and no further examination of the area was possible. The only other road engineer in the country, Victor Albert Williams, was occupied on the other major route, the Kemp Welch road. But the economic relief offered by the copper mines and the Sogeri plantations led to the Sogeri Road gradually assuming priority. The road out to as far as Sapphire Creek had been gazetted a 'main road' in September 1917, and in August 1918 the Acting Director of Public Works, William Robert Smith, concluded another attempt should be made:

> I am not satisfied that it [a vehicular route to Sogeri] has been proved impossible, and I propose shortly transferring Mr Williams from the Rigo–Kemp-Welch road to make a further investigation.

Despite the Public Works Department only having a staff of no more than five at any one time during the 1918/19 period, by July 1919 some positive steps had been taken. An arrangement had been arrived at with the copper miners they be responsible for the road's maintenance during the dry season when they used it. This resulted in several deviations being put in to reduce curvature and grades for the steam-driven prime movers. The company generally upgraded the road along its entire length to the extent it was now a genuine motor-road (in the dry season at least) to out as far as the copper mines just past the Sapphire Creek crossing. Victor Williams was recalled from Rigo and after four months had a new route up the Laloki Valley marked out from the limit of the miners' responsibility at Sapphire Creek to Rouna, the same route taken by about two-thirds of the Sogeri Road today. Smith was very satisfied at the work done and believed this time, the mistakes made in the past with other routes had been avoided:

> I am convinced [Smith reported] that the route now pegged out is in the correct place, though it is not all easy going. A start is to be made immediately on the construction of a good mule track along this route, which can eventually be improved to carry vehicular traffic. Even this, although only a mule track, will be a great boon to the planters, as the existing track [up the side of Hombrom Bluff] contains many almost impossible grades.

Two mule-handlers and their animals which were used for carting rubber and coffee from the edge of the Sogeri Plateau to the road head below the Hairpin Bend.

This photo was taken in 1938.

PNG National Library.

But staff shortages and a dearth of funds for capital works meant a slow start to the project. In the 1919/20 year, a sum of £1,142 was expended on clearing scrub and other work associated with upgrading the surveyed route to a mule track, but only about 2 kilometres of actual road were constructed. In the following year however, not even this was achieved, the government's financial outlook being so uncertain staff had to be reduced, and in many cases, native work contracts were cancelled and the native people returned to their villages. New works stopped altogether and 'only absolutely necessary works of maintenance' were carried out.

This situation continued until November 1922 when, under a new Deputy Director of Public Works, John Thomas Bensted (previously Government Storekeeper), work was recommenced with an initial party of 50 natives being allocated to the project. Within twelve months, over 150 native labourers, four white overseers and Williams were working full time on the road. With such a large team at work, a new motor road out to within one and a half kilometres of Rouna Falls was able to be officially opened on 1st December 1923. The road terminated at the present site of the Rouna settlement, which was known unofficially as the 'Grass Plot' or the 'Grassy Flat' at this time. (The area of the Rouna settlement was later included in land set aside for a town, to be called Migagi, which was proclaimed on 6th August 1924). From this point, the way degenerated into a mule track. Williams could see no way of continuing. An obstacle known as the 'Hairpin Bend' covering a very steep section of about 3 kilometres prevented the road being constructed around and above Rouna Falls. Once over this portion however, the motor road was to be continued to Sogeri. In anticipation of this, the Laloki River was bridged above the Falls in November 1923.

The construction of the new road—specifically, the section from Sapphire Creek to Rouna—had consumed the greater part of the construction funds over the period and the Public Works Department of the day no doubt did their best. But it was really only a wide horse track able to be used by motor vehicles in dry weather. However, in comparison with other major trunk routes in the country, the Buna to Kokoda track for example, it was seen with some justification as a major achievement. A report in the *Papuan Courier*, caught the feeling of the time:

> The construction of the Sogeri Road during the past twelve months provides an illustration of engineering skill and patience under difficulties, that, met with elsewhere, or read about, would fill those interested with admiration ... From Sapphire Creek to within one mile of Rhona [Rouna] Falls, there is almost completed a definite and permanent road, besides which any round Port [Moresby] are insignificant.

There are a number of references to the condition of the road to Rouna, particularly in the first few years after it had opened. Charlotte Cameron, in her *Two Years in Southern Seas*, published in 1923, did not have a very high opinion of it at all. 'The only road is 20 miles [32 kilometres] long', she wrote, 'and in very bad condition, which in a very short time would rattle any machine to pieces. I motored out to Rouna Falls from Moresby over this vile road'. An article by Elinor Mordaunt in the London *Daily News* in 1925 thought the road 'looks as though it was and forever would be, in the process of being made'.

The local residents complained too. A correspondent to the *Papuan Courier* in March 1924, with the pseudonym 'One of the Sufferers', was upset at 'the dangerous state of the road to Sapphire Creek'. This person was one of many who wrote letters to the editor to voice his displeasure at the lack of maintenance. Despite all this however, the Public Works section was proud of its achievement and Murray was particularly enamoured of the road, regularly taking evening trips 10 to 15 kilometres out of town in his Model T Ford.

Over the remaining 16 years of Murray's rule in Papua, the route to the Sogeri Plateau was systematically improved as finances allowed, though Murray himself never saw the completion of the final three kilometres of motor road over the Hairpin Bend. Technically, it was a single trunk route but for practical purposes the Public Works Department considered it as two separate roads—the motor road from Port Moresby through Sapphire Creek to the Rouna settlement, locally called the 'Rouna Road', and the mule track from a point above Rouna Falls to as far as Javarere (then Iawarere). A side track, which was eventually to form part of the 1942 Kokoda Trail route from Port Moresby, led off north, from a point a half kilometre past the Laloki River bridge above the Falls, to link with the old mule road snaking its way up the side of Hombrom Bluff.

The vehicular ('Rouna') road tended to receive the most attention and in the 1924/25 period was kept open to increasing motor traffic throughout the year, in spite of an abnormally wet north-west season. One trouble-spot highlighted by the heavy rains was the Sapphire Creek crossing. Bensted thought a properly constructed bridge to carry heavy traffic was 'an absolute necessity at this point'. Financial resources were becoming even further curtailed by the end of 1924 so it was somewhat unexpected when Bensted was authorised to go ahead with the bridge's construction almost immediately. But, as with the Buna–Kokoda route, the indifference of the New Guinea weather often got in the way of necessary projects. Bensted reported in the Public Works report for 1924/25:

> Unfortunately, the concrete and steel bridge for Sapphire Creek crossing could not be completed owing to the abnormal rains from October [1924] onwards. After considerable delays and losses of material through flood waters, the first abutment was completed,

> but, although every possible precaution was taken against damage, operations had to be suspended. The whole of the form work for the concrete for the second abutment was ultimately swept away and the material mostly lost just prior to being ready for the pouring of the concrete.

The bridge was eventually completed the next year after Bensted had waited for the succeeding dry season to pour the second concrete buttress. The year 1926 also saw a programme of regular maintenance of the Sogeri Plateau mule track (from Rouna to Koitakinumu plantation) being introduced with the Government agreeing an arrangement with the Plateau's commercial plantations on a £1 for £1 basis.

In the following year, the last major trouble spot on the lower road, the swampy ground north of Mount Eriama about 19 kilometres from Port Moresby, was traversed with permanent 'Armco' culverts. This enabled Bensted to proudly announce the road out to some distance beyond Sapphire Creek was now open at all times, irrespective of the weather. By mid 1928, upgrading of the Sapphire Creek to Rouna section extended this claim to the entire vehicular road. 'At no time during the wet season', reported Bensted, 'was motor traffic on this important highway interfered with, or even inconvenienced'. However, the unusually wet *guba* season of 1933 revealed the unsealed route was still susceptible to the affects of the tropical weather. In February of that year it was reported 'the road up to the Grass Plot by Rona [Rouna] Falls on the steep slopes of Warirata [Varirata] is difficult to manage after many inches of rain, and the other further on [the Rouna-Koitakinumu section, via the Hairpin Bend] is impassable'.

The upgrading of the track to Rouna also allowed the first vehicles to be taken onto the Sogeri Plateau though this was surrounded by some minor intrigue (or so it seemed to the local press) in early November 1928. Some weeks earlier, the Public Works Department had announced it had begun work on upgrading the mule track over the Hairpin Bend with the intention of attempting its traverse in the Department's Morris six-wheeled 'roadless' truck. Concurrently with this, as the *Papuan Courier* of 2nd November 1928 reported, 'the local agents of the Ford Motor Company ... conceived the idea of driving a Ford Roadster from Port [Moresby] to Itikinumu [on the Sogeri

Plateau above Rouna Falls] as a test of the power and reliability of that make of car'.

The Ford Roadster to do the trip was owned by Percy John ('P.J.') McDonald, at that time a general contractor and sawmiller, but later the owner of Ilolo Rubber Plantation on the Plateau. It was intended to make the attempt on the late afternoon of Thursday 1st November 1928. When McDonald arrived at the end of the road at Rouna, he found 'a barricade of earth and stone about three to four feet [about 1 metre] high and about nine feet [about 3 metres] deep had been built right across the track ...'. It transpired Bensted had found out about the proposed private attempt and had deployed a labour team working through the previous Wednesday night to construct the obstacle. Bensted had published a warning in the *Gazette*, stating the track was 'not safe for ordinary vehicular traffic', and another notice in the *Papuan Courier*, which cautioned to attempt the traverse 'with an ordinary type of four-wheeled vehicle would, in the Department's opinion, prove extremely dangerous to both life and property'.

PREVIOUS PAGE:

▲ The Laloki Valley taken from above Rouna Falls in 1939, looking back towards Port Moresby. Though lacking sharp detail, this photograph is clear enough to suggest how the undeveloped Laloki Valley would have looked to early road builders, originally MacDonald and then, in 1923, Bensted.

Bensted's 'road'(indicated) can be faintly discerned running in a slightly undulating line from the lower left corner of the photograph to the centre. The mountain in the background (at right) is the western end of Hombrom Bluff.

University of Papua New Guinea.

▼ The same view in 1989, 50 years later, with a portion of the Hairpin Bend visible at left. The upper road follows the line of the mule track that connected the settlement at Rouna with the Sogeri Plateau via the Hairpin Bend.

Though work was sporadically carried out on the Rouna–Sogeri route during the 1920s and 1930s, its upgrading to carry vehicles was really beyond the manual labour teams available to the government. The route was not much more than a horse track until 1942.

The lower road in this photograph was established in the late 1950s by contractors working on the construction of the Rouna hydro-electric station. This too, followed an old track that had existed from at least the mid 1880s, and which went down to the river just below the base of Rouna Falls.

Author

It may have seemed Bensted wanted to retain for his Department the honour of making the initial vehicular crossing of the Hairpin Bend. However, following discussions with the Ford agents on the Friday, Bensted had the stone wall removed at first light on Saturday 3rd November 1928 to allow McDonald to make the attempt. At 7.40 am that day, McDonald, accompanied by three passengers (one next to McDonald in the front and two behind in the rumble seat), became the first person to drive onto the Sogeri Plateau. They were followed at about 9 am the same morning by the six-wheeled Morris truck which carried a one tonne load and 23 passengers, including Bensted and his two young sons, all cheering wildly. The truck was driven by Denzil Williams. As to the test of the car, one of the passengers was reported as saying 'the car pulled wonderfully, you couldn't hold her back'. The Ford agents could not have hoped for a better testimonial. Two weeks later they were able to run an advertisement in the *Papuan Courier* claiming with some justification the Roadster was 'The Car with Outstanding Performance under local conditions'.

Though these initial crossings showed passage over the Hairpin Bend was technically feasible, it remained a hazardous journey for only the most intrepid of drivers. For this reason, it was not a trip drivers undertook regularly. However, Port Moresby residents were so eager for a proper road to be constructed whenever anyone did drive over the Hairpin Bend, it was reported at length in the local paper. About six weeks after McDonald's first crossing, a man named Vieusseux, driving a Ford Phaeton, made the trip to Itikinumu on Christmas Eve 1928. He reported though he did not consider it a normal road, he thought 'it could be made so with comparatively small expenditure'. This plea was taken up by the *Papuan Courier* who asserted 'the track to Itikinumu as it now exists could be made a road fit for ordinary motor transport at comparatively small cost and without any great engineering difficulties'. But these exhortations were not to succeed and it was to be well over a decade before resources were found to construct a permanent vehicular way over the Hairpin Bend.

Despite the difficulties of the Hairpin Bend link, a new portion of the overland mail route was constructed at the end of

1930 on the Sogeri Plateau itself. It was put through by P.J. McDonald, who took up a tract of land at Ilolo on the northern edge of the Sogeri Plateau. The plantation house was situated to take in the truly magnificent vistas over the northern edge of the Sogeri Plateau, over the valleys of the Hiwick and Goldie Rivers and Ebealue Creek. The property was originally intended as a timber lease but McDonald later decided to switch to rubber growing. A portion of the 'road' connecting the Hairpin Bend mule path with the Hombrom Bluff track, already went about one-eighth of the way towards his estate, which was about another 7 kilometres distant. From the Hombrom Bluff turn-off, and with no government assistance, McDonald constructed a new road, which was intended from the outset to be a route suitable for motor vehicles. In 1934, McDonald and Fred Turner took a Dodge truck up the Hairpin Bend and along this road to Ilolo plantation. The road constructed by McDonald was to become part of the wartime Kokoda Trail.

Meanwhile, back in Port Moresby, Bensted had been fortunate funds had been made available when they were and such work which had been authorised had been completed. The economic depression of the late 1920s and the 1930s hit the dependent economy of Papua particularly hard, plunging the Territory into almost ten years of acute financial strain. Cruelly, the market prices for those commodities which had spurred the work on the Sogeri Road fell away sharply. Improved access to the mines and plantations now existed but the expected profits were no longer there to be made. New Guinea Copper Mines Ltd, the company formed in 1920 to work the Astrolabe field near Sapphire Creek, closed down in 1927 (temporarily at first but the company was never to re-open the mine). In the following twelve months, with still falling commodity prices, Murray was reporting with frustration the 'rubber [sale price] fell so low that the trees were hardly worth tapping'.

But things were to get even worse. In April 1928, the *Papuan Courier* reported 'Papuan rubber is now practically unsaleable in Sydney for Australian consumption'. By July 1929, the price had fallen to ten and three-quarters pence per pound and in the next 12 months fell to only three and seven-eighths pence per pound. Given the lowest cost to produce was around 10 pence per pound, it is easy to understand a press report of the time which said of the latter price 'the rubber producers find this fatal'. The price briefly fell to its lowest point in May 1931 when a rate of only 2 3/8 pence per pound was reached. In June 1930, moves were made to close down Koitaki Para Rubber Estates Ltd on the Sogeri Plateau due to the uneconomic conditions; however, a reprieve was in order when the rubber price improved to some extent towards the end of 1930. The only sources of optimism amongst all this gloom was the promise of a sisal hemp industry (a plantation had been started at Rigo, and one was later started at Fairfax Harbour near Port Moresby), and the formation of a company to grow sugar at Sangara, on the Buna–Yodda Road, though, as it turned out, neither proved to be the economic salvation it was hoped for.

For the individual too, black or white, it was also a difficult time. A correspondent to the *Pacific Islands Monthly* of September 1930 observed 'the average [white] settler is taking things fairly calmly—perhaps the calm of despair'. Individuals in Port Moresby to large extent avoided patronising local businesses, preferring to order direct from Australian suppliers. Even with the addition of shipping and landing charges, costs were less than the marked-up prices from the local stores, and this practice put a number of merchants in a precarious trading position, eventually forcing them to review their often excessive profit margins. The effect on the native inhabitants was not so critical since a cash economy was not central to their daily lives. Indeed, there was tendency to refuse to sell their produce for the low returns being offered by the buyers. This gave them less cash to spend and this rebounded on the white trader, who made his living by selling trade goods to the natives.

The effects of the declining local conditions were compounded by similar conditions in Australia and this led to the annual Commonwealth Government grant of £50,000 being successively reduced from July 1929, this falling to only £34,000 in the 1932–33 period. Despite people having less money, local charges and taxes had to be increased and government expenditure ruthlessly cut back. With the transport of copper (from Sapphire Creek) and rubber (from Sogeri) practically stopping altogether, and with public works seriously curtailed, all new work and major improvements on the road to Rouna stopped. White technical staff who left were not replaced and the employment and training of lower-paid native artisans and overseers was accelerated. In 1934, for the first time in over twenty years, groups of native prisoners were used to provide 'bare maintenance' of the Rouna road. 'Public works have practically ceased, as a result of the financial situation' was the Public Works Department report for the 1931/32 period and this was typical of every year from 1928/29 to 1936/37. Towards the end of 1937, after Harris, the Treasurer, expressed his belief Papua had emerged from the depression period, Public Works activity finally began to pick up. For the Rouna road though, this did not mean much more than an improved maintenance programme and it was to be another five years before the imperatives of World War Two brought about changes to this route.

12

The Buna–Kokoda road (1918-1933)

Ironically, in the years from about 1918 up to World War Two, road building operations at the northern end of the overland track were generally more successful than at the southern end, though it took some years to find the right solution. This was despite the desertion of the Yodda field in 1910 in favour of the Lakekumu, and the demands on white population numbers wrought by the First World War. As a consequence, the district remained seriously underpopulated and gold production was significantly down on previous years. From November 1919 to April 1920, only one white miner was working on the Yodda. The earlier plans for large dredges to be employed had not eventuated and the field was still being worked with the old alluvial methods. Supplies still cost a great deal to transport there and the few miners still in the country generally avoided it.

The slower tempo and the economic stringencies placed upon Government officers resulted in a further change to the administrative structure of the north coast Divisions. On the 25th May 1920, the Kumusi and Mambare Divisions were re-amalgamated into a single Northern Division. Charles Theodore Wurth was appointed Acting Resident Magistrate and the old Kumusi Division's main base at Buna was retained as the new division's headquarters. By the end of 1920, Wurth and his officers had, with considerable effort, significantly improved travel along the Buna to Kokoda track. The worst part, a three kilometres section crossing a swamp just inland of Buna, was traversed with a 'log road'. This was a platform raised on stumps about a metre high to keep the route open when flooded during the wet season. The five wire suspension bridges on the route were refurbished, and it was announced each village with a village constable could offer a clean rest house which was regularly maintained by that village. The 'regularity' of maintenance was ensured by introducing the rule rest houses would be inspected within the week following each full moon.

Following the success of trial plantings, the government had started a rubber plantation of about 60 hectares at Kokoda. This venture was recognised as a new and viable direction for the area and this prompted work to be done on cleaning up and generally improving the township. Murray visited Kokoda in May 1921 and was very pleased with the results, recording it was looking 'extremely well' and 'far better' than he had ever seen it before. But these small improvements were not sufficient to attract permanent settlers. Though the number of miners initially rose to seven, by the end of 1921 only three of them remained.

During the 1922 wet season, very heavy rains caused widespread inundation, with much structural damage being done to the built-up parts of the Buna–Kokoda track. All three kilometres of the painstakingly-constructed log road were swept away and the Kamo (now Komo) bridge connecting Kokoda with the Yodda field was destroyed. There was nothing for Wurth to do but start again, though it took almost two years, fortunately aided by milder wet seasons, to get the road back to the 1921 standard. In September 1925 however, there was another long period of heavy torrential downpours that 'totally obliterated' the 33 kilometres of track between Kokoda and the Kumusi River as well as, again, the section of log road near Buna.

One can imagine Wurth's frustration after almost five years of toil and it is to his credit he did not give up the struggle. In fact, he decided to try something new. He did away with the log support staging and replaced it with 'earth embankments well drained at the sides' though, in the absence of road metal, the corduroy surface had to be retained. It took over six months for this work to be completed. It proved to be a worthwhile expenditure of effort, George Zimmer, the Acting Resident Magistrate in July 1927 being able to report it gave 'every indication, after nine months of intermittent rain, that it will be a lasting piece of work'.*

The 1920s decade was a dismal one for gold mining on the Yodda field and for the three years from 1926 to 1929, no mining at all was reported. In the 1930/31 period, the single miner on the field extracted a meagre 128 grams of gold, worth only £18, in the entire year. But rather than gold, the Government was achieving more success with the progress of the Kokoda rubber plantation. This had grown from a small number of seedlings planted as an experiment a few years earlier to 1,524 trees in mid 1925. Within 12 months, this had doubled to 3454 trees which was sufficient to keep 10 tappers occupied, and by June 1927, some 11,948 trees had been established and 20 tappers employed. Though rubber was collected during the Depression years, as already noted profits were non-existent as the price fell to an uneconomic level. However the Government was well rewarded for its perseverance in the late 1930s when the world market price for rubber rose sharply.

In 1930, a new company, the Sangara Sugar Estates Ltd, took up 8,100 hectares of land at Sangara on the Buna–Kokoda road about 43 kilometres inland. It was perhaps a measure of the desperation felt during the Depression years this venture was attempted since there already was an oversupply of sugar, particularly on Australia's protected market. But the scheme's promoters were confident the climate and soil were so conducive to large quality harvests, and their labour costs much lower than elsewhere, they would be able to trade on the world's markets without protective subsidies. Sixteen hectares of the local Badilla cane were planted as an experiment and by the end of 1932 had produced 191 tonnes of cane to the hectare, comparing more than favourably with the best output from the North Queensland fields of 151 tonnes per hectare. This

* This idea was later taken up in other wet areas of the country with good results. In 1934 for example, it was reported from Ioma, which had a network of five 'red gravel causeways', that there was 'no affect to travel' after days of continuous rain at an average rate of 75mm per hour.

demonstration of the district's potential was sufficient incentive for three other concerns to show interest but the industry was never to go any further. Lobbying from the depressed Australian sugar industry claiming their quota under the Imperial Preference Scheme would be affected made it impossible to obtain the necessary finance, and by the end of 1935 all the projected schemes for a Papuan sugar industry had been abandoned.

One outcome of the sugar venture however was the construction of a corduroy road from Sananända Point, where Sangara Sugar Estates had a storehouse and jetty, inland for about 25 kilometres towards the Sangara plantation. The capture of this road was one of the first objectives of the Japanese when they landed near Sananända in July 1942.

Sangara was also the first inland station for the Anglican Mission in Papua, and was established by Henry Holland in 1922. Holland, then a lay preacher but ordained in 1938, was instrumental in putting in a permanent track from the church's base at Gona to Sangara in 1924. Using only local labour, Holland's work over swampy ground near the coast was remarkably well-done, as evidenced by his route being still in use today. Holland, with others from the Anglican Mission, was captured and executed by the Japanese at Buna in August 1942.

By 1930, the Buna-Kokoda road had become well-travelled by government staff and villagers living along the way. It promoted peaceful inter-village communication which contributed significantly to the gradual disappearance of the old hostilities and rivalries. All supplies for Kokoda Station were carried along the road, and this was still generally true even after the Kokoda airstrip was opened in 1932. This occurred about every six weeks, with large numbers of carriers employed to up-lift the stores direct from the hold of the supply ship at Buna. The largest party ever appears to be one of 248 persons which left Buna on the 17th September 1930 and arrived at Kokoda on the 22nd, though the usual, though still large, number of carriers was between 100 and 150.

Employment as a Government carrier on one of these occasions was much sought after and was enjoyed with much effusiveness and laughter by Northern Division villagers. Such work gave them an opportunity to travel and to earn a cash income. A genuine peace had now been established in the region and the days of government resident magistrates and patrol officers having to wear side-arms had now gone for ever. To work off any residual aggressiveness, the popularity of team sports was promoted. Team sports had been introduced into the region by the Anglican Mission at Sangara in about 1924 and was actively supported by the Government as an acceptable and pleasant way of promoting the integration of the different tribes of the area. 'There will doubtless be many fights over disputed goals', wrote Murray, 'but I do not anticipate any serious results'. Nevertheless, Murray made sure it was soccer and not the full-contact rugby code that was encouraged. (Given these origins, it is interesting to note Papua New Guinea is the only country in the world which has rugby league as its national game).

Kokoda Government Station, 1925. By this date, the Kokoda Trail had been in use as a mail route for twenty years.
University of Papua New Guinea (New Guinea Collection)

By the mid 1930s, these occasional matches had become regular organised contests with the three stations of the area, Kokoda, Ioma and Buna, all fielding cricket and soccer teams. Ioma had the best cricket pitch and won most of the matches played there, though Buna seemed to be the most successful at soccer. It is indicative of the extent of the changes in the Division even newspaper reports of these meetings, compiled by native correspondents, were framed as all such articles are in any sport-playing country of the world, in a happily and deliberately biased fashion towards the particular reporter's favourite team:

> Well [wrote Asagi Awagi in the *Papuan Villager* of October 1937] I've never dreamt that Mambare team were going to beat Buna team, since I've never seen Mambares playing football much. Matter of fact, the Mambares were playing very hopelessly ...

How truly different this friendly banter is from the days, only some forty years earlier, when the football players' fathers had met Clarke, Simpson and others first ascending the Mambare in their whaleboat.

In 1931, dredging on the Yodda finally became a reality when J. Ward Williams, an American mining engineer, took up a large tract of land and commenced 'scout boring' operations. Actually, it was William's arrival with his drilling equipment that prompted the construction of the Kokoda airstrip. Many of his supplies and some machinery were later flown direct from Port Moresby in December 1932. The transport of Williams' stores to Kokoda indirectly led to one of the early aviation tragedies in Papua New Guinea. Williams had hired a Guinea Airways Junkers G34 transport aeroplane away from its usual Port Moresby–Salamaua–Wau run servicing the Bulolo goldfields and had walked overland from Kokoda to Port Moresby to arrange the loading of his stores. Between the 16th and 20th December 1932, the aeroplane, under the command of Frank Drayton, made seven return trips between Port Moresby and Kokoda. Following the eighth Port Moresby to Kokoda trip, the final load was landed at Kokoda and Drayton then continued on to Salamaua with one passenger but the plane crashed on the way, killing all on board.

The Resident Magistrate's quarters at Buna in 1932.

This building along with every other man-made structure in the town, was completely destroyed by Allied bombers in 1942.

PNG National Library.

In 1934, Williams* sold out to Yodda Goldfields Limited, a Sydney company formed specially to take over his claim. This company, the sole occupant of the field, was operating 'not unsuccessfully' from 1934 to 1936, though the returns were apparently well down on earlier years of the field. Additional equipment had to be imported in an attempt to increase output. The expense of operating and maintaining the heavy machinery in such a difficult area consumed much of the profits. Murray noted in the 1935/36 Annual Report it had turned out just as expensive for the company to fly in most of the supplies direct from Port Moresby as it would have been to utilise the old method of porterage from Buna Bay. In the year ending June 1939, only 37 kilograms of gold were mined and in the following 12 months, the company was only marginally more successful at 46 kilograms. (The meagreness of these returns can be appreciated by a comparison with the 70 kilograms of gold extracted as a by-product of copper production on the Astrolabe field in 1926, the last full year of production before the mine was closed. The Astrolabe area was considered at the time to be

* Williams, in company with two others, Wallace Kienzle and a man named Bourke, spent the next two years searching for gold in other areas of Papua, particularly on the Fly River to the west. Though traces of gold were frequently found, they concluded at that payable gold was not there to be mined. Williams left Papua in August 1937. In the following year, he was able to use the method he developed in Papua, of employing aircraft to support remote mining operations, in a similar venture in Nicaragua, where the buildings for an entire town were flown into the interior of that country.

The travels of Evelyn Cheesman, an English entymologist and writer who visited Papua in 1933.

The fact that Cheesman was permitted by the government to range as far as indicated here accompanied only by her native assistants is evidence of the scale of the social changes achieved in the area in less than 40 years.

PNG National Library.

uneconomic for gold mining by the Government Geologist Evan Richard Stanley. However, later, in 1937, though smelting was not recommenced, mining resumed on the Astrolabe field simply to obtain the gold bound within the copper matte).

Concurrently with the establishment of the dredging company, the year 1934 also saw the arrival at Kokoda of brothers Wallace and Herbert Kienzle, who established the Mamba rubber estates. Wallace spent the next two years with Ward Williams prospecting in other areas of Papua, before returning to Kokoda. Herbert Kienzle was later to play an important part in the Kokoda Trail campaign of 1942. During the war, Herbert Kienzle was to cross the old mail route eight times.

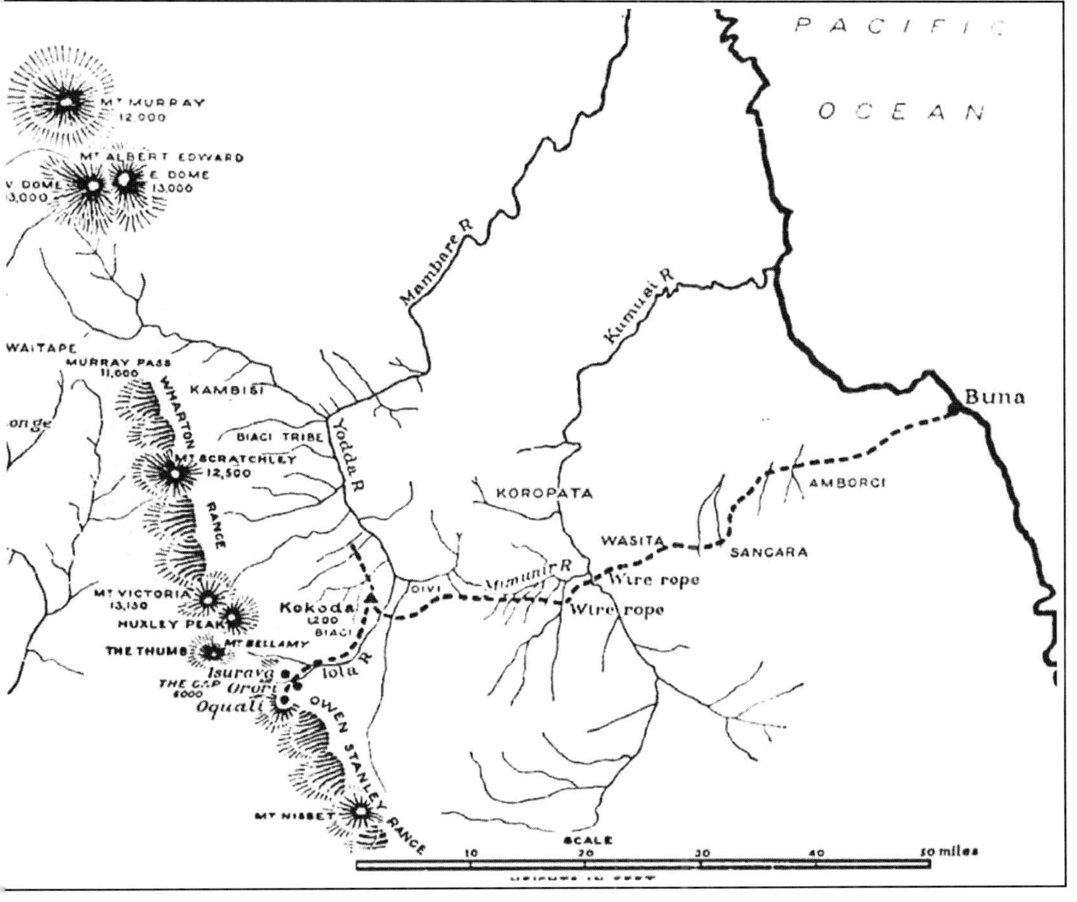

The overland track between Kokoda and the Sogeri Plateau was less regularly travelled as reliable delivery by sea and porterage from Buna became the norm and the opening of the airstrip at Kokoda introduced the option of air deliveries. However, this did not mean it was abandoned completely. The most regular Government travellers for the remainder of the 1930s were medical patrols which, in addition to the Port Moresby-Buna route, covered all other 'bush' areas of the country each year, from about 1920. The Treasury annually allocated £3,000 for these expeditions and staff, with titles such as Travelling Government Medical Officer and Travelling Native Medical Assistants, were specifically recruited to attend to these roving duties. A typical composition of a medical patrol was a European Medical Assistant with three native medical orderlies.

In November and December 1932, such a group walked from Port Moresby to Kokoda, then on to Buna, then back to Port Moresby in six weeks, (in doing so, establishing another early 'double' crossing). Perhaps not as impressive though as the patrol nine years earlier lead by Allan Stewart Graham, a Senior Medical Assistant. This group was on the road from June to October 1923. Starting from Port Moresby, Graham's patrol travelled via the overland route to Kokoda, on to Buna, then calling at various settlements on the north coast to Samarai, then along the south coast to Port Moresby.

Murray was a staunch supporter of these expeditions. In his view, they not only achieved medical and health improvements in remote villages, but were also important for 'showing the flag'. At the time of the introduction of motor transport into the Territory, and again when air transport was introduced, Murray had expressed some reservations about adopting these faster forms of transport. He believed travellers were really only aware of where they started from and where they completed their journey. He cited experiences in British colonies where these modes of transport had been introduced. The reduction in contact by the authorities with the general population had resulted in measurable changes in social attitudes.

This was of some concern to Murray and he had developed a specific policy on roads for Papua which differed in fundamental respects from policies established in other British colonies of the time. In a 'Review of the Australian Administration in Papua from 1907 to 1920', published in about 1923, Murray noted in other places the first existence of a bridle track was sufficient incentive for 'Malays, Chinese and Indians to put up houses in the middle of a few acres of land', and, citing Sir Frank Swettenham of the Federated Malay States, 'a bridle road was no sooner completed than small houses, plantations, and fruit and vegetable gardens sprang up along its whole length'. Murray attributed the lack of this process in Papua to the absence of an 'intermediate race', since 'it would not pay a white man to do so'. Murray seems to be pointing, somewhat obliquely, to the fact the native inhabitants of Papua of that time were extremely insular in their outlook. They lived only within their traditional tribal boundaries and it was literally risking life and limb to go outside them. With a few historical exceptions, the concept of internal migration was not known in the country, and the notion of settling in new districts and of commercial exploitation of new communications routes, was beyond the comprehension of the traditional native mind of the time.

> Thus [Murray concluded] it would be a wrong policy in Papua to build roads vaguely, on the general principle that they will 'open up the country'. They will not, in fact, have this effect, and no road should be constructed except with a definite purpose, either to provide access to a plantation or to a known mineral field, or to open up a district which contains good land that is certain to be developed; the expense of construction and maintenance is so great that, with a small revenue, it is not wise to take any risks.

In any event, as Murray added, nearly all the plantations in the country were on or near the coast and therefore 'traffic by sea will be preferred to traffic by land'. To a certain extent, Murray's policy on roads still holds good today. The terrain and climate of the country are such the construction of roads and bridges into the mountainous interior would incur considerable capital expenditure. As Murray intimated, there would have to be substantial economic or social benefit to justify these costs.

Murray had another experience of new technology in 1933 when he visited Kokoda to inspect the recently opened airstrip constructed by the station's officer-in-charge, Mack Rich. Rich had a 'wireless' set with which he regularly communicated with the Government station at Samarai, which in turn passed his messages on to Port Moresby. Some weeks earlier, the radio had featured in an incident involving an aeroplane on the Kokoda airstrip. It had flown from Port Moresby heavily laden with stores for mining engineer Williams and had become bogged on the soft surface. By using his radio, Rich was able to explain why the craft had not returned to Port Moresby.

The Kokoda detachment of the Armed Native Constabulary on parade in November 1929.

University of Papua New Guinea.

But Rich was left with the problem of getting the aeroplane airborne again. Lacking rollers or similar equipment, he solved the difficulty in a novel way. He paraded all his prisoners from the Kokoda lock-up and these, with others from the village who wished to be in on the fun, he walked up and down the airstrip until the trampling of the many feet had compacted the surface to the required solidarity. The aeroplane was able to take off without further delay.

During his inspection visit afterwards, Murray expressed interest in the 'apparatus' Rich had used, and Rich offered the Lieutenant-Governor, by way of demonstration of the radio's capabilities, to send a message from Murray to the Australian Prime Minister. Murray's record of this occasion evokes a stark picture of the extent to which his country and his people had been overtaken by the outside world.

> The next morning I set out on my return journey to the [northern] coast. I camped that night at the Kumusi Bridge, 20 miles [32 kilometres] down the Buna Road, and about 9 p.m., just as I was going to bed, a native arrived from Kokoda with an answer from Canberra to my telegram. The messenger had left Kokoda in the afternoon, and had done the 20 miles [32 kilometres] in good time, for the last two or three hours of his journey were over a rough track, and in pitch darkness relieved only by the fitful gleam of the firestick which he was carrying.

The guest house at Kokoda Station in 1933.

PNG National Library.

With these words of Murray's, we come to the end of the old ways for Papua, to the conclusion of a unique period in history, and to the end of the Kokoda Trail's heyday. Events of the outside world, inexorably, were sweeping in and incongruencies like radio messages carried by barefoot runners with firesticks could not be sustained. Murray, by now an old man, had a sense of this. 'It was a strange experience', he said, 'to receive a message from the Federal Capital in the middle of the Papuan bush' and, in this regard admitted 'we live rather out of the world in this Territory'.

Murray died in February 1940 and never saw how the events of 1942 affected his beloved Papua. But before his death, in any event, the demands of his position meant he had little time for overseas events of the 1930s, even though the signs of unrest were becoming evident. Already, in Europe, Nazi Germany was carefully laying the groundwork for its later aggressiveness towards its neighbours. In Manchuria too, Japanese forces were gaining the confidence they needed to extend their ambitions towards south-east Asia, the Pacific, and Australia. When these aspirations of Japan were put into effect in the 1940s, they were to inflict upheavals of such magnitude upon Papua the slow, paternalistic, old-world ways of Hubert Murray were to be lost forever.

Detail from a 1932 map illustrates the extent of development adjacent to the old gold mining areas on the north Papuan coast up to the time of the Japanese landings in 1942. The many names of the settlements and plantations along the Buna–Kokoda road illustrates how the emphasis had shifted from mining to agriculture in the Northern Division. In areas not as amenable to agriculture, such as those about Ioma (previously Tamata Station), far less development had taken place.

The particular tragedy of the Japanese invasion of the Papuan mainland was that it was concentrated on, and devastated, those areas of the country that were most advanced in their social and economic development.

University of Queensland.

Part 3

Later days

1938-1992

We trudge along in the rain and sludge
And there is no turning back;
Upward and onward, into the night,
Of the Owen Stanley Track.

Howard Tilse, 1943

Port Moresby in 1938. To the right is Paga Hill where the first artillery pieces were install ed in early 1939.

University of Papua New Guinea.

13

Last days of peace (1938-1942)

Despite the deteriorating political conditions in Europe and Asia, life in Papua in the late 1930s saw the gloom of the Depression years being displaced by a relative prosperity and a more optimistic outlook. Indeed, it was the international tensions which spurred the demand that revived the markets for Papua's agricultural produce, though the basis for improvements, in the rubber industry at least, had been established in 1930 and had begun to show results as early as 1933. By 1938, the strong demand for rubber from Australia was leading the economic recovery in Papua, and in just 24 months from the beginning of 1937 to the end of 1938, an additional 20,235 hectares of land was taken up for plantations, almost quadrupling the area under rubber in the country. The whole of the 1938 rubber output was taken by the Australian market, as well as all of the copra and desiccated coconut output. In just these three items alone, the value of exports increased from £97,163 for July-December 1938 to £128,741 in January-June 1939, or a rise of some £32,000 in just 6 months. Coffee, too, was sought after and the entire crop for 1938, worth £2,000, went to Australian consumers. Gold and copper continued to lead exports—the £180,00 returned for the 1938/39 period accounted for over 36% of the £490,000 total exports for the Territory—but it was the rising fortunes in the agricultural sector which gave the real boost to life in Papua at the time.

ROAD FROM
PORT MORESBY
MULE TRACK
TO SOGERI

The settlement at Rouna (Migagi) in 1939, with the road from Port Moresby and the mule track to Sogeri indicated. Rouna was as far as vehicles could go until 1942.

University of Papua New Guinea (New Guinea Collection)

Most of the gold exported came from claims on the eastern islands though the two remaining mining concerns at Kokoda, Yodda Goldfields Ltd and the Yodda Prospecting Syndicate, persevered with their dredging operations to make their smaller, though still significant, contributions. But it was hard work: a 1938 report showed a mean of 30 cubic metres of gravel wash had to be processed to retrieve just one ounce of gold. In comparison with the average return for the same period for the Lakekumu field (by now virtually abandoned), of 1 ounce of gold for every 1,949 cubic metres, the Yodda's returns may have seemed more than adequate. Yet, when the expenses invested in equipment and maintenance were taken into account, the returns for the companies operating on the Mambare bordered on the uneconomic. Yodda Goldfields appears to have been the better-founded concern (the Syndicate was not reported on after October 1938) and continually expressed optimism about the Yodda field, though perhaps this was principally for the benefit of shareholders.

Houses at Rouna, 1939.

University of Papua New Guinea (New Guinea Collection)

In 1938/39, Yodda Goldfields estimated their leases had a remaining life of about seven and a half years. In this period, they extracted gold worth £7,480, and in the 1939/40 year, 43 kilograms valued at £12,053 was obtained. But the gold was running out as the falling indicator figure, the 'average value per cubic yard' well illustrated. In 1939/40 this was three shillings and two pence (about 32 cents) and this fell to only 2/11 (about 29 cents) in 1940/41. The mean monthly return between December 1938 and October 1941 was about 80 ounces though, somewhat ironically, in the last months of operations, this started to increase. The best return obtained was in August 1941 when 127 ounces were extracted, though it was back to 82 ounces a month later. The dredging company well understood the indications and had reported in mid-1941 'if no further payable ground is found, the prospect for 1941–42 is anything but bright'. Though the approaching war was to force the closure of mining operations in April 1942, the Yodda goldfield had by now been well and truly exhausted, and military operations only hastened the inevitable end.

On top of minerals and agricultural produce, by 1938 optimistic prospects for a local petroleum industry were being entertained. There had been a continuing but sporadic interest in oil since its discovery by Thomas and Lett in the Gulf of Papua in 1911, though the extent and commercial viability of the oil deposits were not known. But the engineering and logistic problems posed by the remote and inaccessible country, the risk-oriented and capital-intensive nature of the industry, and the hard times of the 1920s meant further exploration was delayed for 15 years until the international situation made it worthwhile. Several large consortiums took up permits from mid-1936 to search in both the Territories of Papua and New Guinea. Papuan operations were confined to the Gulf of Papua. At Kariava on the Vailala River, where scout boring commenced in March 1941, a depth of over 5,000 feet had been reached by October 1941 and it was anticipated the maximum depth of 10,000 feet would be reached by mid-1942. At the time, great hopes were held for this well.

The revival of interest in Australia in the primary products of Papua came about because of the general push for rearmament that was occurring worldwide towards the end of the 1930s. Actually, the intimacy of the Western powers' relations with Japan had been steadily diminishing since the 1920s when both Britain and the United States of America had adopted a less friendly stand over Japan's aggressiveness towards China. The withdrawal of the commercial patronage of these countries was acutely felt in Japan in the 1930s. This led to a deep-seated resentment in Japan against Britain and America. The consequent discontent enabled the militant factions to convince the less radical ones, as Hitler had done in Germany, that military aggression and the occupation of someone else's country was the answer to the economic ills of the day.

In 1932, Japanese soldiers took by force the Chinese state of Manchuria and the subsequent uproar in the League of Nations gave Japan the opportunity to dissociate itself from this organisation and its restrictions. Japan had earlier opted out of other international agreements with the West and in 1936, clearly demonstrated where its sympathies lay by withdrawing from the London Naval Conference but joining the Anti-Comintern Pact with Germany and Italy. In the following year,

Japanese forces further trespassed on Chinese territory by invading North China.

All these movements of Japan, and her declared dislike of Britain, the United States of America, and their allies, were sufficient inducement for the Australian authorities to take a closer look at the defence arrangements for their own country and this, ultimately, led to the large increase in demand for Papua's products, as already noted. And as the significance of the Territory of Papua (and the Mandated Territory of New Guinea too, but particularly Papua) as a source of raw materials came to be appreciated, this only emphasised the strategic importance the country already had as a consequence of its geographical location. By 1937, the possibility of a Japanese push southward towards Australia through the New Guinea island had been openly discussed in newspapers and journals (and in even a book, Willard Price's *Japan Reaches Out*) for some time, and the importance of Australian, British, and French possessions in the south-western Pacific was widely accepted. The editor of *Pacific Islands Monthly*, Ralph Robson, was later to write these possessions 'lie, as if placed by Providence, in a position to be used as a protective barrier for the northern ... coasts of Australia'. The prevailing view of the time was perhaps best summed up in an article in the London *Daily Herald* on 2 January 1939 which referred to Port Moresby as Australia's 'Gibraltar'.

The Australian Government at first seemed to favour the appeasement approach taken in Britain and refused to take official cognisance of what so many others could see, hoping the problem would go away of its own accord. In a press release issued on the 7th May 1938, the view was

> the Government strongly deprecates published statements that Australia intends to fortify Papua ... or New Guinea. Such [anti-Japanese] reports, for which there was no justification, might have extremely damaging effects ... [and that] the Government was anxious not to take any action which might be seized upon by another Power as an excuse to extend fortifications in the Pacific. The real position is that Cabinet has never contemplated establishing defences in Papua.

Fortunately, this view did not persist and it was only a matter of months before moves were made to do something in the Papuan and New Guinean Territories. But even in this, initially at least, there seemed to be a flow-on from this earlier reluctance to make a full commitment. Lieutenant-Governor Murray was reported in the *Papuan Courier* of 24th February 1939 as privately favouring 'the formation of a militia force composed of Papuan natives to assist in the defences of the territory'. This report was intended for local consumption only and Murray did not forward the proposal to Canberra for official consideration. However, his suggestion became known in Australia and triggered an immediate reaction from the Australian Defence Minister, G.A. Street. Street pointed out conscription from among the natives had never been considered and '... steps already taken for the defence of Papua were considered adequate'. It is true under the League of Nations Mandate, natives of the Mandated Territory of New Guinea could not be recruited as soldiers, but this restriction did not apply to natives of the Territory of Papua. Street's refutation, made in February 1939, seems at odds with a report in the *Pacific Islands Monthly* only three months later that a plan to enlist native soldiers (in Papua) was under discussion. It does not appear as if this assertion was later challenged by the Government in any way.

The preparations made to defend Papua, the ones Street considered 'adequate', involved the provision of 'fixed coastal artillery, an air squadron,* and naval boom defence ... at Port Moresby'. A small party of army engineers had journeyed to the

---

* A newly-established unit of the Royal Australian Air Force, No. 11 Squadron, under the command of Flight Lieutenant Alexander (later Air Commodore, OBE), commenced service in Port Moresby on 25th September 1939 equipped with two Short 'C' flying-boats requisitioned from QANTAS. By mid-December 1939, there were supposed to have been two RAAF squadrons in the town, No. 11 and No. 20, each equipped with six Catalina flying boats. However, it appears the 12 aeroplanes were not physically where they were supposed to have been. A diary entry of a member of the 15th Battalion noted that between the time of his arrival in Port Moresby in July 1940 and 23rd February 1941, there was only one RAAF flying-boat permanently stationed in Port Moresby. The first fighters to arrive in Port Moresby were the ex-USAF Kittyhawks of RAAF No. 75 Squadron, on 21st March 1942.

town in February 1939 to survey sites for the installation of the artillery pieces. The first site chosen was at the top of Paga Hill, at the southern end of the peninsula upon which the actual port of Port Moresby is situated. A team of 140 prisoners from Badili goal were set to work building a road from the town to the Paga summit and had largely completed this by the 24th March 1939 when a detachment of 38 soldiers from 13th Field Regiment, under Major K.D. Chalmers and a Lieutenant Cape, arrived on *MV Bulolo* to prepare the emplacements for the guns. Only one gun, of 6 inch calibre (about 150 millimetres), was installed (completed in June 1939) though provision was made for a second.

All of the preparations in Port Moresby in 1939 were based on the premise of a sea-borne attack. It was widely held attack from the north was not viable and any threat to the town would only come from the sea. Such threat, it was believed, could be repelled relatively easily, given the appropriate naval and air force resources. A paragraph from an article in the *Pacific Islands Monthly* for January 1939 which noted (correctly) the outer Moresby and the inner Fairfax Harbours were 'capable of sheltering the biggest fleets in the world', illustrates the popular (mistaken) belief of the time:

> The topography is such that the port could be easily defended against approach from the sea. At the back are the foothills leading up into the high mountains—there could be no approach from there.

Australian soldiers being inspected at Konedobu by Acting Administrator Champion on their arrival in Port Moresby on 24th March 1939. These were the first of thousands of troops that were later to pass through the town.

PNG National Library.

This view was accepted as correct for at least two reasons. Firstly, the white man had been in the country for over 60 years and still there was no 'road' over the mountains. This suggested the Owen Stanleys were far too rugged and inaccessible to allow a route to be readily established. There is some truth in this, as earlier chapters have suggested, though the absence of 'roads', in particular between Port Moresby and Buna through Kokoda, is also due in considerable part, to deliberate policies established by Murray in the early 1920s. Some more enlightened members of the public appreciated the fact there were many foot tracks across the mountains, but these were believed to be native footpads which wandered interminably and were completely unsuitable for moving large numbers of troops.

The second reason why the possibility of a successful overland advance was considered unlikely was even if such an attack was mounted, it was believed the attacking force could easily be halted by a relatively small opposing force at The Gap. People were misled by the name of this feature into believing it was like a gorge or mountain pass, passage through which could be infinitely delayed by military or physical obstruction. The Gap is actually about 15 kilometres wide, consisting in many places of reasonably open and flat country. It is restricted to a certain extent to the west by the sharply rising slopes of Mount Bellamy but is somewhat more open to the east. The Gap simply could not be held by a small force at all.

While one may accept the general public may perpetrate whatever fiction it fancies, it is difficult to believe the military planners should have so readily accepted an overland advance was unlikely or could be easily blocked, without checking further. It is amazing no military survey team was sent into the mountains to obtain first-hand intelligence prior to work starting in Port Moresby in February 1939. As late as August 1942, that is *after* the Japanese had landed on the north coast of Papua, it was still believed by some Army engineers the 'pass' could be blown up to block the cross-country passage of an invading force. Sadly, the superficial approach to defence arrangements, given their agreement with (erroneous) popular sentiment and the absence of any professional military appreciation, reeks of political expediency.

The end of an era: a March 1939 photograph of Acting Administrator Champion (seated, left) with Major K.D. Chalmers (seated, right) and Lieutenant Cape (standing). Champion was acting for Lieutenant-Governor Murray who was absent from the country.

The intrusion of the Pacific war into Papua brought to an end the long-entrenched 19th century style of colonialism of the Murray years. After WW2 (from 1949), a new approach—which eventually led to PNG becoming independent in 1975—was taken. This picture captures the beginning of the end of the old colonial period.

PNG National Library.

Having said this, it is not true to say *no* provision was made against an overland attack, since the military planning process more or less automatically considers all possible contingencies. But the arrangements put in place were more in the nature of an afterthought than a deliberate tactical provision, and were viewed by Lieutenant-Governor Murray with some cynicism. In a letter dated 13th July 1939 to his grand-daughter Mrs Marie Pinney, Murray wrote:

> We are up to our neck in preparation for a Japanese invasion. They have worked out an elaborate Defence Scheme which we have to put into force. It is a fine piece of work, but has little relation to reality. For instance one of the Government Secretary's duties is to look after the carrier pigeons, and an anticipated advance on Kokoda from Buna is tc be opposed by a Company of Infantry with machine guns ...

So entrenched was the view the threat to Port Moresby would come from the sea and not from the north that a plan was announced in Port Moresby at the end of September 1939 that in the event of attack upon the town, all non-combatants would be moved inland to a camp at a 'selected place'. To facilitate this, the town was divided into three zones, each zone being in the charge of a warden. In overall charge was a Head Warden, 59-year old Robert Dugald Bertie, who had been a solicitor in Port Moresby since 1916. Gladys Nicholas, who was Bertie's secretary, recalls as part of the preparation for evacuation, food caches were established 'in the Sogeri ranges', though the main camp was actually to be on Hombrom Bluff, not the Sogeri Plateau proper. According to the late Fred Turner, a pre-war resident of Port Moresby, the camp was to be on the northern edge of the Bluff, and the 1910 Laloki River bridge near Sapphire Creek was supposed to have been blown up in the event of invading troops moving inland. (In the same vein, Mrs Nicholas' husband was to assist in dynamiting the Port Moresby power station in the event of a Japanese landing). An observation post was also to have been established on the western end of the Bluff. The food supplies mentioned by Gladys Nicholas may possibly have been established privately. The version of the arrangements reported in the October 1939 *Pacific Island Monthly*, suggest the authorities did not intend to allocate many resources to this plan. Given 'non-combatants' implies a majority of women and children, the preparations did not appear to be very practicable.

> Transport to the encampment will be supplied by the Government, but little else can be provided beyond shelter. Should a preliminary warning be possible, non-combatants intending to make for the encampment should collect beds, bedding, tables, chairs, cooking utensils, etc, also a week's provisions, and hold them ready for transport.

As it turned out, the plan to retreat into the hills was never actioned. Bertie was evacuated to Australia in February 1942 and died there in October the following year.

Murray's poor view of the military preparations may well have originated some months before he wrote to his grand-daughter. Major Chalmers had wished for the residents of Port

Moresby to take more interest in the defence of their town. On the 11th May 1939, he convened a meeting of the white male population in the Library Institute building to discuss the raising of a Papuan militia unit. Thirty-nine volunteers came forward at the meeting though 80 were required. Murray's aid was enlisted in the recruiting of the balance but he was openly critical of how effective such a small force would be. Indeed, even without hindsight, one tends to agree with him. Murray was never to see the results of his reluctant recruiting on the parade ground, for nine months later, on 27th February 1940, he died at Samarai during an official inspection tour.*

Despite Murray's misgivings about the local militia unit, plans for its formation proceeded. It was to be known as the Papuan Infantry Battalion (PIB) and the first Company was formed in June 1940 under Major L. Logan, only weeks before the first Australian units arrived in the country. In July 1940, a detachment of the 15th Battalion, under Major W. Oliver, disembarked at Port Moresby to assist in the defence work about the town. These soldiers were joined by two companies of the 49th Battalion on 21st March 1941.† These men, with the detachment of the 13th Field Regiment to man the gun on Paga Hill, constituted Port Moresby's (and Papua's) entire defence force at the time of the Japanese attacks on Pearl Harbour and other strategic ports on the 7th and 8th December 1941. The force totalled 1,088, all ranks. The deficiencies did not stop here, but extended to essential military supplies as well. The gunners had only six shells for the Paga Hill gun, while the infantry soldiers had sufficient small arms ammunition for only five minutes rapid fire.

---

* Following Sir Hubert Murray's death on 27th February 1940, Papua was governed firstly by Herbert William Champion (later C.B.E.), the Government Secretary, as Acting Lieutenant-Governor until 18th September 1940, and then as Acting Administrator until 16th December 1940, when Murray's Private Secretary (and nephew), Hubert Leonard Murray, was permanently appointed as Administrator.

† The detachment of the 15th Battalion was composed of volunteer militia troops from Queensland with the army serial numbers Q1 to Q168. These soldiers were the first militia infantry troops to serve outside the Australian mainland. This detachment was incorporated into the 49th Battalion on 1st November 1940.

Despite this gloomy picture, the defence work was to eventually bring about some changes to the Port Moresby end of the overland mail route, and some long-delayed work about the town was finally undertaken, much to the sardonic amusement of civilian residents. Following the work done on the Paga Hill road in early 1939, the Port Moresby correspondent for the *Pacific Islands Monthly* wrote caustically in April 1939 under the banner 'Roads at last!':

> After several years of ecstatic contemplation, or hypnotic trance, or perhaps the coma of despair, the Public Works Department has begun to face the urgent matter of road maintenance in and about Port Moresby.
>
> There may have been a definite objective in the policy of masterly inactivity followed for about eight years. One suggestion was that scientific research demanded data as to just how far roads could deteriorate without becoming impassable by modern traffic. Another supposed that the intention of the Department was to impose an elimination test with the object of discovering the world's most robust car; while a third imagined that the idea was to promote trade through the importation of spare parts and new tyres.

Actually, there was some basis for this disenchantment since pressure by local plantation owners for improvement to both the Buna–Kokoda Road and the Sogeri Road to facilitate the transport of agricultural produce from inland plantations had been building as demand for agricultural products in Australia had increased. As early as February 1936, when difficulty had been experienced in exporting 85 bales of rubber from Kokoda, pleas for better transport avenues were being made. But though regular pick and shovel maintenance of these routes was re-established in early 1937, no real improvements were undertaken. In 1937, an approach was made to Australian authorities for financial and engineering help in putting the vehicular road across the Hairpin Bend at Rouna to the Sogeri rubber plantations but, again, as was usual, nothing came of the request. The cynicism of local residents stemmed from this long-standing saga of delayed and deferred public works.

As the 1930s proceeded and more concern was given to the two ends of the overland route, particularly the Port Moresby end, the middle portion, from Ilolo to Kokoda, experienced a corresponding decline in attention. By 1939, the inland track had largely reverted to providing only inter-village communication. The expanding use of coastal shipping services, aviation and radio resources meant the last regular users of the track, the travelling Government medical teams, no longer exclusively required foot patrols to carry out their work. This is not to say the Government wholeheartedly embraced the newer, and more expensive, forms of communication. Though the Government Anthropologist, F.E. Williams, was the first government officer in Papua to travel by air on official business, on 20th December 1932 on a trip from Port Moresby to Kokoda (ironically, Williams was later killed in an aircraft accident in New Guinea during the war), it was not until the 13th and 14th March 1941 the first formal government inspection visits were made to Kokoda and Ioma stations by aeroplane. As it happened, events overtook the government's slow and steady ways, and these were also the last to be made under the pre-war Administration.

In response to Murray's earlier request for assistance in extending the roads about Port Moresby, a substantial grant of £20,000 was received in July 1941. However, most of the original projects for which it had been requested were to miss out including, again, the Hairpin Bend. There were two reasons for this. The first was the heavy construction equipment needed was simply not available. Before March 1942, the only earthmoving plant in the town consisted of a small, and ancient, coal-fired roller and a light scraper, and the biggest crane in the country, installed in April 1939 on the wharf of Steamships Trading Company in Port Moresby, could lift only 10 tonnes. This limited the scope of any projects to mostly pick and shovel work.

The second reason was by this time, the town had become comparatively busy, with additional Australian military units arriving. The *Papuan Courier* of 25 July 1941 reported 'the existing roads in and about Port Moresby, while suited to the comparatively light traffic of a year or two ago, could not stand up to the heavier and faster moving traffic of to-day'. Thus, though the work was to be a joint effort between the military forces and the civilian Public Works Department, the requirements of the military authorities were given priority over civilian claims. The original object was the maintenance and upgrading of existing routes (as opposed to new work), specifically to upgrade and seal a number of the more heavily used roads 'in the town and for some miles outside it'. However, some new work on the Rouna road was found to be necessary as a result of a second project aimed at developing a new airstrip.

At this time, Port Moresby's aerodrome was at Kila Kila, to the east of the town. The circumstances surround the founding of the 'Kila Drome' are of interest because the acquisition of the land gave rise to the first native land case in Papua. This is unusual in itself since, under the regulations established by Scratchley at the start of white government, land generally could not be alienated from its traditional native owners; the government was the only party allowed to do this. At Kila Kila, development had occurred from about 1933 to provide a permanent landing ground for the increasing number of aeroplanes servicing the interior goldfields. Prior to this, aeroplanes had used Ela Beach, on the ocean side of the promontory upon which Port Moresby is situated. In 1937, it was proposed to lengthen the runway at Kila and the Government used the opportunity to formalise arrangements by officially leasing 89 acres from the owners for 10 years. However, in 1939 an ordinance allowing the land to be resumed was passed. Following the issuing of a formal resumption notice in January 1940 and the offer of £3 per acre, the native owners lodged a claim in the Central Court for £50 per acre, or a total of £4,450. The result of the case was not what the owners had hoped for though they did manage to double the amount the Government had been prepared to pay.

Kila Drome, in any event, had been recognised as being an inappropriate site as early as December 1934 and plans to construct a new aerodrome to the north of the Rouna road about five and a half kilometres from town (approximately where the Port Moresby suburb of Hohola is today) were drawn up. These plans did not eventuate and in March 1939 when it was obvious the Kila Drome could not accommodate military requirements, it was planned to construct a larger airfield at another site about 11 kilometres out of Port Moresby. This was to be on the site of a horse racing track constructed during the First World War. It was found the western end of the new airfield would cut across the Rouna road, which had originally been established as the Sapphire Creek road in 1905. Accordingly, a portion of the maintenance funds was used to fund the construction of about 3 kilometres of new road, eventually completed in September 1941. This new section linked the parallel-running Brown River road to the Rouna Road, about 5 kilometres further out. This was the route to Sogeri used during the War and remains so today.

The new airfield was originally called 7-mile Strip but was later named Jackson's Field (though also marked on wartime maps as Jackson's Drome). This commemorates Squadron Leader John Jackson, DFC, Commanding Officer of 75 Squadron, who was killed when he was shot down by Japanese fighters over Mount Lawes, to the north of the airstrip, in April 1942. Today, Jackson's Aerodrome is Port Moresby's international airport. The wartime Marston-matting strip remained in use up until the 1970s and still exists, flanked on either side by newer tarmac runways. Port Moresby had seven aerodromes during the war, and one of these used for fighter aircraft, Ward's Strip, was near the site of the aerodrome which had been planned in 1935 to replace the Kila Drome.

Another important outcome of the defence preparations in Port Moresby was it precipitated a long-dormant scheme to provide reticulated water from the Laloki to the town. Following a feasibility study in the 1920s, the residents of the town had agreed to borrow £20,000 from the Australian government to cover the cost. But with procrastination from Canberra, and with the fluctuating fortunes of the town during the Depression years, the scheme was never actioned, the town's residents making do with rainwater, supplemented by water carted into the town by the government. In July 1939, the increasing defence population was used as justification to raise the matter again (by August 1940, the population of Port Moresby was 11,025; in 1938 it had been about 600), and by May 1940, tenders for the pipes and water purification equipment had been called. The cost had now risen to £70,000, of which the Papuan Government had to meet £36,500. The pumping station on the Laloki came into operation in August 1941, though it was not until December of the same year water was flowing from Port Moresby taps.

It is not surprising many of these long-delayed projects had been taken up in Papua in the two years from early 1939, given the Australian Government's unfolding realisation of the situation. By February 1941, Australian authorities were actively displaying concern at likely Japanese invasion of New Guinea. Some weeks later, on 18th March 1941, eight and a half months before the Japanese attacks on Pearl Harbour, they thought it necessary to direct 'women and children not engaged in essential work in New Guinea ... be encouraged to leave unobtrusively for Australia'. There was only an intermittent response to this and it was not until the Pearl Harbour attack on 7th December 1941 the white Territorians were jolted out of their colonial complacency. The next day, Brigadier B.M. Morris, who was in command of all troops in the country, received orders to mobilise the New Guinea Volunteer Rifles, that Territory's equivalent of the Papuan Infantry Battalion, for full time duty. On 12th December, he ordered the evacuation of all white non-combatants to Australia.

Events began to move quickly from this time. On 3rd January 1942, two militia battalions of the 30th Brigade (39th and 53rd), disembarked at Port Moresby to bring its garrison up to brigade strength. Eighteen days later, Japanese war planes bombed Kavieng, Lorengau, Madang, Salamaua, Lae and Bulolo, and followed this up on 23rd January with the occupation of Rabaul and Kavieng. On 25th January, a general call-up of all eligible white males was ordered in New Guinea, and two days later in Papua. Kokoda was bombed on the morning of the 31st January 1942 and on 3rd February, Port Moresby was bombed and machine-gunned, killing one and injuring two. Eleven days later, at noon on 14th February 1942, civil government ceased. The long-expected war had eventuated.

Bomb damage in Port Moresby, February 1942.
Australian War Memorial 25638.

14

On the track (February–September 1942)

The first troops to cross the Kokoda Trail (in fact the entire mail route, from Port Moresby to Buna) appear to be members of a platoon of the Papua Infantry Battalion under Lieutenant H. J. Jesser (later Major, Military Cross), in early February 1942. They had orders to patrol the northern coast from Buna Station to the mouth of the Waria River and to look for white refugees from the Japanese-occupied towns in New Guinea.

Jesser's platoon arrived on the northern shore area only a week before the first action involving the Japanese on the northern coast of Papua, in which they were participants. On the 10th March a lone Kawanisi float plane on reconnaissance along the north-eastern coast aimed its two bombs, both of which went wide of their target, at the Anglican mission's boat *Maclaren King* while it was anchored in Buna Bay. The ship had just arrived at Buna and its two passengers, Bishop Phillip Strong* and missionary John Duffill, were proceeding ashore in a small launch when the plane arrived. They were in the process of scrambling up the beach and into the cover of trees when the pilot landed his aircraft on the waters of the Bay and

* Later Archbishop Sir Phillip Strong, Bishop of New Guinea until 1963, then Archbishop of Brisbane and Primate of the Anglican Church of Australia to 1970.

commenced machine-gunning the launch and beach. When small arms fire was returned by Administration officials and Jenner's men from further up the shore, the pilot hastily charged his engines and departed. No-one was hurt, but Bishop Strong reported his Office Book was 'almost shot to pieces in the encounter'.

In June 1942, a detachment of Engineer officers journeyed to Buna by flying-boat to conduct an inspection of the country inland from the township with the view to the construction of a forward airstrip for Allied aircraft. An American Engineer Regiment was assigned to undertake the earth-moving tasks. Morris' New Guinea Force was asked, on the 23rd June, to provide a detachment of infantry as a protective force. On this day as well, a second patrol of the Papuan Infantry Battalion, this one of forty officers and men under Major W. T. Watson, who had succeeded Major Logan as Commanding Officer of the PIB in early 1942, set off over the track to Kokoda and beyond with orders to patrol from Ioma (previously Tamata Station) to Cape Nelson. Two weeks later, on 7th July, the detachment selected to provide protection for the aerodrome construction unit also departed for the northern shore. This was B Company of the 39th Battalion under Captain S.V. Templeton, the first Australian unit to set foot on the track. They were ill-equipped, and being members of a battalion raised in Victoria, ill-prepared for the difficulties of the tropics.

> B Company were all young chaps under Captain Templeton, then 42 [recalled former Warrant Officer John (Jack) D. Wilkinson in a letter to the Papua New Guinea *Post-Courier*]; I was then 35 years, the next oldest. All the first troops walked in leather leggings but later on others had the gaiters of the AIF.

The 39th Battalion was a raw and inexperienced unit. Formed in Victoria from a mixture of volunteers and draftees in October 1941, the Battalion was in Port Moresby by 3rd January 1942, only 11 weeks later. In the first five weeks in Papua, the Battalion lost one-third of its strength to dysentery. The Battalion's Commanding Officer, Lieutenant-Colonel H.M. Conron became so ill he had to be replaced, by Lieutenant-Colonel W.T. Owen, on 7th July 1942. It was to be a fateful appointment for Owen.

Kokoda airstrip and village, photographed on 14th July 1942, a week before the Japanese landings near Buna and Gona.

Australian War Memorial 128400.

Templeton and his men reached Uberi on the 7th July to meet Lieutenant H.T. Kienzle (later Captain, M.B.E.), formerly a rubber planter and miner at Kokoda but now an officer in ANGAU.* He had orders to establish staging camps and food dumps along the track and had intended going ahead of Templeton's group. As it happened though, they departed Uberi together on the 8th, with 120 carriers transporting the soldiers food and equipment. A further twenty tonnes of supplies had been despatched by sea to Buna on the lugger *Gili Gili*. Kienzle

* ANGAU: Australian New Guinea Administrative Unit. A unit formed in March 1942 by amalgamating the Papuan Administrative Unit and the New Guinea Administrative Unit. These organisations were formed predominantly from staff of the civil administrations of the Territories of New Guinea and of Papua. The formation of ANGAU is significant because from this point in time the previously separate Territory of Papua and the Territory of New Guinea were considered as a single unit and is the origin of the ethnically diverse Papua New Guinea of today.

sent an additional 130 carriers under police Sergeant-Major Maga ahead of the main party, and at Ioribaiwa and Nauro the soldiers were able to rest and feed themselves in the comfortable camps Maga had set up. From Nauro, 131 carriers were sent on to Efogi to prepare rest huts there. On 15th July, B Company reached Kokoda whereupon Kienzle immediately set off back towards Port Moresby to consolidate the rest camps established on the outward journey. Templeton went on towards Buna accompanied by Private John McBride, leaving the remainder of his men to rest.

The soldiers resting at Kokoda were amazed life on the station appeared to be almost untouched by outside events. Jack Wilkinson later recorded:

> Kokoda suited us, while we were there. There was plenty of native fruit and vegetables and the men were in good shape. The climate was good. Mosquitoes were few. Housing was good. We had radio communications with the outside world. Life looked sweet—for a full week.
>
> Rubber production was still going on and, apart from an occasional plane seen from afar, the war was far away. It was just as in peace-time, except for the khaki hats everyone wore. The native prisoners went out every morning from Kokoda calaboose [gaol], and were carefully locked up every night. Lieutenant Brewer, as magistrate, had cases every day.

On the 18th July, Templeton and McBride joined up with Staff Sergeant A.L. Collyer who was proceeding to Kokoda from Buna in charge of the native porters carrying the *Gili Gili* shipment of stores. By the 21st July, all three had returned to as far as Awala, a village equidistant from Buna and Kokoda, where they met Major Watson and his PIB patrol. Here, a runner dispatched by ANGAU Sergeant Harper at Buna brought the news the Japanese had landed at Buna and Gona shortly after 4 pm that day. Templeton immediately sent back a message to Kokoda ordering one of his platoons to join him while Major Watson's men took up defensive positions about Awala.

Though that night was a quiet one, events began to move swiftly the next day. At 11am on the 22nd, and after marching all night, the platoon ordered forward from Kokoda (11 Platoon under Lieutenant H.E. Mortimore) arrived at Awala simultaneously with a Japanese attack from the north. The quickly-moving Japanese troops dispersed the PIB soldiers, and the weary troops of Mortimore's platoon withdrew across the Kumusi River. Here, Sergeant Collyer and Private McBride cut the main cables of the Wiarope suspension bridge while their comrades withdrew further to another wire rope bridge across Gorari Creek. Leaving this intact, Mortimore's platoon quickly prepared an ambush centred on its approaches.

The next day, 25th July, the small group at Gorari Crossing (numbering less than 80 all ranks) was joined by Lieutenant-Colonel Owen, Commanding Officer of the 39th Battalion. Shortly after his arrival, the Japanese attacked in strength and though the Australians were successful in checking the enemy's advance for a time, they were compelled eventually to fall back to avoid being outflanked. Reinforcements were desperately required and D Company was despatched the next day in commandeered civil aircraft. Only two aircraft containing one platoon (about 30 men) were able to get through, the balance of the Company being in aircraft which could not land at Kokoda because of the weather.* The nearest additional fresh unit was C Company under Captain A.C. Dean, which had left Ilolo on foot on 24th July.

Owen's problems were further compounded on 26th July when Templeton, while seeking to make contact with the D Company platoon, was lost, presumably being ambushed and shot at Oivi by a Japanese patrol which had circled about the Australians' position. Enemy gunfire was heard but no-one actually saw Templeton being shot. It is believed Templeton died of wounds though his body was never found and it was later suspected the local Orokaivas may have been involved in

* The first use of air transport to move a substantial body of Australian troops by air occurred only about 9 weeks earlier, on 23rd May 1942, when most of the 2/5th Independent Company and other elements of Kanga Force, a commando-style unit under Major N.L. Fleay (later Lieutenant-Colonel, D.S.O.) were flown from Port Moresby to Wau. However, the carriage of D Company by aircraft to Kokoda on 26th July is reportedly to be the first time Australian troops were airlifted directly into battle. The group that was set down at Kokoda was 16 Platoon under Lieutenant D.I.H. McClean. Another early flight of Australian troops straight to the 'front-line' also took place in New Guinea, when the 2/10th Battalion was air-lifted from Milne Bay to Wanigela in September 1942.

Templeton's disappearance. The D Company platoon was led to safety by Lance-Corporal Sianopa Simemi, of the Royal Armed Native Constabulary, who had been attached to Templeton's group.

Owen's position at the close of the 26th July was not an enviable one, being in immediate command of only five officers and 74 men to hold an estimated 2,000 of the enemy. He realised it would be futile to attempt to defend Kokoda. He decided therefore to abandon the township itself but to occupy what is known in military parlance as the 'ground of tactical importance'. In this case, this was the high ground of the Deniki plateau which overlooked from about eight kilometres distance both the station, and more importantly, the airstrip. Owen's withdrawal to Deniki had been completed by the 27th. On the morning of the 28th, when it was seen the Japanese had still not entered Kokoda, Owen's men descended from the hills and re-occupied the station without firing a shot. Unfortunately, Owen's urgent requests to Port Moresby for reinforcements to consolidate his tenuous possession of the vital Kokoda aerodrome were never acted upon, for the daylight hours of the 28th July were the only opportunity the Japanese gave the Australians to fortify their position. At dusk that evening, the Japanese launched a determined assault, inflicting twelve casualties among whom was Owen himself, seriously wounded in the head. By 9 o'clock next morning, Kokoda had been abandoned again, with the small force of Australians regrouping at Deniki for the second time.

There is no more direct evidence of the tenaciousness of the 79 Australian soldiers who fought this first battle for Kokoda, who were, by virtue of distance and weather conditions cut off from all outside help, and who were outnumbered twenty-four to one, than in the words of one of their opponents. A Japanese officer, 2nd Lieutenant Hidetaka Noda, recorded of this engagement in a document later captured by the Allies, that

> our Advance Force has been engaged in battle with 1,200 Australians, and has suffered unexpectedly heavy casualties.

The average age of the Victorian militiamen in B Company of the 39th Battalion was eighteen and a half years and they had been in the army for less than 10 months.

Clearings for staging posts along the Kokoda Trail were hacked from virgin forest.

Australian War Memorial 7374.

An Australian staging post on the Kokoda Trail, 1942.

Australian War Memorial 13162.

When the men of B Company set out from Ilolo on the 7th July, they had no medical officer with them. However, a doctor did catch up with them in time to render assistance following the attack by the Japanese on the Australian positions at Kokoda on 28th July. This was Dr Geoffrey Vernon, who had received the Military Cross for First World War service as the Regimental Medical Officer of the 11th Light Horse. After World War 1, Vernon spent ten years on Thursday Island as the Queensland Government Medical Officer. During this time, Vernon regularly visited Dutch New Guinea and Papua, coming to like the country so much that in 1935, he moved to Daru in the Gulf of Papua to establish a kapok plantation, to continue to practise as a doctor and to continue his cherished explorations of the Fly River region. But Vernon was a restless soul and he eventually moved to Misima Island and then, later, took up land at Kokoda to start a rubber plantation.

'Doc' Vernon was a capable and cultured man who relished the challenges of life and was widely known, liked and respected in pre-war Papua. On the outbreak of war, he tried to enlist in the Australian Imperial Force but was not accepted because of his age (he was born in December 1882) and because he had suffered concussion deafness since 1915. Undeterred, Vernon secured for himself firstly an ANGAU appointment as Medical Officer for carriers at Ilolo and then, with Bert Kienzle's assistance, had this extended to carriers working along the entire track. One of Vernon's first actions was to have the carriers' maximum load officially reduced from 50 lbs (23 kilograms), transferred over from pre-war days, to 40 lbs (18 kilograms).

On 20th July (13 days behind B Company, and the day before the Japanese landings at Buna and Gona), Vernon set out along the track to go as far as Kagi to inspect the condition of the carriers at the staging posts Kienzle was establishing. He reached Kagi on the 25th where a policeman brought a note informing him of the Japanese advance inland. Vernon later wrote of this: 'As I knew the 39th Battalion had no M.O. [medical officer] with them, I decided to hurry on and try to join up with them near Kokoda'. Vernon reached the Australian soldiers at Deniki on the 27th, as they withdrew for the first time from Kokoda, and was in Kokoda by 4.30 pm the following day after the troops had re-occupied the town. Vernon, being nearly deaf, slept through most of the battle that night and was awoken at about 1 am on the 29th July to attend to Colonel Owen's head wound. They got Owen back into shelter but

> ... then [Vernon later wrote in his diary] we had some 4 or 5 casualties in rapid succession, who, when dressed, were told to get back to Deniki as soon as they could. [Sergeant Jack] Wilkinson [the medical orderly who had been a pre-war friend of Vernon's on Misima] held the lantern for me and every time he raised it a salvo of machine gun bullets was fired at the building. Owing to this particular enemy M.G. [machine gun] being as yet a little below the edge of the escarpment ... its range was bound to be too high and, while the roof was riddled, those working below could feel reasonably safe. I was very glad to have Jack Wilkinson with me.*

The situation for the soldiers at Kokoda was deteriorating quickly and the decision was taken by Watson to withdraw. Lieutenant-Colonel Owen was unconscious and on the point of death when the last of the Australians had to leave and Vernon estimated Owen did not survive another 15 minutes. By mid-morning of the 29th July, the Australians were back at Deniki, leaving the Japanese in possession of Kokoda. Despite the situation, the adventurous Vernon was in his element. Earlier, during the withdrawal, he had let the bulk of the soldiers pass him by, waiting at the edge of the plantation for Watson and the last of the Australians to leave. Standing in the shadows to gaze

---

* The copy of 'Doc' Vernon's diary from which the citations in this book are sourced is a photocopy of Vernon's original typescript and was obtained from John Wilkinson by Fred Turner and later passed to the present author. This version of the diary contains additional original comments (c. 1972) by Wilkinson who at the time was a resident of Samarai. One of these marginal notes gives a different perspective on the urgent events following Owen's wounding.

> C.O. Col. Owen was pulled out by Maj. Watson and myself with Dr. Vernon at his feet. We hauled him up the top of the escarpment and then put him on a stretcher. I went ahead and prepared the R.A.P. [regimental aid post]. From then on wounded came in fairly rapidly but it was dreadful having a deaf Doctor who wanted to do major operations.

A further insight into this event is contained in an article written by Wilkinson which appeared in the *Pacific Islands Monthly* of September 1943. This article dealt with the early days of the Papuan campaign. Wilkinson reveals the extent of Vernon's bravery under fire in going forward to Owen's assistance, but in doing so modestly downplays his own courage. He wrote: '... "Doc" Vernon, ignoring Jap[anese] snipers, crawled forward to where the officer [Owen] lay. "Doc" and a couple of men brought back his body'.

down on the now-silent battleground, he was moved to later record his own poignant interpretation of events:

> It was an experience I would not have cared to miss, and among the impressions of that exciting night none stands out more clearly than the weirdness of the natural conditions—the thick white mist dimming the moonlight, the mysterious veiling of the trees, houses and men, the drip of moisture from the foliage, and at the last and almost complete silence, as if the rubber groves of Kokoda were sleeping as usual in the depths of the night, and men had not brought disturbance and death to this quiet little Papuan outpost.

The Japanese who landed on 21st July belonged to the South Seas Detachment. The Yokohama Advanced Force, consisting of one battalion of the *144th Infantry Regiment*, the *15th Independent Engineer Regiment*, and a battalion of the *55th Mountain Artillery Regiment*, were the first units of the Detachment to land. In a 1980 study of Japanese operations in New Guinea, historian Kengoro Tanaka makes a surprising revelation. He reported the final decision to attack along this route was taken only 10 days before the landings, and was made 'leaving out any study as to whether or not it was possible'. Tanaka admits the Japanese did not really have any idea how long it would take them to capture Port Moresby. In fact, they held the old view, long discarded by explorers, that once the 'top' of the Range was attained, it would be an easy downhill walk to the far coast. The first troops carried rations for 16 days but the deceptively gentle slopes inland from Buna gave little indication of the difficulties which lay ahead. On 27th July, the commander of the Yokohama Advanced Force reported to his superiors in Rabaul the road from Buna to Kokoda was already good enough in places, or could be improved sufficiently, 'to permit the movement of mechanised units'. The view was once Kokoda was under Japanese control Port Moresby could be taken in 8 days. No mechanised transport was landed in the first days but on 2 September 1942, two transportation companies, which had on their strength light trucks, bicycles and 500 horses, arrived. This raised the total numbers landed to 8,000 army and 3,430 naval personnel. Of this force, six battalions of infantry and one of mountain artillery were available for the advance on Port Moresby.

In the days immediately following the loss of Kokoda, the battered Australian force holding on at Deniki was reinforced by the balance of the 39th Battalion. Captain Dean's C Company arrived on 30th July, A Company under Captain N.M. Symington on 1st August, and the remainder of D Company under Captain M.L. Bidstrup five days later. The extra troops brought the front line Allied strength up to 507 (39th Battalion: 31 officers, 433 other ranks. PIB: 5 officers, 38 other ranks). This was considered a sufficient force for Major A.G. Cameron, who took over command of the forward troops on 5th August from Major Watson (who in turn had taken over after Owen's death), to take the offensive and on the 8th, mounted an attack on the Japanese at Kokoda. This coincided with a Japanese thrust on to his own positions at Deniki, during which Captain Dean was killed. Captain Symington in the meantime, was able to re-enter Kokoda and resume occupation of the old Australian positions, though he was unaware the other units of the Battalion who were to have supported him were locked with the enemy. The Japanese tried to dislodge Symington's A Company that night, and again early next day, but his men stood fast. The local Japanese commander, Lieutenant-Colonel Tsukamoto was then obliged to weaken his main advance by detaching a company of the *144th Battalion* to add some weight to his counter-attack. Still the Japanese could not dislodge the Australians.

By this time however, it had become evident to Symington there was little prospect of being supported. As he was running short of ammunition and food, he decided to withdraw while he was still able to fight his way out. About 7 pm on 10th August 1942, after holding Kokoda for almost 72 hours, the Australians abandoned the township for the third time in 16 days. The darkness and the mist of the tropical rain-forest, the rain and the rough terrain, made command communications difficult and an ordered exit almost impossible. The Company quickly became dispersed and scattered to the south and west of Kokoda as it withdrew. It was not until two days later the first of Symington's men regained contact with their battalion.

On the 13th, Deniki fell to the Japanese, with the Australians falling back to dig in at Isurava. Here, the Japanese advance was momentarily checked, the Australians holding out for the next sixteen days against very heavy attacks which saw the most bitter fighting of the entire Kokoda Trail campaign. Both

Australian and Japanese commanders sought the upper hand by bringing in reinforcements. For the Australians, the 53rd Battalion was brought up from Port Moresby, as were the first units of the 21st AIF Brigade, the 2/14th and 2/16th Battalions, recalled from African service. Neither side was prepared to give way and, as the battle developed into a war of attrition, casualties rose. Total Australian casualties at Deniki were almost 700, of which the 2/16th Battalion accounted for 350 and the 39th Battalion, 180. The Japanese had the entire *144th Infantry Regiment* ranged against the Australians. However, it required the addition of a battalion of the *41st Infantry Regiment* to finally get the advantage and increase the pressure of attacks on the Australian positions.

Although it was some weeks before the Australian troops were to get the upper hand, in retrospect it is reasonable to say the combination of the initial resistance at Kokoda and this battle at Isurava was the turning point for the Allies in New Guinea. It provided that short, vital, period of time for the authorities in Port Moresby to get their arrangements in order and to permit the reinforcements, already on their way from Australia, to get that much closer to the country. It also significantly put back the Japanese timetable to take Port Moresby and this delay subsequently had a critical detrimental effect on the Japanese supply position. As well, the feeling of military superiority enjoyed by the Japanese land forces since their Manchurian campaigns in the mid-1930s had been seriously undermined. The outcome of the advance upon Port Moresby may have been very different if the speed of the Japanese thrust had not been first slowed at Kokoda and then checked at Isurava. None of this of course was evident at the time to the Australian forces, who laboured under woefully deficient supply arrangements. It was virtually a case of not being able to bring forward more troops because they simply could not be supported in the field.

Under such circumstances, the Australians were obliged to retreat further. At midnight of the 29th August, the three forward companies of the 2/14th Battalion holding the forward-most areas with the remnants of the 39th Battalion were ordered to commence withdrawing back to a point half-way between Isurava and Alola, with the other units falling back to take up station about them. However, by 3 pm the next day, that position had become so untenable in the face of the relentless Japanese thrusts, a general withdrawal to Eora (or Iora) Creek was ordered. (It will be recalled it was here, many years previously, Henry Stuart-Russell and John MacDonald were first greeted by a native waving a taro branch as a sign of peace). By dawn on the 2nd September, the Australians had pulled further back, through The Gap, and by the 5th had retreated back through Kagi to Efogi, the mid point of the Kokoda Trail. The Japanese were deliberately maintaining the momentum of their advance to deny the Australians the opportunity to regroup and to make a stand from a firm base. By the 8th September, the Australians had been forced back to Menari, but this was subsequently abandoned the next day in favour of a position further south between Nauro and Ioribaiwa. By the 12th, the Australians had consolidated their position on the Ioribaiwa Ridge itself, and for the next three days beat off heavy attacks.

Stretcher bearers—'Fuzzy Wuzzy Angels'—Kokoda Trail, 1942.

Australian War Memorial 14240.

15

Logistics problems (1942)

While the front line troops were engaged, much activity had been taking place further south in an effort to keep them supplied. Lieutenant Kienzle had been particularly active in organising his lines of carriers to the forward areas, being in charge of as many as 500 porters at a time. To attain these large numbers, and in the Army's desperation to keep the fighting troops supplied, the rubber plantations on the Sogeri Plateau were almost completely stripped of their workers. Yet, as the campaign progressed, the increasing numbers of soldiers being sent northwards began to outstrip the capacity of the carrier lines to supply them.

This eventuality had been anticipated in some measure by Kienzle who had suggested to Morris as early as 24th July supply by air, in addition to native carriers, was the solution to their logistic problems. Although there was a dearth of transport aircraft at the time, Morris was able to arrange for the first experimental drops at Kagi and Efogi three days later. This method of supply, or rather the manner in which it was first attempted, was not very successful. The rough country meant a high loss rate initially but as the dispatchers became more experienced their proficiency at unloading their cargoes into small jungle drop zones improved considerably. Despite this, it was prudent to be wary during a drop. There are several reports of soldiers and carriers being killed or injured by free-falling cargo. Major Watson had his leg broken in such a manner.

The unpredictable weather over the mountains was also a constant hindrance to a reliable supply service. Food and other 'soft' cargoes were dropped without parachutes, these being kept for weapons and ammunition, but even these suffered severe impacts on landing. There were many instances of bent rounds jamming in weapons, and mortar bombs failing to fire or exploding prematurely. The food bundles were more often than not smashed open upon landing and scattered over a wide area. An innovation developed in pre-war New Guinea was later employed with some success. This involved the use of an outer bag to contain the contents after an inner bag had burst open on impact, though this did not stop the contents from being damaged.

The supply problems were compounded by the loss of seven DC3 transport planes following a raid by the Japanese on 7 Mile Strip (Jackson's Strip) on 17th August. These had been earmarked to build up stores in the forward area in preparation for substantial reinforcement of the troops at Isurava. However, after the raid, no airborne supply was possible for five days and only one aircraft was available for the next two days; that is, only one plane was available for resupply tasks during the week 17th to 23th August 1942. As the Australians holding at Isurava since 14th August had become desperate for resupply, the loss of the transport planes could not have happened at a more critical period and was the major factor in the need to withdraw from that position on the 29th and 30th August. Kienzle, in a September 1942 report, (in an echo of Monckton pointing out the difficulties of keeping Kokoda Station supplied in 1904), pointed out it would be impossible to maintain sufficient troops in the mountains without air supply. He wrote:

> The establishment of small food dumps for a small body of troops was now under way as far as Kagi. This ration supply was being maintained by carriers over some of the roughest country in the world. But with the limited number of carriers available maintenance of supplies was going to be impossible along this route without the aid of droppings by plane. A carrier carrying only foodstuffs consumes his load in 13 days and if he carries food supplies for a soldier it means 6½ days' supply for both soldier and carrier. This does not allow for the porterage of arms, ammunition, equipment, medical stores, ordnance, mail and dozens of other

> items needed to wage war, on the backs of men. The track to Kokoda takes 8 days so maintenance of supplies is a physical impossibility without large-scale cooperation of plane droppings.

One problem with drops at Efogi and Kagi was carriers were still needed to take the supplies forward. This difficulty became even more acute by the end of July 1942 with the arrival of the additional companies at Deniki. Much equipment and food had been lost to the Japanese when Kokoda was abandoned and the Australians holding on at Deniki were critically short of essential supplies. Kienzle therefore determined to locate a dropping zone nearer to the front (as it was then). On 1st August, he set out from Kagi to locate some dry lake beds he had recalled seeing on pre-war flights over the Owen Stanleys and which he had named (in 1936) Myola after the wife of a friend.. These lakes, which are geographically the source of Eora Creek, were found ideal for the proposed supply area as their beds were reasonably firm and dry and covered with coarse brown kunai grass. His track out from Kagi, about 10 kilometres to the west, was the first major alteration to the old mail route since Captain Barton's expedition met Griffin at The Gap in December 1904. Kienzle cut a further track north from Myola to rejoin the old track at the Eora Creek crossing, this junction being given the name Templeton's Crossing in honour of Captain Templeton. The first airdrops at Myola were made on 5th August 1942.

Further south, the road out from Port Moresby had also been undergoing some alterations. Since the time when Bensted had put the road from Port Moresby up to as far as the Hairpin Bend at Rouna in 1923, regular vehicular access to the Sogeri Plateau had been difficult, though still possible, by traversing the mule track. This could be achieved only by backing and filling around a group of massive conglomerate boulders which lay in the way. Certainly, the plantations on the Sogeri Plateau had had vehicles in use for over a decade, and as early as 1940, 13 cwt army trucks had occasionally been driven all the way to Ilolo Plantation (McDonald's Corner). However, it still was not suitable for regular traffic and though the necessity for upgrading was recognised, no work had been possible due to the absence of heavy earth-moving equipment. On 18th (or 19th) February 1942, advanced elements of No 1 Section of the 2/1st Mechanical

Equipment Company, Royal Australian Engineers under Captain (later Major) Frank Graham Vidgen (later in charge of the Commonwealth Department of Works in post-war Papua New Guinea) arrived in Port Moresby. Preliminary work commenced almost immediately on determining the extent of the work to be done.

Less than four weeks later, on 10th March 1942, the *M.V. Macdhui* docked at Port Moresby to unload 2 non-commissioned officers, 19 sappers and the vital heavy plant of the Company. They immediately went to work on several tasks, including the Hairpin Bend, which by 7th May 1942 (but possibly up to two weeks earlier) was in intermittent use by single-lane traffic. By 9th June 1942, the engineers had provided clear one-lane access to the Sogeri Plateau for jeeps, utility trucks and other small vehicles. Larger trucks could get through but were required to back-up at least once to get past the almost 180 degree switch-back corner of the Hairpin Bend. Upgrading continued and after a further six weeks, the road had been widened sufficiently to enable vehicles to pass at several points. This was the link in the Sogeri road, completed in less than twelve weeks, the pre-war Public Works Department had coveted for two decades.*

The new road leading up to the Hairpin Bend, June 1942. This section of the Sogeri Road, which the Papuan government had tried for more than 20 years to traverse, was completed in 12 weeks by Army engineers.

There is a steep drop off the right side of this road. Fourteen soldiers were killed when a truck they were travelling on went over the edge here on 9th March 1943.

University of Papua New Guinea.

(The 2/1st Mechanical Equipment Company later worked on what has been recorded as 'one of the most ambitious engineering projects ever undertaken by the Australian Army'. This was the surveying and construction of another trans-New Guinea route, the Bulldog Track, from Bulldog at the head-waters of the Lakekumu River to Edie Creek, which was already connected by road, through Wau, to Lae. To date the Bulldog Track† has been the only motorable route ever put through over

---

* A personal comment (in 1992) by Colonel Bill McKell throws an unexpected light on the social implications of the Hairpin Bend road being completed. McKell recalls, as a Lieutenant with the 49th Battalion's Intelligence unit, walking up the Hairpin Bend mule track to visit the rubber plantations on the Sogeri Plateau in February 1942. He found the Seftons at Koitaki and the Loudons at Eilogo to be extremely hospitable and generous to him and his men. But he recollects clearly that the planters did not want the road over the Hairpin Bend to be built, preferring to remain isolated, as far as was possible, from Port Moresby.

† It is of interest to note a connection between the settlement at Bulldog and the Bulldog Track, and the early days of the northern goldfields, which gave rise to the Kokoda Trail. Plying between Samarai and the Mambare and

the Owen Stanleys. It is regrettable it was never maintained and improved upon after 1945. The route, of 93 kilometres (compared with 96 kilometres of today's Kokoda Trail), was surveyed in October 1942 by Captain Vidgen, Lieutenant Fox, a Corporal Swanson and a Sapper Cribb. Work began on 1st January 1943 and was opened for single-way traffic on 31st August 1943).

Kumusi Rivers around 1907(?)–1910, the *Bulldog* was a steam-powered vessel used to keep the commercial stores on the Mambare and Kumusi Rivers supplied with merchandise. Following the declaration of the Lakekumu River goldfield at the end of 1909 and the consequent desertion of the northern fields, the *Bulldog* was switched to ferrying miners and stores to the Lakekumu. The main miners' settlement on the Lakekumu subsequently became known as 'Bulldog', after the vessel.

The route on the Sogeri Plateau itself also received some attention. In fact, it was one of Lieutenant Kienzle's first tasks to develop a motor road from the (then) new end of the Port Moresby road, at Ilolo rubber plantation, to Kokoda. This was to be done by the end of August 1942. Kienzle soon realised this was futile, and said so, and with his skills being better employed elsewhere, he was switched to take charge of the carrier lines. The section of the track from Ilolo to Nauro however, was seen as the most difficult stretch of the route over the mountains. In August 1942, another officer, Lieutenant (later Captain) Noel Owers of the New Guinea Volunteer Rifles, was given the task of surveying a road which would bypass Uberi, Imita Ridge with its 'Golden Stairs', and Ioribaiwa. Owers had been a surveyor with New Guinea Goldfields at Wau since 1935. The 2/14th Field Company, and later with elements of the 7th Field Company and of the 2/1st Mechanical Equipment Company, started construction of the road forward of Ilolo on 19th August 1942. It was an impossible task and the project was dropped in early October 1942 after the jeep route had been developed only as far as the Goldie River. The junction of the new road and a walking track, which formed part of the original overland mail route coming in from Sogeri and Subitana further to the west, was called 'Owers' Corner'. The other end of the new road, where it struck out from the old road end at P.J. McDonald's Ilolo Plantation, was officially recognised as 'McDonald's Corner', a name already bestowed unofficially by the troops.

Also working in this area was a section of the 1st Independent Light Horse, which had been pack-transporting supplies into the mountains. (This unit had their main camp and stockyards at Kila Kila to the north of the airstrip and this gave rise to the term 'Horse Camp' as the popular name for the locality in the post-war period). Belying their Light *Horse* name, the men of the unit preferred to use the mules from the Sogeri rubber plantations. These had been used to transport rubber bales across the Hairpin Bend at Rouna before the war. Wild horses from the Bootless Inlet area near Port Moresby were also caught and broken in for service in the mountains, though the better-footed mules were favoured for this duty if they were available.

Carriers move down the new road between McDonalds's Corner and Ower's Corner, surveyed by Lieutenant Noel 'Jerry' Owers in September 1942. This road allowed vehicles to be taken almost to the Goldie River.

University of Papua New Guinea (New Guinea Collection).

Animals of the 1st Independent Light Horse on the pack track from Owers' Corner down to the Goldie River crossing during 1942.

Bushwalkers today still follow the same zigzag path down to the river.

Australian War Memorial 27025.

Horses are not indigenous New Guinea animals and those captured and broken by the Light Horse soldiers descended from three sources: from the horses brought to Port Moresby by gold miners during the gold rush of 1878, from the animals imported by the copper miners on Sapphire Creek, and from a herd established by Murray in November 1910 as the nucleus of a 'Government Stud Farm'. (The Government Stud Farm started from listed stock: 'Abdel Kadir', a two-year old, and 'Consolation', a six-year old, as sires, and 17 mares purchased from Queensland stations. The herd consisted of 47 horses in June 1912 and had grown to over 70 animals by December 1916, at which time all stock was auctioned and the Stud Farm closed). Some horses were also imported from Australia by the Army, though these seemed to find the tropical conditions uncomfortable and were often sick. Working initially from just past Ilolo (McDonald's Corner), and then from Owers' Corner, across the Goldie and to Uberi village, where the packs were transhipped to carriers, the Pack Transport section had transported over 643,000 kilograms of stores by the time the packing period ended in November 1942. When it ceased duty, the unit consisted of 1 officer and 110 men, with 43 mules and 135 horses. Remarkably, only one animal, a white mule called 'Bombhead', was lost, being killed after slipping fully loaded off the track.

One of the better known features of the track during the war was the 'Golden Stairs', the section of the route which traversed the southern slope of Imita Ridge. Imita Ridge lies between the villages of Uberi and Ioribaiwa. Here the soldier, already exhausted from the climb up from the Goldie River, was required to further climb upwards almost a kilometre in less than four kilometres. Engineers cut an estimated 3,204 steps into the side of the mountain. Whether these made the going easier appears to have been only of theoretical importance as W.B. Russell, the 2/14th Battalion's chronicle intimated:

> The golden stairs consisted of steps varying from ten to eighteen inches in height. The front edge of the step was a small log held by stakes. Behind the log was a puddle of mud and water. Some of the stakes had worked loose, leaving the logs slightly tilted. Anyone who stood on one of these skidded and fell with a whack in the mud, probably banging his head against a tree or being hit on the

> head with his own rifle. Those who had no sticks soon acquired them, not only to prevent falls, but allow the arms to help the legs, especially with the higher steps. After the first half dozen steps, it became a matter of sheer determination forcing the body to achieve the impossible. It was probably the weight more than the climb, though the climb would have been enough to tire even a lightly loaded man. The rear companies, where the going is always hardest, took twelve hours to complete nine miles [about 14 kilometres].

A portion of the 'Golden Staircase' on the southern slopes of Imita Ridge.

Some 3,204 steps were cut into the mountain in an attempt to make the going 'easier'. About 110 of those steps are shown here.

Australian War Memorial 26837.

The term 'Golden Stairs' appears to have been originated by Colonel S.F. Legge, who accompanied Brigadier A.W. Potts of the 21st Brigade on a reconnaissance from Owers' Corner to Imita Ridge on 11th August 1942. He is reputed to have gasped out the words a short distance from the summit of the Ridge while taking a breather.

The climb over Imita Ridge was not a unique section of the journey either. Indeed, the next main obstacle, the Maguli Range, which lay between Ioribaiwa and Nauro`, was almost a straight climb of 640 metres. The Maguli had its own staircase, 'Japs Ladder', of close to 3,000 steps. The agony of the Golden Stairs remained in the soldier's memory because it was such a gruelling overture to what lay ahead, and required the walker to attune his attitude of mind to travelling over such terrain. It was (and still is) a sobering thought to top Imita Ridge only to realise there is much more of the same still to come. The main problem with the Golden Stairs is the track never levels out to give the walker some respite—it is uphill all the way. None of the actual steps survive today.

It is difficult to say which part of the Trail would have been 'worst' in 1942, as the heavy traffic over even level stretches made travel difficult. Several wartime references and the recollections of some soldiers of the time indicate the long, steep gradient of the climb up from Templeton's Crossing was far from popular and 'Doc' Vernon targeted this stretch as the worst for carriers bringing back wounded soldiers. He wrote:

> The hardest work allotted to our boys was that of carrying out the wounded on stretchers. Right at the start of the homeward trail [as it was on 1st August] from Iora, there rose one of the roughest and steepest hills on the whole route, and even without a load it was a strain to clamber up the almost vertical slopes and flounder on over roots and boulders. A double set of bearers, eight in all, had to be sent [with each stretcher] as less could not have done the work.

In the early part of the Kokoda Trail campaign, the condition of the carriers gave Vernon more concern than the wounded soldiers. Their having to work in such rugged country was bad enough but the harsh circumstances were exacerbated by the treatment meted out by the military authorities. Both Vernon and Kienzle, along with many of the other ANGAU men on the track, were appalled at the lack of consideration for the carriers and the lack of understanding of their working conditions shown by senior officers in Port Moresby. Vernon observed it was typical for heavily-laden carriers to toil over the steep slopes from dawn to dusk, at the end of which they received a meal of nothing but rice, 'and none too much of that', and then faced a cold, wet night trying to sleep in the open. This would have been a miserable prospect since most of the carriers did not possess any clothing for the upper body. The heavy pack they had carried all day may well have been of tinned meat or blankets, yet these were rigidly assigned only to the troops. Of course, these were desperate days and military objectives had to take priority. Yet, as Vernon found, even if only from a military point of view, it was self-defeating to abuse such a vital lifeline in this way. Vernon came across a dreadful case of exploitation of native manpower while he was camped at Eora in mid-August 1942:

> One evening a decrepit old native who had been a storeman at B.Ps [Burns Philp, a large shop] in [Port] Moresby tottered in and collapsed on the ground. I was shocked when I tested the weight of his load. An officer standing by told me he was only shamming, but I could see that a few more days of overwork and exposure like this and he would have left his bones in the mountains. The age of this old chap showed me how desperate was the call for carriers, he was far too old and weak for such work. I put him off duty and later on took him into [Port] Moresby where I got a more suitable job for him.

Vernon was determined to ensure such abuses did not happen again. Unexpectedly, this turned out easier to achieve than he had anticipated. On his return to Port Moresby on 27th August, he was invited to lunch with General Rowell, at which he was able to voice his concerns and lay out his plans for the carriers. Vernon did not know Rowell but it turned out Rowell had served with the 3rd Light Horse in the First World War

(Vernon had been with the 11th) and this helped in extracting an early promise from Rowell to better the lot of carriers on the Kokoda Trail. Twenty days later, on 16th September, formal orders to this effect were issued, and enforced, Vernon recording later the carriers' working conditions were improved 'very much' as a result of Rowell's directions.

The contribution made by the native carriers before the use of the Kokoda airstrip was regained was enormous. It is certain the recapture of Kokoda could not have been achieved when it was without the transport of supplies and the evacuation of the wounded they provided. It is regrettable the initial recommendations of Vernon, Kienzle and others were so quickly dismissed, and it took so long for the proper care of the labour lines to become a matter of official concern. For in those shameful first weeks particularly, when they were worked virtually as slave labour, the carriers and labourers on the track, more so than in any other New Guinea theatre, literally saved the troops who saved Australia.

Carriers bringing a wounded soldier up the almost vertical gradient at Templeton's Crossing: 'one of the roughest and steepest hills on the whole route'.

Australian War Memorial 13286.

16

On the track (September 1942–January 1943)

Meanwhile, the Australians holding at the Ioribaiwa position had been having a difficult time, having to repel vigorous attacks on three fronts. On the 16th September, Brigadier K.W. Eather, who had taken over command of the fighting force on the 14th, began to feel his position was weakening. The constant Japanese pressure prevented efficient deployment of his resources and although he was well aware of the gravity of withdrawing further to the south, he had to have room to deploy his men. Accordingly, he sent the following message to Major-General A.S. Allen, G.O.C. 7th Division, in Port Moresby:

> Enemy feeling whole front and flanks. Do not consider can hold him here. Request permission to withdraw to Imita Ridge if necessary.

One can imagine the apprehension this message would have wrought at Headquarters in Port Moresby, for Imita Ridge was the last major feature before the Goldie River and the Sogeri Plateau, less than 50 kilometres away. General Allen allowed Eather what he wanted* but (as reported by Ken Clift in his book

PREVIOUS PAGE:

▲ This still from Damien Parer's documentary film *Frontline: Kokoda* shows the difficult conditions underfoot on the Kokoda Trail.
Australian War Memorial 13290.

▼ A Beaufort of the RAAF heads back to Port Moresby in 1942 after attacking Japanese forces at Buna. The aeroplane is flying through The Gap—the mountain in the background is Mount Bellamy.
University of Papua New Guinea.

* There was considerable pressure from General MacArthur not to allow the withdrawal to Imita Ridge. Nevertheless, it went ahead. MacArthur exacted retribution some weeks later by having Allen and two other Australian generals removed from their appointments. This was despite the fact that there were sound military reasons for withdrawing to Imita, particularly in that it would seriously restrict, to the Australian advantage, the deployment

The Saga of a Sig) the accompanying conditions were realistic and blunt:

> 'There won't be any withdrawal from the Imita position, Ken,' Allen insisted. 'You'll die there if necessary. You understand that?'
>
> 'Yes,' said Eather. 'I understand that.'

Eather wasted no time in establishing his position on Imita. By 4.30 pm the same day, the Ioribaiwa Ridge, in the Maguli Range, had been noisily abandoned. There was much apparent confusion and long haphazard bursts of gunfire in a pretence of panic. Unbeknown to the Japanese however, was C Company of the 2/33rd Battalion under Captain L. Miller had been left behind in an ambush position. For the rest of the day and into the night of the 16th, Miller's men waited:

> No sleeping during the night [recorded 'NX9717'] was the order. We cursed those who couldn't sleep without snoring. An occasional firefly floated and darted weirdly against the blackness. Perhaps they should have been long anxious hours, but we were tired and fatalistic ...
>
> [Next morning, the Japanese started to move forward down the southern slopes of Ioribaiwa]. Some came further down the hill. A full company of men lying for a space of time must make some noise. They must have thought there were a few stray Australians peering at them between the blades of kunai grass. A coolie walked across the path in full view and back again. A sing-song Japanese voice shouted: 'Fire, fire'. But we waited. We'd heard of Japanese tricks to draw fire.
>
> Forward of us, one on the left and another on the right flank, they brought up two machine-guns. The one on the right flank was set up a few yards in front of a burly, black-headed countryman. That was close enough. He fired a burst from his Tommy [sub-machine gun] through the brown man's chest ...
>
> That burst was the general signal for an orchestra of fire ... It was a hell of a din. On the left the other machine-gun was wiped out ... It was all instantaneous, sudden, surprising...

The ambush company then began to withdraw towards the crest of Imita Ridge, each platoon leap-frogging back through the others, enticing the Japanese to follow. This they did, only to be caught in deadly mortar fire from the Ridge. None of the Japanese survived.

A patrol of the Papuan Infantry Battalion, 1942.

The Battalion rendered valuable service to Australian and American forces in the New Guinea campaigns under conditions that normal units would have found difficult to accept. One PIB company was on continuous front-line operations for a year and a half with a total of only three weeks rest.

The Battalion was disbanded in 1946 but in 1951, with the New Guinea Volunteer Rifles (disbanded in 1943 but resurrected in the post-war period as the reserve unit, PNGVR), was the foundation of the Pacific Islands Regiment and later, the PNG Defence Force.

Department of the Prime Minister, Port Moresby (A/H/157).

---

of Japanese troops. As well, the summit of Imita Ridge to road-end at Owers' Corner was only 4 hours away by porter, enabling easy re-supply.

This particular action marked the end of the withdrawal phase for the Australians. The Japanese came no closer to Port Moresby than this point (notwithstanding the few stragglers who did get onto the Sogeri Plateau) and it was the last action fought in the defensive mode by the Australians. An active patrolling programme, with 50 man patrols, was immediately commenced. On the 21st September, two 25-pounder artillery pieces of the 14th Field Regiment, firing from Owers' Corner, came into service to provide support for the infantry.

The heavy guns would not have made life easy for the Japanese but they were already in an untenable position, being dangerously over-extended and without fresh supplies. Allied air attacks on the Buna beachhead meant few military or food stores were landed, and continuous attacks upon the track itself prevented any daytime movement along it. The Japanese attempted moving supplies by night but gave this up when many of their forcibly conscripted native carriers simply took the opportunity of darkness to dump their loads and escape. The result was no supplies were reaching the troops at the front. Indeed, their commander Horii had concluded a week before the Australian artillery began their barrage, on 14th September 1942, the South Seas Detachment had 'been placed under such a difficult situation that it was impossible for them to further hold out at Ioribaiwa and, needless to say, to advance any further. This was due to the supply of provisions. No provisions were sent from Kokoda at that time'.

Coinciding with their Kokoda Trail misfortunes was the disastrous defeat suffered by the Japanese on Edson's Ridge on Guadacanal on 13th and 14th of September. During this fighting, nearly their entire force on the island was annihilated. Coming on top of the earlier reversals in the Battle of the Coral Sea and at Milne Bay, this forced the Japanese High Command to review their priorities, leading to an immediate switch of emphasis away from Kokoda Trail operations. The paramount objective for the Japanese now was the re-establishing of their position in the Solomon Islands and the retaking of Guadacanal. This left the South Seas Detachment in New Guinea completely unsupported—that is to say, the Japanese forces on the Kokoda Trail were, literally, abandoned by their commanders. No further attempts would be made to send supplies or reinforcements from Rabaul.

Accordingly, Horii (the Japanese commander on the Kokoda Trail) decided 'the capture of Ioribaiwa was the last part of their attack and thereafter the Detachment was to re-group on the north side of the Owen Stanley Range'. Horii's decision had anticipated orders, which he received on 23rd September, to fall back to Kokoda. He had actually begun the withdrawal of his troops on the 16th, a week earlier. By the 26th, with the withdrawal of the last battalions of the *144th Infantry Regiment*, the Japanese retreat had begun in earnest. There had been a plan established for an orderly Japanese withdrawal, by which the separate units would leap-frog back through each other to Buna. However, the Japanese soldiers had nothing to eat at all and, as soon as the senior officers left, they withdrew northwards in uncoordinated movements in a desperate search for food.

Thus, the Australians initially enjoyed rapid advance. On the 28th, the abandoned Japanese battlements at Ioribaiwa were in their hands, and by 3rd October Nauro had been reached. The following day, the vanguard was reporting Efogi, the mid-point of the overland route, all clear, and on the 7th October, Myola was recaptured against light opposition. On the 8th however, the Japanese rearguard was overtaken near Templeton's Crossing and the Australian advance was checked for eight days while they flushed their enemy from carefully prepared defensive positions. This was grim, dangerous work, and was to typify the style of fighting for the rest of the campaign. It took twelve days to take Eora Creek village.

The remains of the Wiarope Bridge. Originally destroyed by members of B Company, 39th Battalion, the bridge was reconstructed a number of times by the Japanese but each time being subsequently destroyed by Allied air strikes. This photograph was taken on 21st October 1942.

Australian War Memorial 128149.

The Japanese were literally fighting to the death but an equally direct view was taken by Brigadier Lloyd, now in command of the fighting force. Ken Clift recorded he (Lloyd) told one 'O' group '... each rearguard, left by the enemy to oppose us, has to be completely destroyed'. At noon on the 30th, Alola was recaptured, and later the same day, the outskirts of Isurava were being cautiously entered. In contrast to the situation only days before, the only resistance now being met was from stragglers and isolated snipers. The bulk of the Japanese force was retreating quickly along the Kokoda–Buna road, though this was not known to the Australians at the time. On 3rd November, a morning patrol from the 2/31st Battalion under Lieutenant A. N. Black, walked into Kokoda to find the place free of the Japanese. By 11.30 am, the town had been secured.*

War damage at Kokoda Government Station, November 1942.
Australian War Memorial 25638.

* For 'Doc' Vernon, re-entering Kokoda was a moment to be savoured and just to simply walk into the town seemed a bit tame. Vernon, always on the lookout for a bit of fun, managed to do it in some style.

> As we drew close to Journey's End, [he wrote] my boys found a derelict Jap. bike that with some pushing was still rideable. It had no tyres and only one pedal, but I hopped onto it and the boys shoved behind, highly excited and showing it in catcalls [and] whoops of delight. It was quite a triumphant entry.

Though the Japanese had held Kokoda and adjacent areas to the south for only 14 weeks, they carried out many improvements to the portion of the overland track near the town and to the south. The extent of the changes were such that Vernon, who knew the area before the war, and who entered Kokoda on the 3rd November, became unsure of where he was. He recorded:

> The tracks between Isurava and Deniki had changed so much now that at times I was at a loss to know exactly how far we had come. This area had been a main base camp for the Japs, and in places there were regular cities of huts and shelters, well hidden from air attack, and a litter of abandoned gear all over the place. The Japs had made a more thorough job of roadmaking up this side of the range than we had, and it was well graded for horse packing; many of the steep little creeks that we had to scramble down and out of, were crossed by high arched bridges such as you see in Japan. The track right down to within a mile or so [about 1600 metres] of Kokoda had been thus occupied ...

There were no permanent materials available to the Japanese and the swing of later military interest away from the Kokoda Trail, and the immediate post-war concentration on the rebuilding of major coastal towns by the civil authorities, meant these improvements deteriorated quickly in the humid climate. No work at all was done to maintain or replace the Japanese bridges and the earth works were allowed to erode and crumble. Only the vaguest suggestions of some of the earthworks between Deniki and Kokoda are evident today.

The recapture of Kokoda with its airstrip greatly improved the supply situation to the forward Australian units. Within hours, ammunition and food supplies, and even Jeeps, were landed there, allowing a build up of stores for the advance towards the northern coast. Stiff resistance was expected for this next stage, this being made evident when it took six days to clear the Japanese from Oivi, a village on the road to the east of Kokoda. An Australian bayonet charge on the 10th November finally cleared the position and turned the Japanese withdrawal into a full-scale rout. At the destroyed Wiarope Bridge on the Kumusi River, which was in flood at the time and over 150 metres wide, hundreds of Japanese soldiers drowned in their haste to escape. The Japanese commander, Major-General Horii also perished, on 12th November 1942.* On the 13th November, the Australians had reached the Kumusi themselves, and by the end of that day, the 2/5th and 2/6th Field Companies, under the direction of Lieutenant-Colonel (later Brigadier) W.D. McDonald, had put across two 'flying foxes' and a small suspension bridge. Within three days, an entire brigade had been transferred to the far side and was advancing on Gona, and four days later, forward elements of the lead battalion were entering that settlement. But they had outstripped their supply line from Kokoda and they were obliged to withdraw to be replenished.

Australian troops crossing the Kumusi River on a makeshift suspension bridge in November 1942.

This bridge is not much different from the first bridges across this river built 40 years earlier by Armit, Monckton and Naylor.

Australian War Memorial 13755.

---

* Kengoro Tanaka, the Japanese war historian cited in these pages, was with Horii on the day he drowned. Tanaka, with Horii and other staff officers, was using a raft in an attempt to reach Girua.

> This raft however, [wrote Tanaka] was caught by a large tree which had fallen on the bank, and brought to a standstill. The Commander then ordered the use of a canoe ... and safely reached the mouth of the Kumusi River. Being far too eager to reach Giruwa [sic], the Commander went out to sea, in spite of the knowledge that it would be extremely reckless. Unfortunately, during the afternoon, a thunderstorm occurred, and strong gusts of winds blew. The canoe was capsized ... 10 km off the coast, and the Commander and his staff officers never returned to land.

Horii's position as commander was taken by Colonel Yosuke Yokoyama.

On the north coast route, 1942.

The carriers in the background are standing on a log-corduroyed road, the same surface laid down to good effect by Resident Magistrate Wurth on this route in 1925. The difference it makes to conditions underfoot can be seen by noting where the soldiers in the foreground are walking.

Australian War Memorial 14187.

The situation at this time in the crescent-shaped area about the Japanese beach-heads at Buna and Gona was very confused, with fast-moving Australian patrols slicing deep into territory previously held by the Japanese. Inland, isolated pockets of Japanese, now cut off from their main force on the coast, remained to impede the progress of the main body of Australian troops. The Australian author, George H. Johnston, who was in the area at the time as a war correspondent, recorded his impressions of the situation:

> It's difficult to know what is going on. Today I was in the front line attempting to get a picture of what was happening ... The soldiers asked me how the fighting was going and I asked them. In this sort of country you can see very little beyond the 10 or 20 feet [3 to 6 metres] of black-shadowed jungle that lies immediately ahead.

In a curious twist of circumstances, Johnston's colleague at the time was Ian Morrison, correspondent for the London *Times*. Morrison's father was George Ernest Morrison, who it will be recalled, led the *Age* expedition of 1883 into the area traversed by the early part of the Kokoda Trail. Ian Morrison survived the

New Guinea campaigns but was later killed while reporting on the Korean War.

On the 24th November, a massive Allied attack was launched against the Japanese positions at Buna, and the day after, a similar thrust was made against Gona. Gona fell on the night of 9th December, Buna village on the 14th, and Buna mission on 2nd January 1943. The Japanese, without reinforcements or a supply line back to their Rabaul base, were now fighting a battle which could only have one result. By the 21st January 1943, with the country to the south-east of Buna being cleared by combined Australian and American sweeps, all Japanese resistance in the area ceased. The Kokoda Track campaign, which had lasted for 6 months and 2 days, was over.

Buna Station, 14th January 1943. Every man-made structure at Buna was totally destroyed by the severity of the Allied bombing of the Japanese entrenched there.

Australian War Memorial 128401.

The cost of the campaign in terms of human life was high. Australian casualty figures for the period from the time the Japanese landed in July 1942 until 16th November 1942 are 103 officers and 1,577 men, of whom 39 officers and 586 men were killed. The 2/1st Battalion, officially classified as 'typical', lost 253 men killed, wounded or too sick to fight, out of a total of 608 in 41 days. Some idea of the havoc sickness alone wreaked upon the troops can be gauged from the experiences of one Signals line party of the 2/3rd Line Section. This unit, without being in direct contact with the enemy, lost, within 12 days, 50 percent of its strength to malaria.* The 39th Battalion, which had returned to take part in the battle for Gona after being reinforced, held a roll call on 23rd January 1943. Only 7 officers and 25 men of the original unit that had faced the Japanese in July of the previous year remained. (The 39th Battalion's casualties exceeded 40% with 132 being killed or missing in action or dying of wounds and 266 being wounded in action. Battle honours included one Distinguished Service Order, one Distinguished Service Cross [U.S.A.], two M.B.E.s, seven Military Crosses, two Distinguished Conduct Medals, ten Military Medals, and two Mentioned In Dispatches).

Estimates of Japanese losses during the Kokoda Track campaign vary, ranging from Brigadier Potts' estimate of 900 killed and 1,400 wounded, to the 1,500 deaths calculated by General Allen's Intelligence staff. These figures are far removed from Tanaka's assertion (compiled 37 years later) 8,000 Japanese were killed in action between 19th November 1942 and 20th January 1943 in defence of just the Buna/Gona beach-head. Tanaka's figures would seem to include deaths from all causes,

---

* The 2/3rd Line Section was responsible for putting through an 'earth-return' telephone line from their Signals Office at Horsley's Gap near Port Moresby (adjacent, today, to the International High School) to Kokoda in 31 days in November/December 1942. This was later extended to Buna, providing for coast to coast communications for the first time, and then to Lae. The Horsley's Gap Signal Office became the largest signals centre in any AIF operational area of the Second World War with 44 trunk lines, 174 local lines and up to 50,000 morse 'groups' being sent in a day. Their 'wireless' network extended back to Australia and a regular air-mail service was provided, as well as a dispatch rider deliveries. Dispatch riders had to travel by foot once past Owers' Corner and in doing so, emulated the mail carriers of pre-war Papua.

including starvation. He cites, for example, 'the amount of food available per day per capita was 0.36 l[itres] at the end of December [1942,] 0.036 to 0.07 l[itres] in the beginning of January [1943], and zero from January 8 to 12. It was literally a battle against famine'.*

The end of the road. Buna Beach, January 1943.
Australian War Memorial 14085.

* The acute shortage of food by the Japanese had horrific consequences. In mid-October 1942, some three months before the campaign ended, the Japanese were already so short of food that some Japanese soldiers resorted to cannibalism of Australian dead. In January 1943, evidence of cannibalism on their own dead was also discovered. Ordinarily, cannibalism is a repugnant practice but it is interesting to note the slightly bizarre rationalisation that emerged from the desperation and stresses of a 'take no prisoners' campaign. Ken Clift reported in his *The Saga of a Sig* that 'the Japs weren't sadists—they were just hungry and determined to keep up their strength to hold their positions. ... They were even shorter of rations than we were. We certainly did not condemn them on this cannibalism'.

With the liberation of Buna and Gona, it was confirmed civilians had also perished at the hands of the Japanese. There were reports of up to 40 Orokaivas being hanged. Several European non-combatants were caught and were either executed or suffered great privations. These latter were people associated with the Anglican missions in the area or plantation families, and included female teachers and nurses. The presence of one group, of 11 people, which included a six year old boy, was revealed to the Japanese by natives from Perombata, about 10 kilometres inland from Buna. All were captured by the Japanese and were later executed, one after the other, on the beach at Buna on 12th August 1942. The young boy was forced to watch the others, which included his father, being beheaded with a long sword, until he too was killed.*

* An account of the fate of members of the Anglican mission stations at Gona, Sangara and Isivita is told in Dorothea Tomkins and Brian Hughes, *The Road from Gona*, Angus & Robertson, Sydney 1969.

17

Post-war developments (to 1972)

The last Japanese soldiers to be cleared from the Papua and New Guinea theatre occurred at Manus Island on 6th February 1945. Nine months later, on 30th October 1945, the civil Provisional Administration of Papua-New Guinea took over Papua and parts of the previous Mandated Territory of New Guinea from the military authorities. The new Administrator was Jack Keith Murray (later O.B.E.) (no relation to Hubert or Leonard Murray). Civil government for the remainder of the old Mandated Territory was restored on 24th June 1946 though it was not until 15th March 1949 Port Moresby was officially designated as the capital of the new, united Territory of Papua and New Guinea.

The process of rebuilding the physical and economic structures of the country was an enormous task, a major difficulty being knowing where to start, since many areas were badly damaged and needed urgent attention. Top priority was given to the rebuilding of Lae, since this important town was almost completely destroyed during the war, and for two years after the return of civil administration, Lae continued to take precedence on the Public Works Department schedule. The re-establishment of local shipping was also considered important and the Department was committed to rebuilding wharves and storage sheds at several locations about the country. But, despite the best of intentions, it was difficult to get much done in the confusion of the immediate post-war period. In December 1946, after 14 months of civil control, it was reported 'extreme shortage[s] of building materials, shipping, plant and equipment; and insufficient native labour' were still seriously impeding restoration work.

In Port Moresby, which underwent extensive expansion and development during the war, the problem was one of a different kind. Frederick Howard, a reporter for the Melbourne *Herald*, found in March 1946 'nearly all of its wartime development is useless for civil purposes' and

> [a] network of wide and finely surfaced roads now leads nowhere. The great air-strips which they served are deserted. The vast maze of telephone communications is valueless. Much of its equipment cannot be converted, because it was designed for a short life.

Howard discovered too, some desperately needed items would have been available, had it not been for a curious policy of the Australian government which required the deliberate destruction of surplus material and equipment by the departing forces. 'The burning of sound timber and bitumen,' he wrote, 'the machine-gunning of parks of cars, trucks and tractors into scrap metal, are among victory's mysteries in these parts'. One has to wonder at the rationale applied by the Australian government in allowing this bizarre waste of resources to occur in a country critically short of everything, and for which resources the Australian Government later had to expend more money to replace.

A further example of the inexplicable attitude of the Australian government was illustrated in the circumstances surrounding the restoration of New Guinea's newspapers. Up to January 1942, there were three newspapers in the country, the *Papuan Courier* in Port Moresby, the *Morobe News* in Lae and the *Rabaul Times* in Rabaul. The plant of the *Papuan Courier* was taken over by the Australian Army and removed, and the printing presses in Lae and Rabaul were lost due to Japanese occupation of these towns. New newspaper printing equipment was unobtainable immediately after the war. However, another press, owned by the Army Amenities Unit, had been brought to New Guinea for the production of Army publications and in

1946, the three publishers of the former newspapers sought to acquire this from the Australian government to re-start newspaper production in the country. But the Australian Government refused to sell; instead, the Government authorised the removal of the press so it could be taken to Japan, where the printing industry had not been affected at all by the war, for use of the Occupation Forces. It was not until 26th September 1950 a new newspaper, the *South Pacific Post* commenced publication in Port Moresby.

Given the need to carefully husband resources, little direct attention was given to the overland route at this time. Some of the new roads about Port Moresby were maintained after a fashion, but more for the local convenience they afforded than for the improved access they may have provided to the Sogeri Plateau. What is clear however, is the southern end of the Port Moresby to Buna route had emerged in far better condition than it had been in 1939. In October 1945, it was a proper two-lane road, though unsealed, to as far as Sogeri and to Ilolo, with single-lane vehicular tracks to the Musgrave River (via Sogeri) and Owers' Corner (via Ilolo). Nominally, it was now an all-weather route though some sections were still difficult, and dangerous, to negotiate after heavy rain, particularly as there were no safety rails. It had seen much hard use however, and needed continuous upkeep. Ethel Ellen (Judy) Tudor, correspondent for *Pacific Islands Monthly*, travelled to the G.A. Loudon's Eilogo rubber estate on the Sogeri Plateau from Port Moresby in October 1946 and mentioned the 'pot-holes, corrugations and water courses' defacing the surface of the road.

In 1947, a major programme for the Sogeri Road was planned, and reconstruction of existing, and erection of new, bridges and culverts began. A new quarry was opened about 40 kilometres along the road from which crushed metal was obtained to resurface the entire 60 kilometres of the route. The object of this was to provide a proper camber to the road so water would flow off quickly, rather than soak into the earth surface. The heavy demand for the services of the public works department elsewhere meant this was to be a drawn out process and the task was still had not been completed by June 1949. At Sapphire Creek, it will be recalled Bensted had erected a bridge in 1926 to replace the original ford crossing established by John MacDonald in 1905. Bensted's bridge had disappeared by 1938 and for 3 years, a gravel crossing was used. In 1941, Army engineers put down a concrete ford and this was in use up until 1970, when a new concrete bridge was constructed to take the Sogeri Road across Sapphire Creek. The road itself remained unsealed until the late 1960s, at which time sections of bitumen road were laid down to keep pace with Port Moresby's urban development which had begun to creep out along the road. Today, one may drive on tarmac all the way to Sogeri.

During the war years, most traffic on the Sogeri Road went straight past the turnoff to the old Hombrom Bluff track established by Henderson in 1910. However, the bridge over the Laloki, completed in April of 1910, afforded easy access to the heavily wooded terraces on the steep southern slopes of Hombrom. It was here General Blamey established his Staff Headquarters, near the small lake part-way up the foot-slope. This site, which was perfectly camouflaged from the air, became known as Blamey's Retreat and after the war was officially designated a botanical garden, to maintain and improve upon the many plants established by the soldiers during their time there. The fact much labour had been expended in developing the gardens particularly irked 'Doc' Vernon, who returned to Kokoda in March 1946. Just prior to his return, he had visited Blamey's Retreat and what he saw there compelled him to write a critical letter to the *Pacific Islands Monthly* (in March 1946, a time when the apparently irrational destruction of surplus Army resources mentioned earlier was most evident), pointing out this further example of a waste of money. He wrote:

> The whole set-up is amazing. Setting aside its undoubted beauty, one wonders ... how many thousands of pounds and units of native labour were expended in its construction ... . Had the money and the work been put into a small experimental tropical garden, on a site not in danger of sliding down into perdition at any moment, and some assortment of useful tropical plants ... collected[,] the expenditure would have been justified on educational and economic grounds. ... the Flora and Fauna Park of Papua is

just another monument to Army Brass-hat love of luxury and waste of public money.

Leaving aside the question of whether the expenditure was justified, Vernon's criticism of the site of the gardens was not entirely misplaced. In 1948, the bridge over the river collapsed under the pressure of a flooded Laloki. Even essential works were being deferred at the time because of a shortage of funds, so repair of an old, non-essential bridge stood no chance of receiving attention. Subsequent wet seasons caused further damage and with no ready access to the area, the proposed development of the botanical gardens never went ahead. Unfortunately, 'Doc' Vernon's sudden death on 16th June 1946 in the hospital at Samarai, only two and half months after finishing his ANGAU service, did not allow him the satisfaction of reiterating his point about wasted effort.

By far the worst damaged area of the Port Moresby to Buna route was at the northern end, with Buna and Gona being totally obliterated by Allied attacks against the Japanese beach heads. Mavis Parkinson, a teacher at Gona Mission who was executed by the Japanese in August 1942, recorded before her capture in a single day, there had been 19 bombing raids on Gona by 3.30 in the afternoon: 'Less than every half-hour there was a raid', she wrote. In 1946, due to Buna's destruction, a new headquarters for the Northern Division was established at Higatura, about 13 kilometres south of the present site of Popondetta. Kokoda was no longer a major centre for gold mining (although stock prices for the Yodda Goldfields company continued to be listed during the war and up until October 1948, at which time they were being offered for sale at one shilling and nine pence per share. During the war, the buying and selling prices were shown as 'not quoted'. Yodda Goldfields stock were not listed after October 1948). The increasing production of rubber however, ensured Kokoda remained an important post. Almost a quarter of a million kilograms of rubber were produced in both 1949/50 and 1950/51 from the plantations there.

The airmail service between Australia and Papua New Guinea was resumed on 2nd April 1945 by Qantas Empire Airways Limited, almost seven months before civil government was restored. The widespread use of air transport during the war had demonstrated its effectiveness and air deliveries of mail to inland stations was to be the norm from now on. It will be recalled before the War, Kokoda had been one of the first government posts to be linked to the Port Moresby headquarters with a regular communications service, first by pedestrian deliveries and then by an air service. Yet, in a curious reversal of circumstances, Kokoda was the only major station not to be an immediate part of the post-war internal airmail service. It was not until August 1949 QANTAS introduced a weekly flight from Port Moresby through Kokoda to Popondetta, the nearest large landing ground to Higatura. Six months later, the traffic on this route had increased to such an extent it was necessary to introduce a bi-weekly service.

The delay in bringing Kokoda into the airmail network and the woeful state of coastal shipping services in the immediate post-war years led to the re-introduction of the pedestrian mail service over the Port Moresby–Kokoda–Buna route. This service, more or less, had not stopped operating since the 1930s, when its days as an advertised scheduled service ceased. During the war years, ANGAU had used police runners to carry military mail over the track and this practice was easily transferred to civilian life when most of the ANGAU staff were transferred to the Provisional Administration in October 1945. Wally McPherson, the first post-war Port Moresby Postmaster, and later Superintendent of Postal Services, recalled the Port Moresby–Kokoda service was well-established in May 1946 when he took up his duties. Even after 50 years, McPherson is still impressed by the pride shown by the mail-carrying policemen on their arrival at Port Moresby Post Office with the mail from Kokoda. He recounts how one of the policemen would correctly report to him, coming stiffly to attention and saluting, before formally handing over the mail bag, showing evident pride in a difficult job well done. As in pre-war times, the policemen were still armed but the articles carried were restricted to letters only. Heavier parcels and newspapers were sent by sea to Buna, from where they were delivered by runner across shorter and easier routes. The mail service along the Kokoda Track may have survived competition from air services in 1932 but it was not to be the case a second time. The introduction of the QANTAS service to Kokoda in August 1949 was the final blow to the overland mail service, and it was shut down for ever in October that year. There were other pedestrian mail services in the country which continued past this time but none could match the Kokoda Track route for length, difficulty and historical significance. Ironically, one of the last pedestrian mail routes to cease operating was the Buna–Ioma track, Ioma (as Tamata Station) being where the seeds of the Kokoda Track were sown in the 1890s. The Buna–Ioma service continued to at least February of 1958 when it too was disbanded.

As the effects of the war years lessened, the northern districts began returning to an easier pace reminiscent of life during the Murray years. Food gardens were re-established and villages rebuilt. Schools were reopened and a more ordered way of life slowly became established. This pleasant picture was briefly interrupted in November 1946 when the whole of the northern coastline between Cape Nelson and the Mambare River mouth was ravaged by a severe cyclone. This caused a tidal surge to sweep inland for some distance, killing eight people and destroying all the carefully restored gardens. But by December 1950, the area had settled back into its somewhat sleepy pre-war existence. At Higatura on Christmas Eve 1950, the staff of the Works and Housing Department sponsored a 'grand' party for all the residents of the district, with each child receiving a Christmas gift. But, again, further turmoil was to be visited upon the region and, tragically, many of these children were to be killed four weeks later when the country's worst disaster, the eruption of the Mount Lamington volcano (also known previously as Berepo) volcano occurred. This caused thousands of deaths and was to interrupt post-war reconstruction activity in the northern region for years.

The first indications of volcanic activity within the mountain, which previously had not been considered active, were earth tremors that began at about 4 pm on Tuesday 16th January 1951. The frequency of these increased to between 60 and 70 a day over the next few days. At about 11 am on the 18th, black smoke and a stream of pumice and hot mud began issuing from the mountain. The Deputy Administrator, Mr Justice Phillips, and District Commissioner Cecil Francis Cowley, who lived in

Higatura, about 11 kilometres from Mount Lamington, made an appraisal of the situation. They came to the conclusion evacuation of the area was not warranted. However, at 10.42 am on Sunday 21st January 1951, a major eruption occurred. This did not occur in the normal way, for the Mount Lamington eruption was to be of the violent *Peléan* type. It exploded sideways with a 'terrific horizontal blast', totally enveloping the Higatura station and killing 2,900 natives and 35 Europeans, including District Commissioner Cowley and several children under four years of age. The noise of the blast was heard 270 kilometres away and smoke and particles were sent over 17,000 metres into the air. The intensity of the blast was such a missionary, the Reverend Dennis Taylor, who was the only person in the Higatura area known to have survived the actual eruption, later died from severe burns he received from radiated heat at a point almost 5 kilometres from the explosion. Reverend Taylor's wife and four young children also perished.

The first patrol into Higatura after the eruption, under Claude Champion, the Assistant Government Secretary, entered the area on Tuesday 23rd January. They found 'iron telegraph poles three inches [75 mm] in diameter were bent over like meccano toys'. They also found 'whole houses were blown off their floors for anything up to a quarter of a mile [400 metres]' and most of the bodies were naked, having had their clothing blown off them. Most of the deaths resulted not from blast or heat however, but from inhalation of the deadly *nues ardentes* smoke, the incandescent dust and gas mixture which usually accompanies a *Peléan* type eruption and which brings about virtually instant death.

On the day following the eruption, the Administration established a temporary headquarters for the Division at Popondetta and a camp for 4,000 native evacuees at Wiarope. QANTAS and private air companies were prominent in making available their entire local resources for the ferrying of medical supplies and food. The Royal Australian Air Force sent two Dakotas which by, by 2nd February 1951, had alone dropped 31,000 kilograms of rice, almost 6,000 kilograms of meat, 1,500 kilograms of wheatmeal and 61 bags of sugar in the Wiarope drop zone. Food deliveries were critical since nearly all food gardens in the area had been destroyed. The situation was so bad that rations to the local villagers were provided by the Administration for nearly the entire year, until 20 December, by which time local agricultural production had been re-established.

The disaster, nevertheless, did bring about some lasting changes, as the movement of evacuees to Wiarope was utilised to establish permanent villages in the area. Plans were drafted to commence the growing of rice along the road to Kokoda to supply these new settlements in the same week the evacuees' camps were established. Minor eruptions and residual rumblings continued for some time after the initial explosion and it was not until January 1953, two years later, the eruption of Mount Lamington was considered to have ceased. The eruption had altered the levels and the courses of many of the streams in the area. As a result, road services between Kokoda and the coast were severely disrupted for months and a substantial proportion of the record rubber production of over 272,000 kilograms that year had to be air-freighted out.

Rubber, which originated in the experimental plantings made in about 1920, was to prove a boon to the district, and to the country, in the immediate post-war years. Bert Kienzle and his brother Wallace operated four plantations about Kokoda and were major producers. Before the war, they had about 360 hectares under cultivation but by 1958 had planted a further 300 hectares. In that year, they alone produced close to half of the 506,000 kilogram yield of the Northern Division, which was a seventh of the total rubber exports of the entire country for 1958. The Kienzle brothers also operated a 400 hectare pastoral lease and by 1958 were running almost 400 head of Aberdeen Angus and Poll Shorthorn cattle. In May 1958, the new Administrator, Brigadier (later Sir) Donald Cleland, inspected the region and expressed the view 'it [had] more agricultural potential than any other district in Papua'. The success of other crops gave witness to this. Guy Pritchard had planted cocoa trees in the area in 1955 and by June 1958 was expecting a yield of about 500 tonnes a year. Several hundred hectares of coffee had also been planted, much of which was owned by the native villages about Higatura. Though this produce was usually sent out through

Buna, the efficiencies of air transport demonstrated in the aftermath of the Mount Lamington eruption had been noticed. With the lift in primary production, there was a corresponding increase in the use of air transport direct to the overseas port at Port Moresby. This set the pattern for the entire country, and in the following three decades, Papua New Guinea was to have one of the highest rates of third-level aircraft use in the world.

Actually, the entire overland route, from Port Moresby to Buna, is well served in the air-age, either as a legacy of the war years or as a result of post-war development. Port Moresby (which, at one point during the war, had seven separate airfields), Kagi, Efogi, Menari (or Manare), Nauro, Kokoda, Popondetta and nearby Girua all have airstrips today. Even Mount Victoria has its own airstrip, at Manumu, as does Ioma. Up until the early 1960s, Sogeri also had a landing field, though it is now covered by the waters of the Sirinumu Dam. The airstrips near Buna and Dobudura on the north coast have now been abandoned. The airstrips are appreciated by modern-day travellers because they enable quick access to a range of destinations in mountainous regions which, in earlier times, required days of walking. This is an important economic point since the old battle grounds are popular tourist attractions and something of a money-spinner for the smaller aircraft operators and the Government.

In a more important sense, because the profile of the old overland route had been raised by the events of the war and was well-known outside the country, it was considered an ideal vehicle to focus external awareness on the emerging national feeling within Papua New Guinea in the years before the Territory became independent. To this end, Bishop Ravu Henao of the United Church, Catholic Archbishop Virgil Copas of Port Moresby, the Anglican Bishop of Papua New Guinea Bishop David Hand, and the Anglican Archbishop of Sydney, Archbishop Marcus Loane walked the track in May 1972, the year before self-government was proclaimed. This brought about repairs to many sections of the route. Log crossings were renewed and safety rails were erected at places where a slip could have led to a dangerous fall. This was the first maintenance work done on the walking track since the war years.

The township of Kokoda in 1973.
Office of Information, Port Moresby 53610 and 53618.

A report of this journey was published in the Papua New Guinea *Post-Courier* newspaper on 9th June 1972 and an accompanying article triggered an interesting sequel in terms of the public debate it triggered within Papua New Guinea. The article, headed 'Let's turn it into a real asset' and sub-titled 'There's nothing like the Kokoda Track', was written by Neville Gare, Executive Director of the Papua New Guinea National Parks Board, and put into words the tacitly understood importance of the route to the country. Gare proposed, with care, it could be promoted as an economic asset without denigrating its wartime history. He wrote:

> No Australian soldier who fought on the Track can forget it, nor can he forget the carriers and stretcher bearers of this land who fought a cruel war there with him. ... The sons and young brothers of these men are bursting to come and try the Track, and I am sure that away in Japan there are others who will want to carry out a similar pilgrimage. And in Papua New Guinea, there are increasing numbers of young people for whom the Track is a challenge to their physical endurance and their tradition as son of the men who gave so much on it to drive back the invaders 30 years ago. So why not a National Walking Track? A rugged and primitive one, for people who are fit and tenacious, and who want to remain resourceful. For men and women who know the true comradeship of long walks and camps in rugged terrain, and the satisfaction that comes with conquering one more hill. ... How about it, Papua New Guinea?

This invitation lay dormant until the Place Names Committee of the Government's Department of Lands decided to take the first step and formalise the route's name. Up until this time, it had been popularly known in Australia as the Kokoda *Trail*. This term was also in use in Papua New Guinea though Kokoda *Track* was used at least as much, particularly by pre-war and long-time Australian residents. In the Government *Gazette* of 12th October 1972, the Committee gave notice they intended to assign the name 'Kokoda Trail' to the section of the old mail route not accessible to motor vehicles, that is, the 'walking path' from Owers' Corner on the Sogeri Plateau to Kokoda. The Committee advised their decision would be final but they would entertain objections to their intention if received within one month. This announcement led to vigorous public discussion in Papua New Guinea. Many letters to the local newspaper were furiously penned and divided schools of opinion within the ex-servicemen's organisations developed. Such was the public interest the Committee was obliged to extend the time for objections by three months. However, the eventual outcome was 'Kokoda Trail' was selected.

This was not a universally popular decision, and in Papua New Guinea at least, most white residents probably would have preferred the main alternative 'Track' to have been chosen. They certainly had a strong argument, based on the length of time 'track' had been in use. It is worthwhile to note however, before the Second World War neither of the specific two-word terms 'Kokoda Track' or 'Kokoda Trail' was in common use. But 'track' on its own, or in combination with other words, was regularly used, even as far back as December 1904 when the route was first established by Barton. It may be recalled as well, before Barton the route was used by other government officers, including MacGregor, Ballantine and Rochfort. In August 1897, after he had utilised this route to go to the Hagari district, MacGregor recorded: 'From the time we left Port Moresby until we arrived at Hagari we used native *tracks* the whole way ... ' (emphasis added). The earliest written use of 'track' to describe any unformed path in Papua appears to be contained in Volume 46 of the Journal of the Royal Geographical Society, published in London in 1876. In this, Octavius C. Stone records 'native tracks are numerous ...' about Port Moresby. In contrast, the earliest written use of 'trail' to describe the Kokoda Trail (or any jungle path in New Guinea) does not appear able to be ascribed to any date earlier than 1935, when Evelyn Cheesman's book *The Two Roads of Papua* was published and in which this term was used.

Despite the sometimes heated public debate, there seemed to be universal agreement 'track' was in general use before the war and through to at least the latter part of 1942. Indeed, access to two military journals of the time, ('Headquarters, New Guinea Force Intelligence Daily Summary' and '1st Australian Corps Intelligence Weekly Summary') was granted to Fred Turner of

Port Moresby, the principal champion of the 'track' camp. He found:

> The first date shown [in the documents] is that of the 1st January 1942 but the important documents start dated 2nd July 1942 and the last dated document is dated the 9th November 1942. Every map that is in the files shows the word 'Track' and all descriptions of the fighting refers to and uses the word 'Track' in every case. The reports on the fighting, victories, withdrawals and ambushes again use the word 'Track' exclusively, and nowhere can I find the word 'Trail' used in any manner or form whatever.

Kokoda 'Track' is also the term used by war historian Dudley McCarthy, who had served in pre-war New Guinea as a Patrol Officer, in the Australian official war history volume *South-West Pacific Area—First Year: Kokoda to Wau*, published in 1959. It is also of interest two other wartime routes which paralleled the Kokoda Trail across the Owen Stanleys, the Jaure (or Kapa-Kapa) Track and the Bulldog Track, retain their 'track' names to this day, as does the Black Cat Track from Salamaua to Wau.

How then, if the word 'track' was so widely used in the country, did 'Trail' obtain such a foothold? Though 'trail' is a standard English word describing a beaten path through the wilderness, many argued against 'trail' because it was an 'Americanism'. American speakers of English do tend to use this word, while Australian and British speakers of English prefer to use 'track' to describe the same entity. Yet the entrenchment of 'Kokoda Trail' in the Australian vocubulary quite likely stems from the use of this term in Australian newspapers during the latter part of 1942. Indeed, one war correspondent of the time, Geoffrey Reading, who reported for the Sydney *Daily Mirror* and the *Sydney Morning Herald*, suggests his dispatches may have been responsible. In the NSW Leagues Club Journal of May 1971, Reading wrote:

> None of the reporters ... knew precisely what to call the track over the mountains ... I found myself typing out messages describing it thus: Port Moresby hyphen Ioribaiwa hyphen Kokoda Track. Because of the relatively primitive communications at the time the hyphens had to be spelt out. In addition, words were relatively dear—one shilling each if I

> remember rightly—and so most of us were under office instructions to economise as much as possible. But the main consideration as far as I was concerned was that typing out a long winded punctuated description ... was simply a bloody nuisance ...
>
> At least half my colleagues in the war correspondent's hut ... were Americans and there were many American servicemen in Port Moresby at the time.*
>
> One night in September 1942, I sat down to my typewriter ... and solved the problem ... by typing out 'Kokoda Trail'. I went back to a game of poker and didn't give it another thought. However, apparently in Sydney, where newspaper people have the problem of fitting headlines in large type in small spaces, the innovation was well received ... Other newspapers with the same problem took it up and the name stuck.

This explanation is plausible and even though Reading's reports were not the first to contain the word 'trail', it is not inconsistent with the findings of this author's review of a number of newspapers of the time (the *Daily Mirror* and *Sydney Morning Herald* in Sydney, *The Age* in Melbourne, and the *Truth* and *Courier Mail* in Brisbane),

As Reading suggests, it was not clear at first how the Kokoda Trail region should be described. 'Track' was an early choice and widely used, though along with other synonyms. The first report of the Papuan campaign in the *Daily Mirror* was made on 27 July 1942 by another correspondent, Barry Young. Young described the Trail as 'a difficult but passable track' and as 'practically the only overland route in the whole of Papua'. On

* The Americans based in Port Moresby were service personnel and, with one exception, no American troops were on the Kokoda Trail proper during the period July 1942 to January 1943 when the campaign was fought. The exception was no less than General Douglas MacArthur. He had driven to Owers' Corner, chatted for an hour or so with various Australian officers, then departed in, as one observer of the time put it, 'a cloud of dust and tobacco smoke'. The nearest that American troops came to fighting the Japanese on the actual wartime Trail took place in an incident on 10th November 1942. A detachment from a unit of the U.S. 126th Infantry Regiment, crossing from Port Moresby to Jaure on the headwaters of the Kumusi, contacted the Japanese eight kilometres south of Wiarope.

following days, his reports contained phrases such as '[Oivi] is on the track to Port Moresby', 'rough bush tracks', 'the Buna-Kokoda area', and that the Japanese may seek 'to penetrate along jungle tracks'. All the other newspapers reviewed used similar descriptions in the earlier part of the campaign and this continued through to the end of August 1942. Occasionally in these reports, the word 'trail' was used as a means of introducing variety into the narrative though the specific two-word term 'Kokoda trail' or Kokoda Trail' was not used. The use of 'trail' as a synonym of equal status to other words appears to have become normal practice by early September 1942 but there was no consensus on a single term and phrases such as 'jungle path', 'Papuan jungle front', 'foothills of the Owen Stanley Range south of Kokoda', 'Owen Stanley front above Kokoda', 'Japanese supply line', 'jungle front', 'Buna-Kokoda area', 'mountain track', 'jungle track', 'mountain supply line' and so on continued to be used with equal frequency.

The first attempt to describe the whole of the Kokoda Trail area by a single term appears to have been made by Osmar White in the *Courier Mail* of 7th September 1942 when he referred to the 'Kokoda road'. However, again, this use seems to have been driven by a need for variety in the text and his reports continued to be liberally interspersed with 'track' and 'trail'. Two correspondents who frequently used 'trail' from mid-September 1942 were L.J. Fitz-Henry and Geoffrey Tebbutt, both of whom wrote for the *Courier Mail*. Barry Young, whose reports appeared in the Brisbane *Truth* as well as the Sydney *Daily Mirror*, also used 'trail' more often than 'track' from about the same time though in the *Truth* of 20th September 1942, he seeks to cover all possible contingencies by referring to 'the jungle tracks and trails that crossed these saw-toothed peaks'.

The distinct term 'Kokoda track' (lower case T) appears to have been used for the first time (in the text, not as a heading) on 23rd September 1942 in both the *Sydney Morning Herald* and *The Age*. The first time the distinct term 'Kokoda trail' (lower case T) was used (again, in the text, not as a heading) appears to be in a report in the *Courier Mail* on the following day though two days later, on 26th September, all of the *Courier Mail*, the *Sydney Morning Herald* and *The Age* were back to using 'Kokoda track'.

By these dates, the Papuan campaign had been reported on for over two months; the country had been described many times and maps showing various places along the Kokoda Trail had been published in newspapers so there was a good general understanding of the area. As well, fighting in other areas in Papua was also taking, or had taken, place so there was a need to specifically differentiate between the various campaign areas. The use of the 'Kokoda track' or 'Kokoda trail' terms did this succinctly, as well as being a sort of contraction of or shorthand for all those cumbersome earlier descriptions that were no longer required by a now-educated public.

From the end of September 1942, there was a gradual but identifiable swing towards using 'track' or 'trail' in the sense of a proper noun (though still without an initial capital T), and increasing use of both these terms in conjunction with the definite article. Thus, instead of long strings of words like 'the track from Port Moresby to Buna through Kokoda', there appeared shorter phrases such as 'the track to Kokoda' or, even more simply, 'the track'. This process seemed to develop quite quickly and by 10 October 1942, *The Age* was able to run a story with the headline 'Kokoda Road Bombed', and the *Sydney Morning Herald* a story on 15th October with the headline 'Japanese Astride Track Pushed Back', confident readers would understand 'Road' or 'Track' referred to the Kokoda Trail region. This would not have been possible earlier in the campaign.

Similar thinking seems to have been employed when the first part of a five-part series on the campaign by Geoffrey Reading was published in the Daily Mirror on 26th October 1942. This was entitled 'DEATH ECHOES LINGER ON KOKODA TRAIL' (all capitals) and was the first time the term was used in a heading. However, whenever 'trail' appeared in the text of this article, it was always spelt with a lower-case T. In the second article of the series however, 'JUNGLE TRAIL NOT MEASURED BY YARDSTICK', published on 27th October 1942, the term 'Kokoda Trail' (with a capital T) appears for the first time as a true proper noun. The second time it was used was in an article by Reading published the following day dealing with the resourcefulness of Australian soldiers in being able to produce tasty meals from Army rations. The third appearance of 'Kokoda Trail', on 29 October, is also associated with Reading, being contained in the caption of a map which accompanied part four of his article series.

Acceptance by other publishers of the term 'Kokoda Trail' from this time is not as straight-forward as Reading's 1971 comments may suggest. Other than the headline in the *Daily Mirror* on 26th October 1942, the term 'Kokoda Trail' does not appear in any headline in the five papers reviewed up to the end of January 1943. Nor was 'Kokoda Trail', with a capital T, used in the text in any of the reviewed papers except the *Daily Mirror* in the same period. Notwithstanding this, there is an evident increase in the use of 'Kokoda trail' in the text in the Brisbane and Sydney papers reviewed from the end of October 1942 (though 'track' lingered on in the Melbourne *Age*). Whether the increased use in other newspapers was directly attributable to Reading's article is debatable. What is clear however, is Reading would seem to be the first person to use the term as a specific two-word proper noun in the sense it is used today and, on this basis alone, would seem to be able to fairly claim a leading role in its adoption.

And so came about the name 'Kokoda Trail'. To the indigenous people however, even though English is the official language of today's independent Papua New Guinea, both 'track' and 'trail' were imported names. A third suggestion offered to the Place Names Committee, that the route be named in the Motu language 'Kokouda Dala' or 'Kokouda Dalana', (which means Kokoda *Road*) had considerable merit, if only to resolve the track–trail impasse. It still is referred to in this manner by the track-side villagers on the southern side of the Owen Stanleys. Notwithstanding this, the formal adoption of 'Trail' has to be seen in context. If the route was to be established as a National Walking Track in an international context, to be promoted as a tourist destination outside the country, it was best to choose the most widely-understood term for its official name. Had it been only a question of which term had been in use for the greater length of time, or which term had been used during the military campaign of 1942, 'track' would surely have been chosen. With all factors taken into balanced consideration, the decision of the Place Names Committee in favour of 'trail' made sense in 1972 and, to large extent, their reasoning still holds good today.

Not everyone at the time was happy with the selection of 'Trail' and even now in Australia, four decades later, some diehards are still insisting 'trail' is wrong, principally on the basis that 'track' was the term commonly used by WW2 Australian soldiers. But, and notwithstanding the significance of the 1942 Kokoda campaign to the Australian perspective, we, as Australians, should be wary of insisting our viewpoint is the only one that matters. Though Papua was still an Australian Territory in 1972 when 'Kokoda Trail' became the official name, the government of independent PNG has chosen to retain it. Parts of the Trail were being explored and developed up to 130 years ago and the 6 months and 2 days of the WW2 campaign constitute about a third of one percent of this long story. The other 99.6 percent of the time belongs to PNG history, entitling the PNG government to call the old overland mail route whatever they like. It shows a measure of disrespect to the PNG government—some Australian newspapers are consistently guilty of this—to continue to maintain the 'correct' name of the route is 'Track'.

It is interesting too, not all old soldiers of the time immediately disagree with the use of 'trail'. Brigadier A.W. Buttrose, D.S.O., who as a Lieutenant-Colonel in command of the 2/33rd Battalion on the track in 1942, walked the whole distance from Port Moresby to Gona. He returned to Papua New Guinea in 1972 on a visit to Port Moresby. 'We used to talk about the Track, and sections of the Track', he said [as reported in the Papua New Guinea *Post-Courier* of 4th August 1972] 'and all official Army documents call it the Kokoda Track. But somehow, I've fallen into the habit of talking about it as the Kokoda Trail'. The entire matter can be put in perspective by leaving the last word to Geoff Reading, the correspondent who provided the explanation of how the term 'Kokoda Trail' was introduced into Australian usage: 'This is how the Kokoda Trail got its name. How it got its fame is another and far more important story'.

18

The track today

In the early 1970s, the Returned Services League of Papua New Guinea proposed the establishment of a museum to honour the exploits of servicemen during the New Guinea campaigns. The fighting on the old Kokoda mail route was considered to be particularly significant and it was intended to erect the museum building on the track itself. As a tribute to the late P.J. McDonald, who was renown for his generosity to troops stationed near or passing through his Ilolo rubber plantation during the 1942–43 period, the museum was to be known as the 'P.J. McDonald Memorial War Museum'. McDonald's family, who still resided at Ilolo Plantation, generously donated a large tract of land at McDonald's Corner for the project, and the League set about raising the money to cover construction costs. The main building, designed in April 1972 by G. Benson, was an edifice of clean architectural line and quiet dignity becoming of its purpose. It was octagonal in plan with a heavy brick buttress at each of the eight corners to support the roof beams. This permitted, aside from a central pole, an uninterrupted internal span of 50 feet (15.25 metres), providing ample space for the intended displays. Unfortunately, after a number of requests from the Returned Services League to the Papua New Guinea Government for support were turned down, the museum project did not proceed.

The idea of a memorial on the track itself however, was not to be entirely lost. On Anzac Day 1994, a $650,000 'Kokoda Memorial Project' was launched jointly by the RSL organisation in Australia and the Rotary Club of Gosford in New South Wales, to provide a health centre at Kokoda and aid posts at nearby villages. The intention of this was to provide not only a memorial to those who fought and died on the Track but to furnish a measure of on-going practical assistance to the indigenous people of the area. The first aid post was established at Waju Village and the second, at Sairope, in October 1994. A hospital at Kokoda was opened in September 1995. There is too, at Bomana, now easily reached by motor road from Port Moresby but the site of an evening camp on the original overland route when travel to Sogeri was made on horseback, the Commonwealth War Graves Commission's Bomana War Cemetery. At the end of hostilities, the remains of servicemen were moved from temporary graves to Bomana. Originally, each grave had a wooden cross but in February 1948, the Port Moresby firm of John Stubbs and Sons were awarded the contract to supply marble headstones for the 4,000 graves. The cemetery was opened by Sir William Slim, Governor-General of Australia, on 19th October 1953. The cemetery is well tended, and its green lawns and dignified trees amongst the dusty brown scrubland surrounding it promote an oasis of quiet peace and personal reflection. The most poignant moments at Bomana War Cemetery are experienced during the annual Anzac Day dawn service. In the still, early hours, the surviving ex-servicemen, dressed all in white, stand in the gaps between the white headstones, and with the cool dawn mist obscuring detail, the impression of the fallen once again being on parade with their comrades is an acutely moving experience.

Due to the heightened interest within Papua New Guinea in the Kokoda Trail, Bert Kienzle, who it will be recalled originally came to New Guinea in 1927, who served on the track as the ANGAU officer in charge of carrier lines in 1942, and who returned to Kokoda after the war, offered a prize in November 1972 for the fastest crossing of the Trail between Owers' Corner and Kokoda, or between Kokoda and Owers' Corner. He offered to sponsor the contest for five years, putting up $200 for each year's winner. As an indication of what was required, he pointed out his two sons, John and Wallace, already appeared to have completed the quickest crossings—John, at 16, doing it in 32 hours walking time and Wallace, at 13, taking only 30 hours. These times compare favourably with what appears to be the earliest interest in setting a record crossing. 'Doc' Vernon mentions Major (later Lieutenant-Colonel) A.G. Cameron's time from Deniki to Port Moresby was 'just under 3 days' in August 1942. Vernon originally wrote 'I doubt if this will ever be beaten for the Range trip' but an inserted comment notes a Major McCann later achieved a quicker crossing. Unfortunately, McCann's time is not recorded. Vernon was at Nauro when Cameron passed him and wisely declined Cameron's invitation to be part of the record attempt.

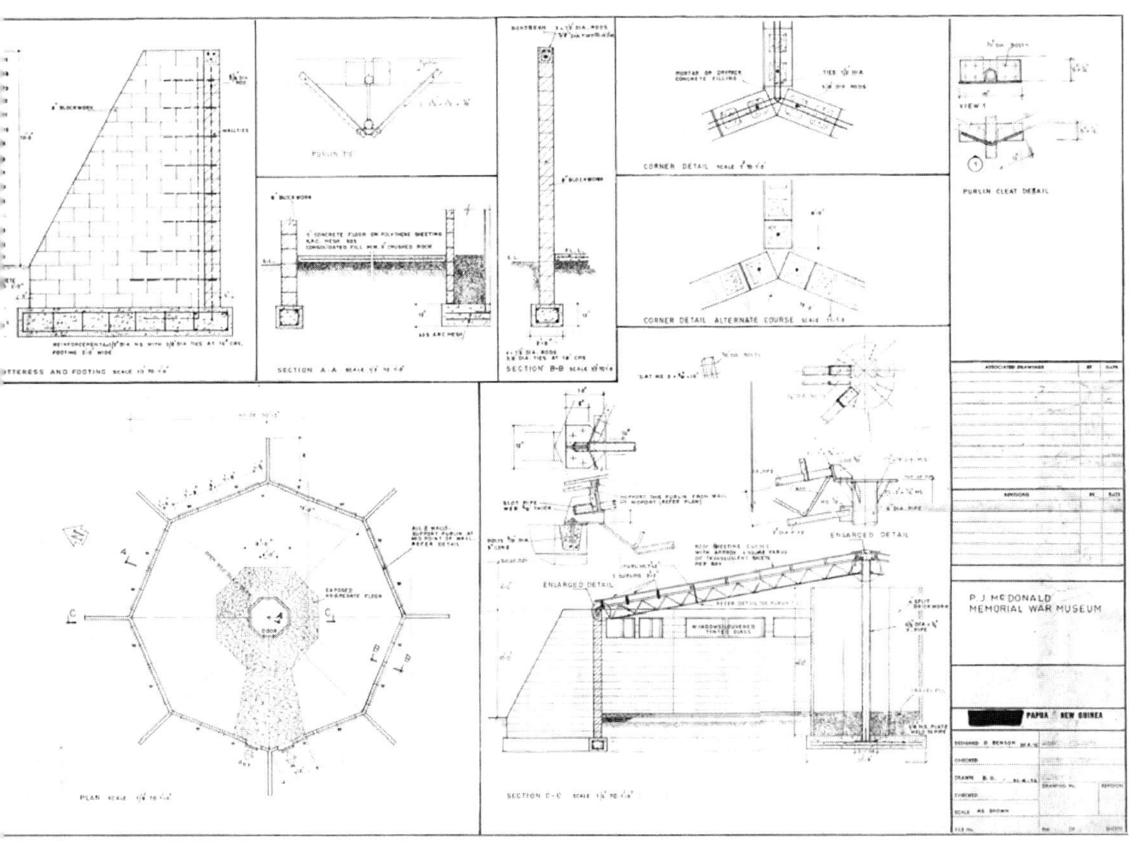

Some detail of the proposed 'P. J. McDonald Memorial War Museum'. It was intended to construct the museum at McDonald's Corner in 1974 but the project did not proceed past the planning stage.

In 1993, a smaller museum was opened at Kokoda to commemorate the achievements of Bert Kienzle on the Kokoda Trail during the war.

RSSAILA., PNG Branch.

Captain H. T. Kienzle, MBE. During WW2, Kienzle walked the Kokoda Trail eight times in six months. This photo taken in 1967. *RSSAILA PNG Branch*.

The first post-war race following Bert Kienzle's initiative, was held in 1973 with a commendable time of 36 hours being achieved. This quantified the challenge and interest in the event was sufficient to establish the contest as a permanent institution with male and female divisions being implemented. In 1975, the fastest time was set in the men's category, 31 hours and 5 minutes, with the first woman coming in at 53 hours 15 minutes. The following year though, saw the still-standing records in both divisions being established. Abau Senesi of Alola Village left Sogeri on 5th August and reached the Kokoda Council Chambers on the 7th after only 27 hours 5 minutes walking time. The new women's record was set by Mabel Mafi of Asimba Village in the Northern Province (previously Northern Division), reaching Kokoda after only 33 hours 15 minutes, breaking the old mark by a huge 20 hours. These times have proven hard to better. In 1986 for example, the remarkable effort of 28 hours 14 minutes achieved by Osbourne Bogajiwai, was still 69 minutes short of the record.

The Kokoda Trail briefly returned to prominence on the front pages of Australian newspapers following the visit of Paul Keating, Labor Prime Minister of Australia, to Kokoda in April 1992. This was the first time an Australian Prime Minister had been to Kokoda. The visit was not notable so much for this as it was for Keating's kneeling and kissing the concrete base of a plinth erected to commemorate the bravery of Australian soldiers. This was reported in the *Australian* of 27th April 1992 as 'completely unplanned' and 'an emotional response' on Mr Keating's part. However, the publicity of the unusual event fitted in well with two domestic political issues, republicanism and a design for a new Australian flag (not containing the British Union Jack), then being advocated in a campaign by the Australian Labor Party. The widely-reported ground-kissing incident was utilised to highlight the 1942 Kokoda Trail campaigns as the first time Australian soldiers had truly fought in defence of Australia. It was therefore, in Keating's view, more significant than earlier military expeditions where allegiance had been to 'the Mother Country and Empire'.

While this is not untrue, in Australia, Keating's posturing was viewed with cynicism by some sections of the public and there was some unease at the use of Anzac Day for political purposes. However, Keating was not the only one engaged in lobbying for his interests. A number of petitions, including one from Raphael Oimbari, who had been recruited as a carrier on the Kokoda Trail in 1942, and who announced he was speaking for 49,500 former carriers, labourers and stretcher-bearers, were presented to Keating. Oimbari's petition sought compensation from the Australian Government for the service given by the Papua New Guinea people during the war. The petitions were received by Keating without comment at the time but if the disgraceful record of all post-War Australian Governments in this regard is anything to go by, the Papua New Guinean people probably will never be rewarded for their efforts. (The people concerned here are not those who were enlisted in the Papuan Infantry Battalion, the New Guinea Volunteer Rifles or the Native Constabulary. Rather, it is the stretcher bearers, carriers, labourers and the like who were summarily drafted into service). The Returned Services League in Papua New Guinea tried for over twenty years to secure recognition of and adequate compensation for the service given by the indigenous people to the Australian Government. The responses the League in Papua New Guinea received from Australian Governments over this period consisted of a remarkable tirade of stonewalling, negation by delay, truth-twisting and straw-splitting. The reasons given why it was not possible for the Australian Government to compensate the summarily conscripted Papua New Guinea people can be reduced, in summary, to two responses. It was either because they had not been formally enlisted or because, and therefore, the names of the people concerned were not recorded.

These issues have been widely discussed in other forums. Suffice to say here in this matter the onus would seem to be on the Australian government. The fact the government has recourse to solutions such as *ex gratia* payments, retrospective legislation, striking of special medals, and so forth, makes hollow the claim some legislative or quasi-legal restriction prevents a morally-indicated action from being taken. The Papua New Guinean Government has repeatedly indicated they can identify those who worked as carriers, bearers and labourers. *Prima facie*, the Australian people owe a debt to the unofficial servicemen, and women, of Papua New Guinea and repayment of this debt has been officially avoided for half a century. The oft-touted argument the debt has been repaid during Australia's colonial governorship of the country, and in the annual grants to an independent Papua New Guinea since 1975, ignores the contribution of the individual. There is no formal individual acknowledgment of the personal effort made, the danger faced, the hardship endured, the injury suffered, the life lost, the family destroyed. This is not to say recognition is lacking. In his 1992 Anzac Day speech in Port Moresby (as reported in the *Australian* of 27th April 1992), Keating himself clearly articulated the sentiments of all Australians. But the shame of it is recognition goes no further than political rhetoric and it is left to belated, though admirable, private initiatives, such as that of the Gosford Rotary Club, to attempt to express the Australian gratitude at the individual level. Keating said:

> ... Above all we should honour and express our profound admiration for the Papua New Guinean carriers whose stalwart support was crucial to final victory. The support they gave to Australian soldiers, the terrible conditions and dangers they endured with the soldiers, the illness, injury and death many of them suffered, constitutes one of the great humane gestures of the war—perhaps the greatest humane gesture of our history. It has never been forgotten and never will be forgotten.

In recent years, the old mail route has lived up to its expectations as a popular bushwalking route though crossings are now often made in 'reverse', with groups flying to Kokoda or Popondetta to walk back to the Sogeri Plateau. The recent commercialisation of the bushwalking route, with organised packages for tourists, has diminished some of its mystery and risk, though these have served to make the journey available to a wider community. It is regrettable however, organisers of most of these expeditions do not seem to be aware of the rich pre-war history of the Track, and give the impression its significant history dates only from 1942. Despite the fast crossings in the annual Kokoda Trail race, the average time for a normal walk is about five days. The best group size for efficiency, safety and

On Anzac Day 1992, the Australian Prime Minister Paul Keating knelt and kissed the plinth at the base of the monument at Kokoda. This was later described as 'an emotional response' and an 'unplanned' action.

While a relative of Keating's did serve on the Kokoda Trail during the Pacific war, the fact that the event was used to raise matters of a domestic political nature caused public unease because of the linking of the Kokoda Trail with party politics. This newspaper cartoon by Mac Vines captures the mood of the time.

Mac Vines.

speed is probably five or six people though much larger groups have made the crossing. In July 1974, a 24-member team from Port Moresby Hash House Harriers, led by Les Waldron, flew to Kokoda and walked back to Owers' Corner in five days. For those with a reasonable level of fitness, and of adventurous bent, it can be a challenging test of stamina and a stimulating experience. Though it is possible to employ carriers for different portions of the journey, in many quarters of the bushwalking fraternity this is not considered good form—one is expected to do the trip through one's own exertions. This in turn invokes the bushwalker's maxim: you may take anything you like with you so long as you are willing to carry it yourself. Some have been known to cut the tags off their teabags or to shorten their boot laces to reduce weight. These measures may appear extreme but at the three-quarter point up the Golden Stairs on one's first crossing, the sentiment is thoroughly understood. Intending travellers who are not experienced in independent self-contained bushwalking in rugged and remote areas should seek advice from a qualified source before setting out.

Members of a May 1973 party breasting the final crest of Imita Ridge on the Kokoda Trail. The actual path can be seen running off into the top right corner. The path is usually well defined under the jungle canopy but becomes indistinct in clearings and at river crossings.

Author.

PREVIOUS PAGE:

▲ Only four hours out from Owers' Corner and already exhausted. Members of a May 1973 party rest at Uberi Village after the climb up from the Goldie River crossing, before tackling the Golden Stairs on Imita Ridge.

Author.

▼ Imita Ridge camp, May 1973. The heavy morning mist was still lingering when this photo was taken at 8.30am.

Author.

On the track, the path is usually well marked where it runs under the jungle canopy or near villages. However, at creek crossings, one may have to hunt about to pick up the track as the thicker plant growth quickly obscures any clearing of scrub that is occasionally done. The crossing of rivers and creeks too, provides most of the physical danger during the trek. This does not arise so much from a risk of drowning as it does from the risk of slipping on ever-moist rocks and logs, particularly the latter. These obstacles are parts of the trek that cannot be avoided. A good solution to this problem is a pair of instep crampons for your boots. A stout pair of leather boots giving firm ankle support is recommended, though some walkers have worn sneakers, studded football boots and even spiked running or golf shoes. Some of the villages offer overnight accommodation and there is an occasional rest hut along the way but be prepared to look after yourself. A walk across the Kokoda Trail can be an enjoyable experience but thorough preparation is essential as the route is still not without its difficulties and most parts of it are a long way from outside help. In April 1969, a female hiker died of exposure and exhaustion and in September 1992, a 53 year old ex-British Army sergeant-major became lost for 16 days during an attempt to walk the Trail alone.

The jungle reveals very little of the past of the Kokoda Trail to the modern bushwalker. Here and there, one may be able to determine crumbling excavations or the occasional cartridge case or piece of mortar bomb or grenade may turn up. For the most part though, a green mantle of foliage covers the wounds of the landscape, and the axe blazes and bullet scars have long been hidden behind the saturated mosses and strangling vines embracing the trees.

Yet, though the past cannot be seen, just being there invokes a sense of days long gone, as if a record of the past lingers imprinted in the ancient landscape. It is easy to imagine someone from another era, perhaps a hundred years earlier, sat equally worn out on the same rock, or drank equally thirstily from the same stream, or gazed with equal wonder across the same vista. In some mysterious way, perhaps simply because you have walked in their footsteps, you are able to appreciate the efforts of the pioneers and pathfinders, and to understand the triumphs and follies of their times, with a clarity not available to others. Indeed, you cannot but be aware of a deep empathy with those earlier fellow travellers, people like Chalmers, Morrison, MacGregor, the irrepressible Monckton, Lieutenant Jesser and David Ballantine, Stuart-Russell and ill-fated Captain Templeton, the mail-carrying policemen, Murray, Major Watson, Bert Kienzle or 'Doc' Vernon; in fact, with any of the weary thousands who have gone before you on their own long day's journey, along this narrow jungle track over the Owen Stanley mountains.

Selected bibliography

The following works are those from which significant items of information have been derived. General and background references have not been listed.

GOVERNMENT REPORTS, GAZETTES AND OFFICIAL CORRESPONDENCE

Annual report on British New Guinea, 1886 to 1906/07, Government Printer, Brisbane and Melbourne. (Papua New Guinea National Library, Port Moresby).

Annual report of the Lieutenant-Governor of Papua, 1907/08 to 1940/41, Government Printers, Brisbane and Melbourne. (Papua New Guinea National Library, Port Moresby).

Annual report of the Territory of Papua and New Guinea, 1947/48 to 1964/65. Government Printer, Port Moresby. (Papua New Guinea National Library, Port Moresby).

'British New Guinea, correspondence, register of outletters, etc., 1884-1900', University of Queensland microfilm MIC7384 (12 reels), MIC7385 (3 reels), MIC7386 (1 reel).

'Further correspondence respecting New Guinea' [C—3617], British Government, May 1883. (Freyer Library, University of Queensland).

'Correspondence respecting New Guinea and other islands, and the Convention at Sydney of representatives of the Australian colonies', Volume 2 [C—3863], British Government, February 1884. (Freyer Library, University of Queensland).

'Further correspondence respecting New Guinea and other islands, and the Convention at Sydney of representatives of the Australian colonies', Volume 4 [C—4217], British Government, October 1884. (Freyer Library, University of Queensland).

'Further correspondence respecting New Guinea and other islands in the Western Pacific Ocean', Volume 5 [C—4273] February 1885; Volume 6 [C—4584] August 1885, British Government. (Freyer Library, University of Queensland).

Government *Gazette* of British New Guinea, of the Territory of Papua, of the Territory of Papua and New Guinea, and of Papua New Guinea, various issues 1888 to 1977. Government Printer, Port Moresby. (Ela Beach Public Library, Port Moresby [originals]; also Gazettes 1903-1906, University Of Queensland microfilm MIC4914).

Murray, J.H.P., 'Review of the Australian Administration in Papua from 1907 to 1920', published with the concurrence of the Commonwealth Government, c.1923; included on University of Queensland microfilm MIC4925 (PMB DOC 307)(2nd half of reel in part identified as 'Papua: miscellaneous published reports').

OTHER REPORTS, PRIVATE PUBLICATIONS, MANUSCRIPTS, NEWSPAPERS AND DIARIES

Proceedings of The Royal Geographical Society, 1877-78. (Papua New Guinea National Library, Port Moresby).

TheJournal of The Royal Geographical Society, Volume 46, John Murray, London, 1876. (Ela Beach Public Library, Port Moresby).

Transactions and Proceedings of The Royal Geographical Society of Australiasia, New South Wales Branch, 1885-86, Volumes 3 and 4. (Papua New Guinea National Library, Port Moresby).

Transactions and Proceedings of The Royal Geographical Society of Australiasia, Queensland Branch, 1888-89, 4th Session. (State Library of Queensland, Brisbane).

Return to Kokoda, The Returned Services League, Papua New Guinea Branch, Port Moresby, 1967.

Ganiga, Daera, 'Daera Ganiga's experience in the Papuan Infantry Battalion', as recorded in Appendix 3h of Robinson, Neville K., *Villagers at war: some Papua New Guinea experiences in World War II*, Pacific Research Monograph Number Two (Fisk, E.K., series editor), The Australian National University, Canberra, 1979.

Tanaka, Kengoro, (translated by Nobuo Kojima), *Operations of the Imperial Japanese Armed Forces in the Papua New Guinea Theater during World War II*, Japan Papua New Guinea Goodwill Society, Tokyo, 1980.

Harris, Edgar B., *William Bairstow Ingham*, (Manuscript OM72-10, State Library of Queensland, Brisbane).

Nicholas, Mrs Gladys, *I was a Before: A story of life in the Territory of Papua prior to the outbreak of the Pacific War*, (Manuscript 870907, Fryer Library, University of Queensland).

The *Age* (newspaper), January-December 1884, Melbourne. (State Library of Victoria).

Argus (newspaper), September to December 1883, Melbourne. (State Library of Victoria).

Pacific Islands Monthly (journal), Pacific Publications, Sydney, 1930-1977. (Ela Beach Public Library [originals]; also University of Queensland microfilm MIC3470).

Papuan Times (newspaper), 1911 to 1916, Port Moresby. (Ela Beach Public Library, Port Moresby [originals]; also University of Papua New Guinea [originals]; also University of Queensland microfilm MIC6188).

Papuan Courier (newspaper), 1917 to 1942, Port Moresby. (Ela Beach Public Library, Port Moresby [originals]; also University of Queensland microfilm MIC4498).

The *Papuan Villager* (newspaper), 1929 to 1941, Government Printer, Port Moresby. (Ela Beach Public Library, Port Moresby [originals]; also University of Queensland microfilm MIC3216).

South Pacific Post, *New Guinea Courier* and *Post-Courier* (newspapers), various 1957 to 1977, Port Moresby.

McDermant, D.A., personal diaries and photograph collection, June 1940-June 1942.

Turner, F.W., file of notes and written comments, copies of letters and press clippings 1971-1973.

MAPS (arranged by date of publication)

'Cape Nelson to Hercules Bay, British New Guinea', British Admiralty, London, July 1886. (Originally in author's possession; donated to University of Queensland Fryer Library).

'Southeast New Guinea embracing its northern and southern waters', Surveyor-General's Office, Brisbane, 1889. (University of Queensland RAB MAP G8160 S285 1889.M36 1889 sh.1).

'Geological observations on British New Guinea in 1891', Geological Survey of Queensland, 1892, GSQ No 85. (Library of Department of Resource Industries, Brisbane).

'Map of the Territory of Papua from the latest surveys 1908', Department of Public Lands, Brisbane, 1908. (University of Queensland G8160 S2027 1908.M36 1908 1).

'Papua', c.1920 (University of Queensland G8160.NS.19**.P3619**, Geology Library).

'Papua', Lands and Survey Branch, Works Department, Canberra, 1932. (University of Queensland RAB MAP G8160 S1267 1932.P35.1932).

'Papua', c.1940 (University of Queensland G8160.S1900.194*.M36194*, Geology Library).

'Cape Nelson, New Guinea', 1:500,000 series, U.S. Army 1942. (State Library of Queensland).

'Port Moresby, New Guinea', 1:500,000 series, U.S. Army 1943. (State Library of Queensland).

'Uberi, New Guinea', 1:63,360 series, 2/1st Aust. Army. Topo. Survey Coy., March 1943. (State Library of Queensland).

Royal Australian Army Survey Corps 1:50,000 Series T784: 'Port Moresby', 5229-IV, 1965; 'Sogeri', 5229-I, 1965; 'Laloki River', 5230-III, 1965.

Royal Australian Army Survey Corps 1:250,000 Series T504: 'Aroa'. SC55-6, 1965;'Port Moresby', SC55-7, 1970; 'Tufi', SC55-8, 1966; 'Buna', SC55-3, 1966; 'Yule', SC-552, 1963.

'Roads - Port Moresby and the northeast coast', Port Moresby, 1983. (University of Queensland G8161.P2.S1000.1983.P36 SH.SW 1983).

BOOKS AND OTHER PUBLISHED WORKS

Austin, Victor (compiler), *To Kokoda and beyond (The story of the 39th Battalion 1941–1943)*, Melbourne University Press, 1988.

Baden-Powell, B.F.S., *In savage isles and settled lands*, Richard Bennett, London, 1892.

Baker, J.N.L., *A history of geographical discovery and exploration*, Harrap, London, 1931.

Bevan, Theodore F., *Toil, travel and discovery in British New Guinea*, Paul, Trench, Trubner and Company, London, 1890.

Biskup, P., Jinks, E., and Nelson, H., *A short history of New Guinea*, Angus and Robertson, Sydney, 1968.

— —, *Readings in New Guinea history*, Angus and Robertson, Sydney, 1973.

George Brown D.D., *Pioneer missionary and explorer* (autobiography), Hodder and Stroughton, London, 1908.

Burton, Rev J., 'The Australian Mandate in New Guinea' in *Studies in Australian affairs*, MacMillan and Company, Melbourne, 1930.

Cameron, Charlotte, *Two years in southern seas*, T. Fisher Unwin, London, 1923.

Chalmers, J., *Pioneering in New Guinea*, Religious Tract Society, London, 1885.

——, *Work and adventure in New Guinea*, Religious Tract Society, London, 1885.

Chatterton, Percy, *Day that I have loved*, Pacific Publications, Sydney, 1974.

Cheesman, Evelyn, *The two roads of Papua*, Jarrolds, London, 1935.

——, *Things worth while*, Hutchinson and Company, London, 1957.

Clift, V.R., *The saga of a sig*, K.C.D. Publications, Randwick, New South Wales, 1972.

Clune, Frank, *Prowling through Papua*, Angus and Robertson, Sydney. 1943.

Cooke, C. Kinlocke, *Australian defences and New Guinea*, MacMillan and Company, London. 1887.

Crocker, Hamilton, *The postmarks of British New Guinea and Papua to 1942*. The Hawthorn Press, Melbourne, 1956.

Franklin, Mark, *Franklin's guide to the stamps of Papua and New Guinea*. A.H. & A.W. Reed, Sydney, 1970.

Geil, William Edgar, *Ocean and isle*, Wm. T. Pater and Company, Melbourne, 1902.

Griffin, Major H.L., *An official in British New Guinea*, Cecil Paplmer, London, 1925.

Humphries, W.R., *Patrolling in Papua*, T. Fisher Unwin, London, 1923.

Idriess, Ion L., *Gold dust and ashes*, Angus and Robertson, Sydney, 1944.

Inglis, Amirah, *Karo: The life and fate of a Papuan*, Institute of Papua New Guinea Studies in association with Australian National University Press, Canberra, 1982.

Johnston, George H., *New Guinea diary*, Angus and Robertson, Sydney, 1944.

Joyce, R.B., *Sir William MacGregor*, Oxford University Press, Melbourne, 1971.

King, Rev Joseph, *W.G. Lawes of Savage Island and New Guinea*, Religious Tract Society, London, 1909.

Lawson, Capt J.A., *Wanderings in the interior of New Guinea*, Chapman and Hall, London, 1875.

Lennox, Cuthbert, *James Chalmers of New Guinea*, Religious Tract Society, London, 1902.

Lett, Lewis, *Papuan gold*, Angus and Robertson, Sydney, 1943.

——, *Sir Hubert Murray of Papua*, Collins, Sydney, 1949.

'Line Triumph on the Kokoda Trail' in *Signals*, Halstead Press, Sydney, 1954.

Long, Gavin, *The six years war*, The Australian War Memorial and the Australian Government Publishing Service (joint publishers), Canberra, 1973.

Lovett, Richard, *James Chalmers, his autobiography and letters*, Religious Tract Society, London, 1902.

MacArthur, Douglas, *Reminiscences*, William Heinemann Ltd, London, 1964.

MacFarlane, Rev S., *Among the cannibals of New Guinea*, London Missionary Society, London, 1888.

MacGregor, W., 'Introduction' in Murray, J.H.P., *Papua or British New Guinea*, T. Fisher Unwin, London, 1912.

Mackay, Colonel Kenneth, *Across Papua*, Witherby and Company, London, 1909.

Mayo, Lida, *Bloody Buna*, Australian National University Press, Canberra, 1975.

McCarthy, Dudley, *South-west Pacific area—first year*, (Volume V of Series 1 of the official war history 'Australia in the War of 1939–1945'), Australian War Memorial, Canberra, 1959 (1962 reprint).

Mair, L., *Australia in New Guinea*, Christophers, London, 1948.

Monckton, C.A.W., *Some experiences of a New Guinea Resident Magistrate*, John Lane, London, 1921.

Murray, J.H.P., 'Australian Policy in Papua' in *Studies in Australian affairs*, MacMillan and Company, Melbourne, 1930.

——, *Papua or British New Guinea*, T. Fisher Unwin, London, 1912.

——, *Papua of today*, P.S. King and Son, London, 1925.

——, *Recent exploration in Papua*, Turner and Henderson, Sydney, 1923.

NX9719, 'Ambush' in *Khaki and green*, Australian War Memorial, Canberra, 1943.

Pacific Islands *Year book and who's who*, 2nd to 6th, 8th to 10th editions, Pacific Publications, Sydney.

Paull, Raymond, *Retreat from Kokoda*, Heinemann, Melbourne, 1958

Pearl, Cyril, *Morrison of Peking*, Angus and Robertson, Sydney, 1967 (1981 edition).

Pitcairn, W.D., *Two years among the savages of New Guinea*, Ward and Downey, London, 1891.

Powell, John H., *The postal history of the Territory of New Guinea from 1888 to 1942*, The Hawthorn Press, Melbourne, 1964.

Robson, William, *James Chalmers, missionary and explorer of Rarotonga and New Guinea*, S.W.Partridge and Company, London, undated (c.1900).

Romilly, Hugh Hastings, *From my verandah in New Guinea*, David Nutt, London, 1889.

Ryan, Peter (general ed.), *Encyclopedia of Papua New Guinea,* Melbourne University Press in association with the University of Papua New Guinea, 1972.

Sinclair, James, *The outside man: Jack Hides of Papua,* Lansdown Press, Melbourne, 1969.

Souter, Gavin, *New Guinea: the last unknown,* Angus and Robertson, Sydney, 1963 (1972 reprint).

Staniforth-Smith, Miles Cater, *Handbook of the Territory of Papua,* Government Printer, Melbourne, several editions, 1907 to 1927.

Stone, Octavius C., *A few months in New Guinea,* Samson Low, London, 1880.

Stuart, Ian, *Port Moresby: Yesterday and today,* Pacific Publications, Sydney, 1970.

Strachan, J., *Explorations and adventures in New Guinea,* Sampson Low, London, 1892.

Thompson, J.P., *British New Guinea,* George Philip and Son, London, 1892.

Tomkins, Dorothea & Hughes, Brian, *The road from Gona,* Angus and Robertson, London, 1970.

VX17681, 'War in New Guinea' in *Soldiering on,* Australian War Memorial, Canberra, 1942.

West, Francis, *Hubert Murray: The Australian pro-consul,* Oxford University Press, Melbourne, 1968.

——, (Ed.), *Selected letters of Hubert Murray,* Oxford University Press, Melbourne, 1970.

White, The Rt Rev B.P. Gilbert, *A pioneer of Papua,* Society for Promoting Christian Knowledge, London, 1929.

Wigmore, Lionel, *The Japanese thrust,* (Volume IV of Series 1 of the official war history 'Australia in the War of 1939–1945'), Australian War Memorial, Canberra, 1957.

Index

A reference to material in a footnote contains an 'n' suffix.
A reference to a person appears in bolded type.
A suffix of 'ff' means all or some of the pages following, up until the next reference or the end of the chapter.